MAINE
FISHING MAPS

◆

VOLUME 1 - LAKES AND PONDS

Maps by
DeLorme Publishing Company

Text by
Harry Vanderweide

ISBN 0-89933-007-X
© 1986, 1984, 1982, 1980 DeLorme Publishing Company
Freeport, Maine 04032
All rights reserved.

INDEX

Legend of Map Symbols . . . . Page iii
Introduction iv
Maine's Record Fish iv
The One That Didn't Get Away Club iv
Waterway Markers v
The Fishes of Maine v
The Lakes:

    Allagash Lake . . . . Map 1
    Androscoggin Lake 2
    Attean Pond 3
    Auburn Lake 4
    Aziscohos Lake 5
    Beaver Mountain Lake 6
    Beech Hill Pond 6
    Big Lake 7
    Biscay Pond 8
    Branch Lake 8
    Brassua Lake 9
    Brewer Pond 9
    Cathance Lake 10
    Caucomgomoc Lake 10
    Chain of Ponds 11
    Chamberlain Lake .11
    Chesuncook Lake 12
    China Lake 13
    Clearwater Pond 14
    Cobbosseecontee Lake . . . .•. . 15
    Cochnewagon Pond 16
    Cold Stream Pond .16
    Crawford Lake 17
    Cross Lake 17
    Damariscotta Lake 18
    Dodge Pond 19
    Drews Lake 19
    East Grand Lake 20
    East Pond 21
    Echo Lake 21
    Embden Pond 22
    Fish Lake 22

Flanders Pond . . . . Map 23
Floods Pond 23
Gardner Lake 24
Great Pond 25
Great East Lake 24
Green Lake 26
Hancock Pond 26
Hatcase Pond 27
Hermon Pond 27
Highland Lake 28
Hopkins Pond 28
Indian Pond 29
Junior Lake 29
Kennebago Lake 30
Kezar Lake 30
Kidney Pond 31
Lincoln Pond 31
Little Jim Pond 32
Little Kennebago Lake 32
Little Ossipee Lake 33
Little Sebago Lake 34
Lobster Lake 35
Long Pond 36
Lovewell Pond 37
Maranacook Lake 38
Matagamon Lake 37
Mattanawcook Pond 39
Meddybemps Lake 39
Messalonskee Lake 40
Millinocket Lake 41
Molunkus Lake 42
Moose Pond (Great Moose Lake) 45
Moose Pond 45
Moosehead Lake 44
Mousam Lake 47
Musquacook Lakes .46
Nahmakanta Lake 47
Nequasset Pond 48
Nicatous Lake 48

North Pond . . . . Map 49
Parker Pond 50
Pemadumcook Chain of Lakes 51
Phillips Lake 52
Pleasant Lake 52
Pleasant Pond 53
Pocomoonshine Lake 53
Porter Lake 54
Pushaw Lake 55
Quimby Pond 56
Range Ponds 56
Rangeley Lake 58
Richardson Lakes 59
Roach Ponds 60
St. George Lake 62
Salmon and McGrath Lakes 63
Scraggly Lake 64
Sebago Lake 65
Sebec Lake 67
Sheepscot Pond 68

Sourdnahunk Lake . . . . Map 69
Spencer Lake 69
Spring Lake 70
Square Lake 70
Third Machias Lake 71
Thompson Lake 71
Threemile Pond 72
Toddy Pond 72
Torsey Pond 73
Tunk Lake 73
Wassookeag Lake 74
Webber Pond 74
West Lake 75
West Grand Lake 76
Wilson Pond 78
Wilson Ponds 77
Wood Pond 78
Wytopitlock Lake 79
Fishing Directory of Maine Lakes and Ponds . . . . Page 80

LEGEND OF MAP SYMBOLS

- Sporting camps
- Boat launch, carry
- Boat launch, trailerable

  (fee may be charged)

ABBREVIATIONS FOR FISH SPECIES

S	Salmon
BK	Brook trout
T	Togue (lake trout)
BN	Brown trout
R	Rainbow trout
BL	Blueback trout
SU	Sunapee trout
BS	Bass
WP	White perch
PK	Pickerel
SM	Smelt
WF	Whitefish
CU	Cusk

All maps are fully indexed to
The Maine Atlas and Gazetteer
to provide easy access and directions.

The information in this book does not imply landowner permission; private property or landowner restrictions must be respected.

INTRODUCTION

Maine has been well-endowed with attractive natural features, none of them, perhaps, more important than her 2,500 great lakes and ponds. This volume is the most extensive effort ever to compile useful information about the best known, most productive, and prettiest lakes in the state.

With a special emphasis on the quality of fishing in each lake, we have mapped and described a wide variety of waters. The lakes covered here range from highly developed spots located in large communities to remote ponds which are difficult to reach. Naturally, we have focused on the largest lakes, but you will find many intimate waters listed here as well. Our idea has been to provide the most accurate and up-to-date guide available which readers will find useful, whatever their preferences for size, scenery, remoteness, or fish species.

Many people have contributed to *The Book of Maine Fishing Maps*. A special thanks is owed to the following for their assistance in research: Steve Takach, Sherwood Chandler, Don Cote, Phil Foster, Wayne Hockmeyer, Dick Drysdale, Calvin Philbrook, Dave O'Connor, Bob Leeman, Wilmot Robinson, Wayne Hooper, Peter Walker, Bob Sanderson, Al Raychard.

A word of explanation is in order here. In Maine, the words "lake" and "pond" are used interchangeably. Although lakes will tend to be larger and deeper than ponds, that is not always the case.

Also, a word of caution: The maps in this book are not intended to serve as primary water navigation charts. Reefs and hazardous rocks have not been marked, and the depth soundings are only approximate.

Harry Vanderweide

MAINE'S RECORD FISH

BROOK TROUT 8 pounds, 8 ounces, James R. Foster, Sr., Howland, Chase Pond, 1979

BROWN TROUT 19 pounds, 7 ounces, Norman Stacy, Fitchburg, Mass., Sebago Lake, 1958

LAKE TROUT 31 pounds, 8 ounces, Hollis Grindle, Ellsworth, Beech Hill Pond, 1958

BLUEBACK TROUT 4 pounds, 4 ounces, Merton Wyman, Belgrade, Basin Pond, 1973

LANDLOCKED SALMON 22 pounds, 8 ounces, Edward Blakely, Darien, Conn., Sebago Lake, 1907

ATLANTIC SALMON 28 pounds, 1 ounce, Howard Clifford, Portland, Maine, location undisclosed, 1980

SMALLMOUTH BASS 8 pounds, George Dyer, Augusta, Thompson Lake, 1970

LARGEMOUTH BASS 11 pounds, 10 ounces, Robert Kamp, Denmark, Moose Pond, 1968

WHITE PERCH 4 pounds, 10 ounces, Mrs. Earl Small, Waterville, Messalonskee Lake, 1949

CHAIN PICKEREL 6 pounds, 11 ounces, Reggie Arsenault, Rumford, Androscoggin Lake, 1976

WHITEFISH 7 pounds, 8 ounces, Neil Sullivan, Worcester, Mass., Sebago Lake, 1958

CUSK 17 pounds, 8 ounces, Kurt Savasuk, Waterville, Moosehead Lake, 1979

THE ONE THAT DIDN'T GET AWAY CLUB

The Maine Sportsman, Box 507, Yarmouth, Maine, 04096, a monthly hunting and fishing publication, operates The One That Didn't Get Away Club. This program recognizes outstanding freshwater fish catches in Maine, and each person who qualifies is awarded a membership card and jacket patch.

The contest is open to anyone holding a valid Maine fishing license. All fish entered must be legally caught in Maine. Fish from a state, club, or private hatchery or pool are not eligible. Weight should be checked by an inland warden, who has the proper entry forms. In remote areas the fish may be weighed and the catch certified by two disinterested persons, then shown to a warden at the angler's convenience. (Some Maine sporting goods stores can provide application cards.)

Minimum weights to qualify for the club are:

Landlocked salmon	6 pounds
Brown trout	6 pounds
Brook trout	4 pounds
Largemouth bass	7 pounds
Smallmouth bass	5 pounds
Pickerel	4 pounds
Lake trout	15 pounds
Atlantic salmon	12 pounds
White perch	2 pounds

Only one patch per species is issued during any calendar year.

WATERWAY MARKERS

The following are descriptions of common Maine freshwater navigation markers:

SOLID BLACK Keep to the left when traveling upstream.

SOLID RED Keep to the right when traveling upstream. (Black and red markers are often used in pairs to indicate narrow channels, and boats should travel between them.)

BLACK AND WHITE VERTICALLY STRIPED Pass by, close on either side.

WHITE WITH BLACK TOP Pass by the north or east to stay in safe water.

WHITE WITH RED TOP Pass to the south or west.

RED AND WHITE VERTICALLY STRIPED Obstruction from the nearest shore extending to the marker. Pass on the outside.

DIAMOND SHAPE Danger. A diamond shape with a cross in the middle means, keep out of the area. A diamond shape with a circle in the middle indicates restrictions in the area, such as a boating speed limit.

SQUARE OR RECTANGULAR SHAPE The marker's information or directions are within the square.

WHITE WITH A SINGLE BLUE BAND A mooring buoy.

ALTERNATE WHITE AND ORANGE FLOATS An organized swimming beach.

RED AND YELLOW ROUND MARKERS A ski slalom course.

WHITE WITH HORIZONTAL BANDS A permanent race course.

RED FLAG WITH DIAGONAL WHITE STRIPE A skin-diver or scuba diver in the area.

YELLOW WITH BLACK VERTICAL STRIPES A sea-plane landing area.

WHITE FLOAT A bait trap float.

Salmon

THE FISHES OF MAINE
LANDLOCKED SALMON
(Salmo salar sebago)

Possibly the most prized game fish in Maine, the landlocked salmon is considered to be identical to the famed Atlantic salmon by ichthyologists. Originally, landlocks were found only in four Maine drainages -- the St. Croix, Union, Presumpscot, and Penobscot Rivers. Now this species has been introduced to waters all over Maine and the world. The current world's record landlock, 22½ pounds, was caught in Sebago Lake in 1907. A handsome, silvery fish which feeds heavily on smelt, the landlocked salmon thrives best in large, deep, cold lakes. While occasional whoppers are taken, the average Maine salmon weighs about two pounds when caught. A 14-inch landlock is about three years old. Spawning takes place in gravel sections of swift-flowing streams, usually in the month of November; however, spawning migrations often occur weeks earlier.

Lake Trout

LAKE TROUT
(Salvelinus namaycush)

Called togue in Maine, the lake trout is the heavy-weight among the state's coldwater game fish, often reaching 20 pounds -- although a 7- or 8-pounder is considered a good catch. This is a bottom-dwelling fish, found in the deep sections of coldwater lakes. The exception is during spawning season, usually in November, when togue move into the shallows to spawn among the rocks. Lake trout have the classic body form of trout and range in color from silver to almost red, depending on their habitat. While lake trout are sometimes found on the surface at ice-out, they are usually fished down deep, with trolling the favorite method (using lead core lines or down-riggers to keep a lure or bait near bottom). The lake trout has a world-wide distribution wherever deep, cold lakes are found.

Brown Trout

BROWN TROUT
(Salmo trutta)

Brown trout are not native to America, and were introduced from Europe. But the brown trout is becoming an increasingly important game fish in Maine because of its ability to thrive in less-than-ideal water conditions. This is probably the hardest-to-catch fish in Maine, since brown trout are wary, often growing to sizes exceeding 10 pounds in lakes and ponds. Their coloration varies widely with the water they are in; when they share a lake with landlocked salmon, it often takes a biologist to tell the two fish apart, so similar is their appearance. One attractive feature of browns up to 3 or 4 pounds is their willingness to feed on surface insects, so they are prime fly rod targets. Browns are active night feeders. They spawn in late fall or early winter in feeder streams or coarse rubble near shore.

Brook Trout

BROOK TROUT
(Salvelinus fontinalis)

Maine has the best population of wild brook trout in the eastern United States. Commonly called the squaretail or brookie, this colorful game fish has red spots surrounded by blue rings on its sides, dark wavy lines on its greenish back, reddish lower fins edged with white, and a milky-white belly. A Maine brook trout weighing over 5 pounds is a real trophy, and most fish caught probably weigh less than a pound. While good wild populations do exist, fishing pressure is heavy for brookies, and they are well stocked in many of Maine's smaller lakes and ponds. Brookies are easily caught, taking bait and almost any lure. Requiring very high quality water, these fish do not compete well with other species. Brook trout spawn in the fall, in the gravel sections of streams.

Blueback Trout (Sunapee Trout has similar appearance)

SUNAPEE TROUT
(Salvelinus aureolus)

This fish is also called the golden trout, and some scientists consider it just a color variation of the blueback trout. Sunapees take their name from Sunapee Lake in New Hampshire, where they were originally found. In Maine, sunapees were discovered at first only in Floods Pond, Bangor, but they have been stocked in other Maine waters since. A small fish (a 5-year-old Sunapee would be only 15 inches long), the Sunapee has much the same habits as the lake trout, living in the depths and spawning in shoreline rocky areas in late fall.

BLUEBACK TROUT
(Salvelinus oquassa)

This a small, slender trout with a steel grey coloration on the back, fading to silver on the belly. Scientists believe that bluebacks may actually be a landlocked form of the Arctic char. Once there were huge numbers of blueback trout in the Rangeley lakes, but by the 1930's they had become extinct in those waters. Bluebacks exist in relatively

few Maine waters today, preferring deep, cold water -- although they feed on the surface in early spring and in the fall. They are stream spawners, and make their annual migrations during the middle of October. Fishing with worms is probably the most effective way to catch them.

Whitefish

WHITEFISH
(Coreogonus clupeaformis, Prosopium cylindraceum)

Two varieties of whitefish are found in Maine. The lake whitefish (*Coregonus clupeaformis*) is the species most likely to be encountered by the angler. These are satiny white, with a green cast to the back. Lake whitefish have weak mouths, but are sometimes taken on flies intended for trout. The fish are most frequently caught through the ice, by using bits of fish or small jigs. Often weighing three of four pounds, they spawn on shoals or in streams in early November. The round whitefish (*Prosopium cylindraceum*), seldom caught by anglers, is an important food fish for lake trout. Whitefish spawn in late fall at the mouths of streams, and are primarily plankton eaters.

Smelt

SMELT
(Osmerus mordax)

The freshwater Maine smelt is a small, thin, silvery fish with an odor like cucumbers. Smelt are deep dwellers in cold, clear lakes and an important food source for salmon and lake trout. In some lakes they are actively fished for with tiny hooks and bits of worm or fish, both in open water and ice seasons. They are also netted during their spawning runs up streams. These runs usually take place just as ice-out begins, most often at night. Smelt feed on insects and tiny fish. In some Maine lakes smelt never grow bigger than four or five inches ("pin" smelt). In other waters they grow to 14 inches ("jack" smelt).

SUCKERS
(Catostomus commersoni, Catastomus catastomus, Erimyzon oblongus)

Three species of suckers are found in Maine. While all are abundant and good to eat, they are hardly

White Sucker

ever fished for, although some are taken by spearing during spring spawning runs on streams. The white sucker (*Catastomus commersoni*) is the most abundant. This bottom feeder (like all suckers) has a vacuum-like mouth which sucks up material, through which the fish sifts for small animals. Small suckers are a prime forage fish for game fish. The longnose sucker (*Catastomus catastomus*) is quite similar to the white sucker, and it is doubtful that the average person could tell them apart. (All suckers tend to be brownish on the back and white on the belly). The longnose sucker is found in deeper, colder parts of lakes than the white sucker. The creek chubsucker (*Erimyzon oblongus*) spawns at lake outlets in late May and early June. These are the least common and smallest of the Maine suckers, measuring up to 12 inches and less than a pound, compared to the five pounds white suckers sometimes attain. Suckers are occasionally caught on earthworms.

Pickerel

PICKEREL
(Esox niger)

The chain pickerel is the only member of the pike family found in Maine, and it is widespread. Sometimes described as a "water wolf," this slender fish with its mouthful of sharp teeth usually lies motionless in weedy shallows, waiting for a bait fish to swim by. With chain-like markings on their sides, pickerel appear either greenish or brassy in color, depending on the water they are living in. Pickerel spawn in the spring in shallow water shortly after ice-out and dwell in the shallows, where they feed on fish, frogs, and just about any other small creatures they can catch.

Hornpout

HORNPOUT
(Ictalurus nebulosis)

Outside Maine, this fish is called a brown bullhead

or catfish. Hornpout are found in the weedy and muddy sections of lakes. These big-mouthed bottom feeders have barbels or "whiskers" which help them to locate their food in the dark, when they are most active. Hornpout are best caught by using worms; watch out for the sharp spines on the fins which can give a very painful wound if the fish is not handled with care. Hornpout are brown to black on their backs and white to yellow on the belly. Sometimes hornpout as long as 15 inches are caught, but a 12-incher is a good length for this fine-eating fish.

Cusk

CUSK
(Lota lota)

The cusk (as it is known in Maine) is the only freshwater member of the codfish family, and it greatly resembles the saltwater codfish – even to having a single whisker (barbel) on its chin. Elsewhere known as the burbot, the cusk is a deepwater fish which spawns in winter underneath the ice, and is most often fished for through the ice and at night. A small minnow or piece of fish left on bottom serves as effective bait. A five-pound cusk is a big one, and a 15-pounder is the state record.

White Perch

WHITE PERCH
(Morone americana)

The white perch is actually a member of the sea bass family, more closely related to the striped bass than any freshwater fish. This is a schooling species, sometimes found in huge numbers in Maine lakes. Big white perch weigh a pound or more, but many Maine lakes have stunted populations which seldom grow to eight inches. White perch are most active at dawn and dusk, when they feed on the surface and can be taken on dry flies or surface lures. The rest of the time, a worm or small minnow fished near bottom is most productive. This fish is excellent, though bony, eating; many white perch are taken by whole families who fish the streams during spring spawning runs, shortly after ice-out. A two-pound white perch is bragging-size.

Yellow Perch

YELLOW PERCH
(Perca flavenscans)

The yellow perch is probably cursed more often than any other fish in Maine. Fishery biologists find it very challenging to trout and salmon populations because it tends to compete for the food and the spawn of these fish. Anglers don't like yellow perch because they are often small in big lakes and wormy when taken in weedy ponds. However, this fish has an excellent flesh for eating, and is easily caught on bait and small lures. Basically a bottom feeder, it is almost never taken on the surface. A ten-year-old yellow perch would weigh about a pound. (Most are smaller than that.) Spawning takes place in spring around the shoreline. Yellow perch have spiny fins, and are yellow with darker bars down the sides.

Smallmouth Bass

SMALLMOUTH BASS
(Micropterus dolomieui)

A fish of rocky shorelines, the smallmouth bass is often called "old bronzeback" because of its coloration. To tell a smallmouth from a largemouth bass, look at the upper lip -- that of the former never extends beyond a line drawn vertically through the eye. The best fishing for smallmouth is during the early part of June when they are on their spawning beds. These circular spots of cleared sand, about three feet wide, are found in four to 10 feet of water. The males guard the nest and will fertilize the eggs of several females on the same nest. This is a powerful fish, known for its leaping ability. The Grand Lake area of Washington County is nationally famous for its smallmouth bass fishing, although the fish is found all over Maine (with the exception of Aroostook County). A two-pound smallmouth is a good fish, and a five-pounder is exceptional.

LARGEMOUTH BASS
(Micropterus salmoides)

The largemouth bass, also called the black bass, is growing in popularity in the southern third of

Maine, where it inhabits almost every sizeable lake and pond. The largemouth is found in warmer water than the smallmouth and is not as fond of rocky areas, often invading weedy shores. These fish are most often found near structures such as logs, ledges, and wharves. Their spawning habits are similar to those of the smallmouth bass, and

Largemouth Bass

June is the best time to fish for them. They bite well throughout the season, but in mid-summer fishing after dark or early in the morning is most productive. All kinds of lures and flies catch bass, and minnows are good bait. Rubber worms are a favorite lure. This strong fish is much given to spectacular, head-shaking leaps. A seven-pound largemouth bass is bragging-size.

Black Crappie

BLACK CRAPPIE
(Pomoxis nigromaculatus)

The black crappie exists in Maine only as a mistake! Accidentally introduced into both Sebago and Sebasticook Lakes, this fish has since been found in several smaller waters in the state. The crappie is a member of the sunfish family, and is basically a minnow feeder. Its habits are much like those of a largemouth bass, and it will be found in the same places. They sometimes reach three pounds, but a two-pounder would be big in Maine. Crappies are also called calico bass because of the black and white markings on their sides.

Redbreast Sunfish

SUNFISH
(Lepomis auritus, Lepomis gibbosus)

Two kinds of sunfish are commonly found in Maine lakes and ponds, with a third (the green sunfish) existing in some waters. The redbreast sunfish (*Lepomis auritus*) is a little fellow which rarely exceeds six inches. As the name implies, these fish have a red breast area. Like all sunfish, they have flattened sides and spiny fins. The redbreast is often

Pumpkinseed Sunfish

found mixed in with the pumpkinseed sunfish (*Lepomis gibbosus*) in the weedy shallows where both fish are found. Both species nest in early summer, clearing depressions in sandy bottom areas in shallow water. The males can often be seen standing guard over the nests until the eggs hatch. Sunfish are a great kid's fish, since they are not shy and will nibble at a hook until caught. Though small and bony, sunfish are tasty.

OTHERS

A number of other fishes commonly found in Maine are seldom caught or hold little interest for anglers. Among these is the eel, an unusual fish in that it lives in fresh water and spawns in salt. Maine eels, when fully grown at three or four feet, spawn in the Sargasso Sea. Alewives are foot-long, silvery fish which, to spawn, enter lakes with streams leading to the sea. Although these are commercially valuable, alewives are seldom caught on hook and line. The sea lamprey is an eel-like parasite which lives by sucking blood from other fish. To spawn, lampreys often enter some lakes with streams leading to the sea. The banded killifish is often called a minnow in Maine, although the small fish isn't, in fact, a minnow. Killifish get to be three or four inches long, and are often used as bait. The swamp darter is the smallest freshwater fish in Maine, seldom exceeding 2½ inches. It looks somewhat like a perch. The freshwater sculpin is another small fish, brownish and mottled, which inhabits deep lakes. And, four species of sticklebacks -- slender little fish with sharp spines on their backs -- are found in Maine.

MINNOWS

The following are some of the species of minnows found in Maine lakes and ponds: Longnose dace, blacknose dace, lake chub, fallfish, creek chub, pearl dace, finescale dace, northern redbelly dace, golden shiner, fathead minnow, common shiner, blacknose shiner, bridle shiner.

Allagash Lake

T7 R14, T8 R14
Piscataquis County, Maine Atlas Map 55, D-3

Area: 4,260 acres. *Maximum depth:* 89 feet.
Fishes: Brook trout, lake trout, lake whitefish, round whitefish, white sucker, longnose sucker, cusk.

SCALE OF MILES

0   5

Tenths of Mile

N

Allagash Lake is part of the Allagash Wilderness Waterway. It is accessible only by foot or portage, being closed to aircraft and motorized transportation. Due to tight bag limits and minimum length restrictions, the lake holds large togue and brook trout. There also is an abundant supply of whitefish. Water below the 30-foot level is cold and well-oxygenated even in the heat of summer. The surrounding area is hilly and covered with northern forest trees. The best fishing is from June 1 to July 4 and during the month of September. Mid-May sees the ice cleared. For information about the Allagash Wilderness Waterway, contact: Maine Parks and Recreation Bureau, State House, Augusta, Maine.

Map 1

Androscoggin Lake

Leeds, Wayne
Androscoggin and Kennebec Counties
Maine Atlas Map 12, C-1

Area: 3,826 acres. *Maximum depth:* 38 feet.
Fishes: Smallmouth bass, largemouth bass, white perch, yellow perch, chain pickerel, hornpout, smelt, eel, white sucker, cusk, pumpkinseed sunfish.

N

North Leeds

Androscoggin Lake has such a good reputation as both a large-mouth and smallmouth pond that a number of fishing tournaments have been held there. Ice-out can be expected April 20. The best fishing months are June, July and September. The lake is surrounded by low hills covered with hardwoods, and the shoreline is heavily developed.

Leeds

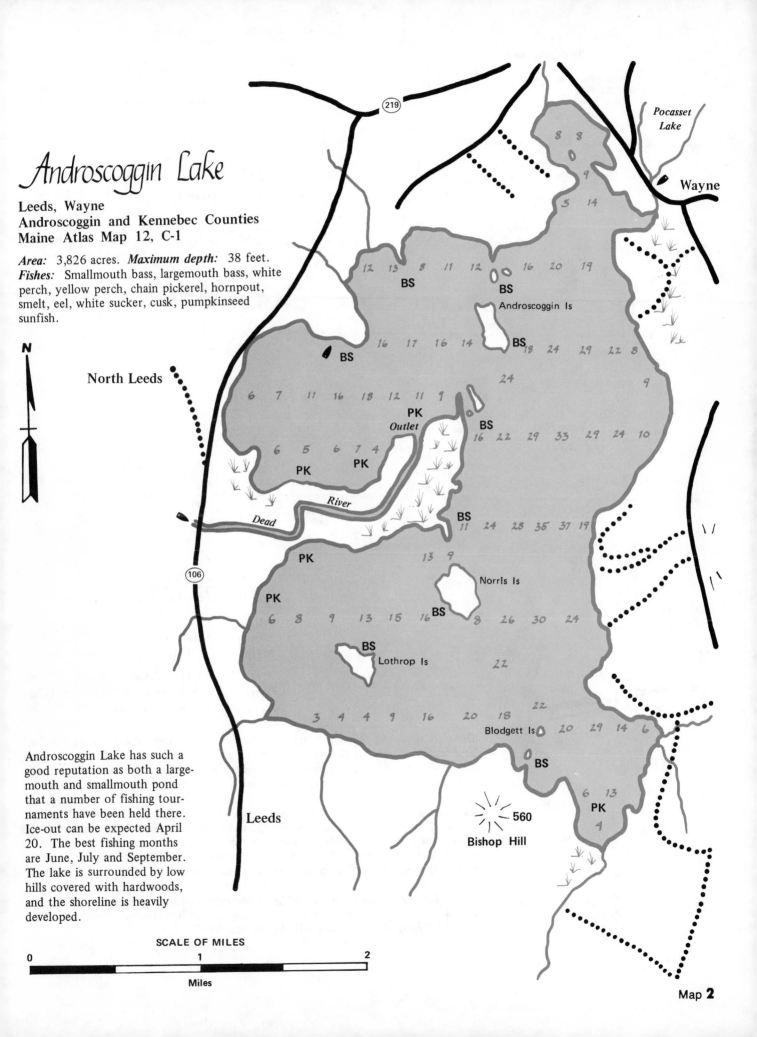

Pocasset Lake

Wayne

219

106

BS
BS
Androscoggin Is
BS

BS

PK
Outlet

PK
PK
PK

River
Dead

BS

PK

PK

Norris Is
BS

BS
Lothrop Is

Blodgett Is
BS

560
Bishop Hill

PK

SCALE OF MILES

0   1   2

Miles

Map **2**

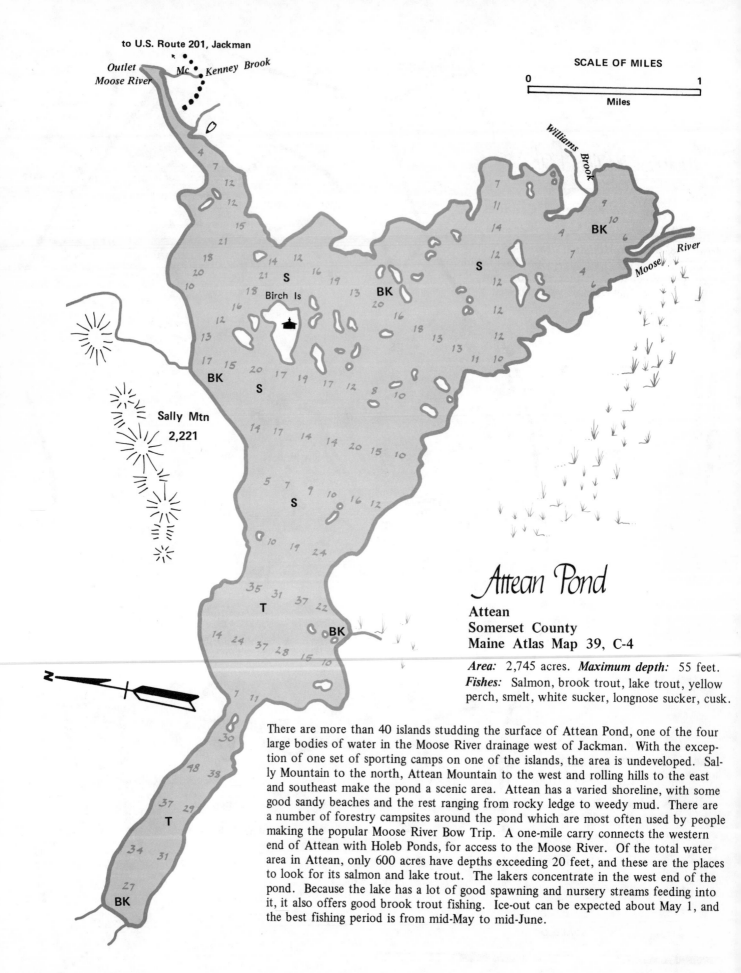

to U.S. Route 201, Jackman

Outlet
Moose River Mc Kenney Brook

Williams Brook

SCALE OF MILES

0   1

Miles

BK

Moose   River

Birch Is

S

BK

S

S

BK

Sally Mtn
2,221

S

T

BK

N

T

BK

Attean Pond

Attean
Somerset County
Maine Atlas Map 39, C-4

Area: 2,745 acres. *Maximum depth:* 55 feet.
Fishes: Salmon, brook trout, lake trout, yellow
perch, smelt, white sucker, longnose sucker, cusk.

There are more than 40 islands studding the surface of Attean Pond, one of the four
large bodies of water in the Moose River drainage west of Jackman. With the exception of one set of sporting camps on one of the islands, the area is undeveloped. Sally Mountain to the north, Attean Mountain to the west and rolling hills to the east
and southeast make the pond a scenic area. Attean has a varied shoreline, with some
good sandy beaches and the rest ranging from rocky ledge to weedy mud. There are
a number of forestry campsites around the pond which are most often used by people
making the popular Moose River Bow Trip. A one-mile carry connects the western
end of Attean with Holeb Ponds, for access to the Moose River. Of the total water
area in Attean, only 600 acres have depths exceeding 20 feet, and these are the places
to look for its salmon and lake trout. The lakers concentrate in the west end of the
pond. Because the lake has a lot of good spawning and nursery streams feeding into
it, it also offers good brook trout fishing. Ice-out can be expected about May 1, and
the best fishing period is from mid-May to mid-June.

Map **3**

Auburn Lake

Auburn
Androscoggin County, Maine Atlas Map 11, E-4

Area: 2,260 acres. *Maximum depth:* 118 feet.
Fishes: Salmon, brook trout, brown trout, lake trout, smallmouth bass, white perch, yellow perch, pickerel, hornpout, eel, smelt, white sucker, pumpkinseed sunfish.

As it is a public water supply, Auburn Lake is closed to swimming, and this tends to keep summer activity to a low level. This lake has a reputation as a producer of big lake trout. As the ice starts to clear in April, a run of smelts goes up the stream which passes under the road to North Auburn. Lake trout and an occasional salmon follow, giving even shoreside anglers a chance to catch the normally depth-loving togue. The preferred bait for this action is a live smelt. After ice-out (about April 20) the lakers will move to deep water again. Fishing is best from April to June. The surrounding land is hilly and largely covered with pines. Much of the shoreline is owned by the water company, and has been left forested.

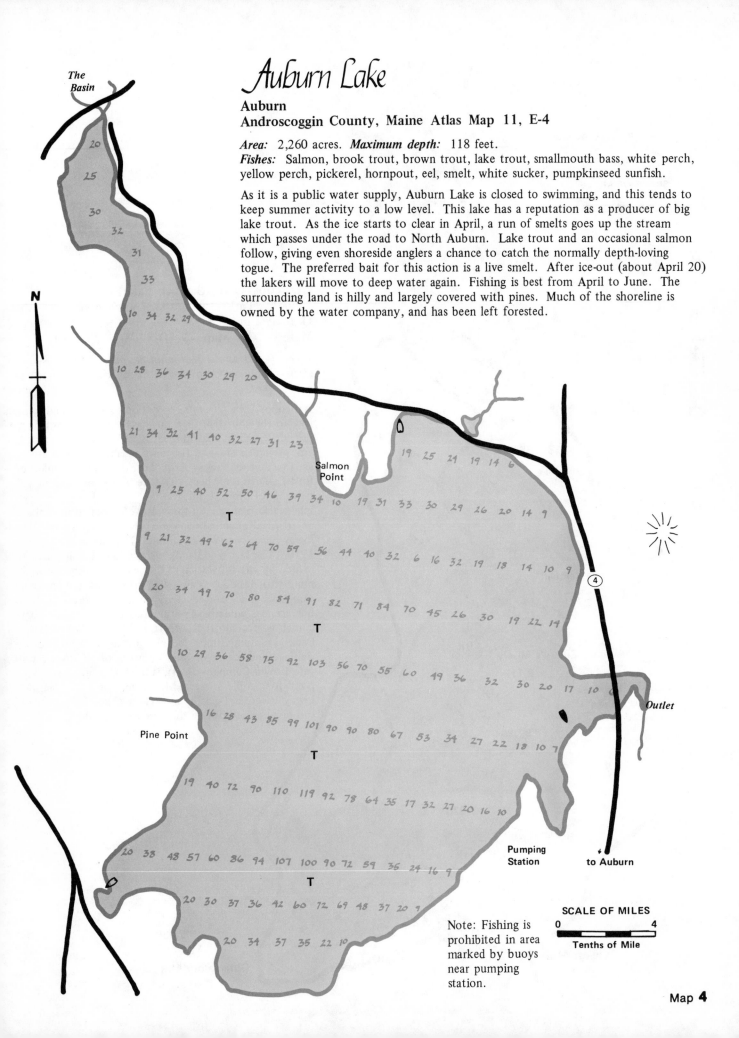

The Basin

N

Salmon Point

Pine Point

Outlet

Pumping Station

to Auburn

Note: Fishing is prohibited in area marked by buoys near pumping station.

SCALE OF MILES
0   4
Tenths of Mile

Map **4**

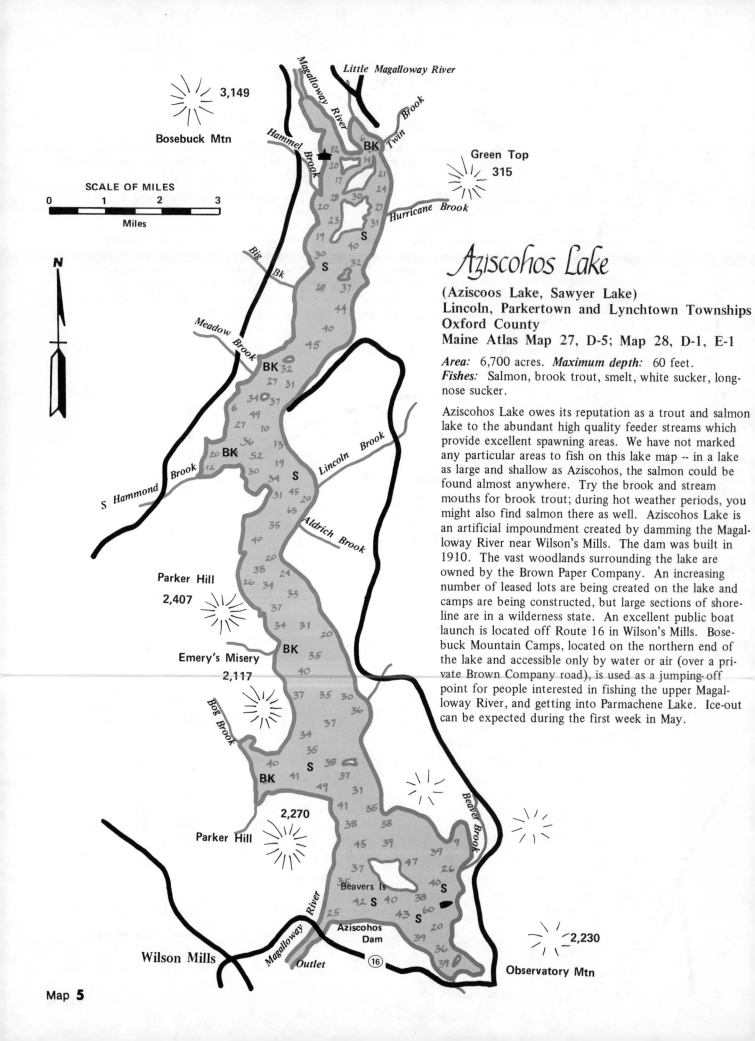

3,149

Bosebuck Mtn

Green Top
315

Aziscohos Lake

(Aziscoos Lake, Sawyer Lake)
Lincoln, Parkertown and Lynchtown Townships
Oxford County
Maine Atlas Map 27, D-5; Map 28, D-1, E-1

Area: 6,700 acres. *Maximum depth:* 60 feet.
Fishes: Salmon, brook trout, smelt, white sucker, long-nose sucker.

Aziscohos Lake owes its reputation as a trout and salmon lake to the abundant high quality feeder streams which provide excellent spawning areas. We have not marked any particular areas to fish on this lake map -- in a lake as large and shallow as Aziscohos, the salmon could be found almost anywhere. Try the brook and stream mouths for brook trout; during hot weather periods, you might also find salmon there as well. Aziscohos Lake is an artificial impoundment created by damming the Magalloway River near Wilson's Mills. The dam was built in 1910. The vast woodlands surrounding the lake are owned by the Brown Paper Company. An increasing number of leased lots are being created on the lake and camps are being constructed, but large sections of shoreline are in a wilderness state. An excellent public boat launch is located off Route 16 in Wilson's Mills. Bosebuck Mountain Camps, located on the northern end of the lake and accessible only by water or air (over a private Brown Company road), is used as a jumping-off point for people interested in fishing the upper Magalloway River, and getting into Parmachene Lake. Ice-out can be expected during the first week in May.

Parker Hill
2,407

Emery's Misery
2,117

2,270

Parker Hill

2,230

Observatory Mtn

Wilson Mills

SCALE OF MILES

0   1   2   3

Miles

N

Map **5**

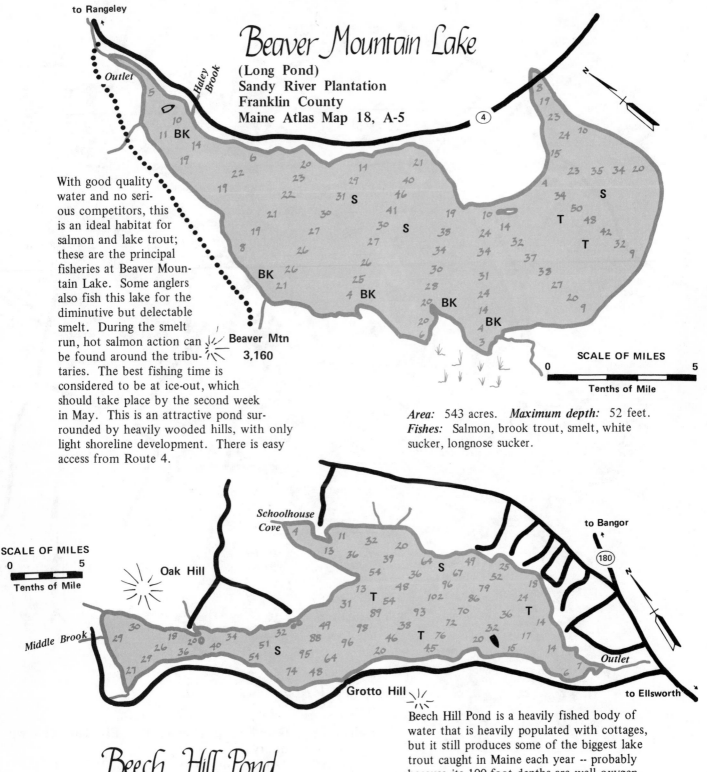

Beaver Mountain Lake

(Long Pond)
Sandy River Plantation
Franklin County
Maine Atlas Map 18, A-5

With good quality water and no serious competitors, this is an ideal habitat for salmon and lake trout; these are the principal fisheries at Beaver Mountain Lake. Some anglers also fish this lake for the diminutive but delectable smelt. During the smelt run, hot salmon action can be found around the tributaries. The best fishing time is considered to be at ice-out, which should take place by the second week in May. This is an attractive pond surrounded by heavily wooded hills, with only light shoreline development. There is easy access from Route 4.

SCALE OF MILES
0   5
Tenths of Mile

Area: 543 acres. *Maximum depth:* 52 feet.
Fishes: Salmon, brook trout, smelt, white sucker, longnose sucker.

Beaver Mtn
3,160

SCALE OF MILES
0   5
Tenths of Mile

Beech Hill Pond

Otis
Hancock County, Maine Atlas Map 24, C-1

Area: 1,351 acres. *Maximum depth:* 104 feet.
Fishes: Salmon, brook trout, lake trout, white perch, chain pickerel, smelt, eel, white sucker, pumpkinseed sunfish.

Beech Hill Pond is a heavily fished body of water that is heavily populated with cottages, but it still produces some of the biggest lake trout caught in Maine each year -- probably because its 100-foot depths are well oxygenated and have an abundant supply of smelt for forage. Located off Route 180 not far from the city of Ellsworth, it has a single privately owned boat launch site. Fishing remains good from ice-out to mid-July, and this is also a popular ice fishing lake. Ice-out averages around April 17.

Map 6

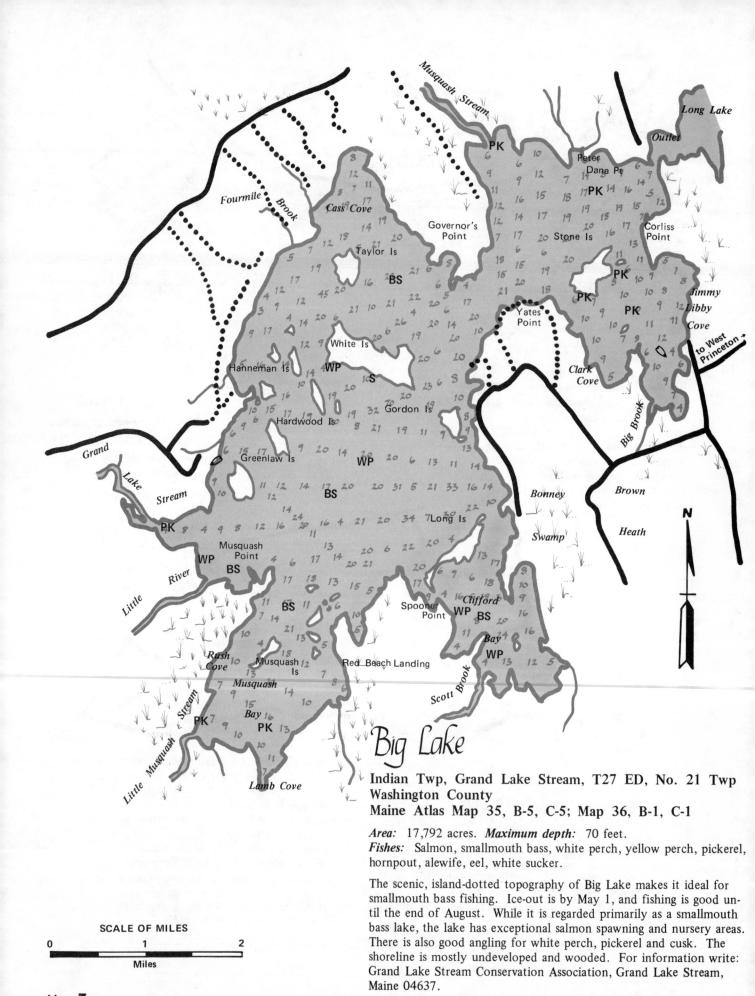

Big Lake

Indian Twp, Grand Lake Stream, T27 ED, No. 21 Twp
Washington County
Maine Atlas Map 35, B-5, C-5; Map 36, B-1, C-1

Area: 17,792 acres. *Maximum depth:* 70 feet.
Fishes: Salmon, smallmouth bass, white perch, yellow perch, pickerel, hornpout, alewife, eel, white sucker.

The scenic, island-dotted topography of Big Lake makes it ideal for smallmouth bass fishing. Ice-out is by May 1, and fishing is good until the end of August. While it is regarded primarily as a smallmouth bass lake, the lake has exceptional salmon spawning and nursery areas. There is also good angling for white perch, pickerel and cusk. The shoreline is mostly undeveloped and wooded. For information write: Grand Lake Stream Conservation Association, Grand Lake Stream, Maine 04637.

SCALE OF MILES

0   1   2

Miles

Map **7**

Biscay Pond

Bremen, Bristol, Damariscotta
Lincoln County, Maine Atlas Map 7, B-4

Area: 253 acres. *Maximum depth:* 61 feet.
Fishes: Brown trout, smallmouth bass, white perch, yellow perch, pickerel, hornpout, smelt, alewife, eel, white sucker, pumpkinseed sunfish.

Best known for its brown trout, Biscay also offers good fishing for smallmouth bass. It has the best quality water in the Pemaquid River chain. A good population of smelt and alewives keeps the brown trout colorful and fat. This lake is heavily fished in April and May; being so close to the coast, ice goes out early, usually between April 5 and 10. After the opening rush, browns can still be caught in the deep brown water down the middle of the pond. The fishing is fair for moderate-size bass. The shoreline is about 60 percent developed, fairly flat with woods and some fields on the southeastern shore.

SCALE OF MILES

0   1

Miles

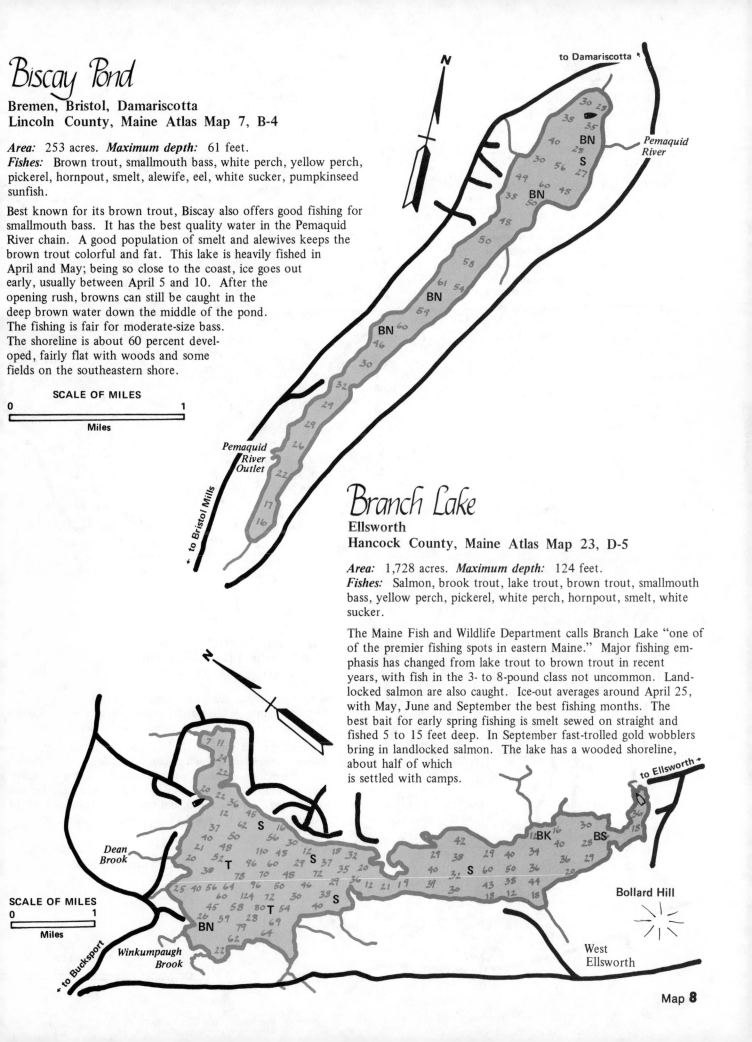

Branch Lake

Ellsworth
Hancock County, Maine Atlas Map 23, D-5

Area: 1,728 acres. *Maximum depth:* 124 feet.
Fishes: Salmon, brook trout, lake trout, brown trout, smallmouth bass, yellow perch, pickerel, white perch, hornpout, smelt, white sucker.

The Maine Fish and Wildlife Department calls Branch Lake "one of of the premier fishing spots in eastern Maine." Major fishing emphasis has changed from lake trout to brown trout in recent years, with fish in the 3- to 8-pound class not uncommon. Landlocked salmon are also caught. Ice-out averages around April 25, with May, June and September the best fishing months. The best bait for early spring fishing is smelt sewed on straight and fished 5 to 15 feet deep. In September fast-trolled gold wobblers bring in landlocked salmon. The lake has a wooded shoreline, about half of which is settled with camps.

SCALE OF MILES

0   1

Miles

Map **8**

Brassua Lake

T1 R1 NBKP, T1 R2 NBKP,
T2 R1 NBKP, T2 R2 NBKP
Rockwood Strip
Somerset County
Maine Atlas Map 40, A-4, B-4

Area: 8,979 acres. *Maximum depth:* 65 feet.
Fishes: Salmon, brook trout, smelt, white
sucker, longnose sucker, cusk.

Part of the headwaters of the Kennebec
River and flowing into Moosehead Lake
via the Moose River, Brassua is a flowed
lake with a drawdown potential of 30 feet.
Brook trout are the main attraction, with
salmon second. Best fishing is in the
spring and fall; ice-out averages at May 15.
The surrounding area is wooded and hilly,
and there are some excellent vistas.

SCALE OF MILES

0   4

Fifths of Mile

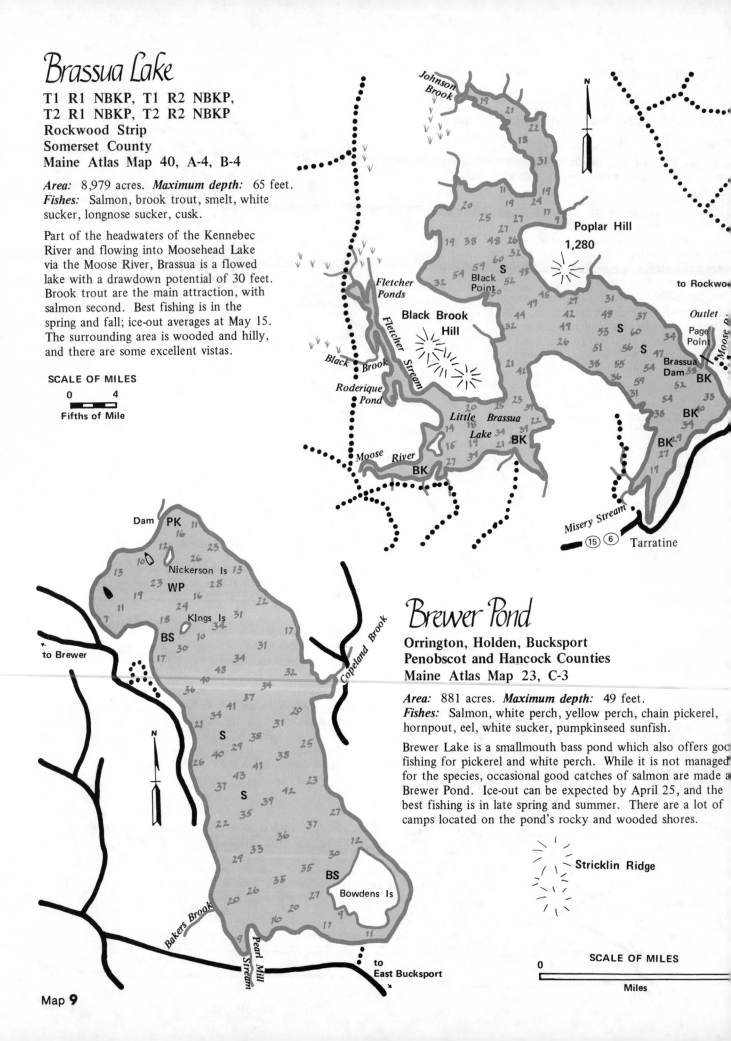

Brewer Pond

Orrington, Holden, Bucksport
Penobscot and Hancock Counties
Maine Atlas Map 23, C-3

Area: 881 acres. *Maximum depth:* 49 feet.
Fishes: Salmon, white perch, yellow perch, chain pickerel,
hornpout, eel, white sucker, pumpkinseed sunfish.

Brewer Lake is a smallmouth bass pond which also offers goo
fishing for pickerel and white perch. While it is not managed
for the species, occasional good catches of salmon are made a
Brewer Pond. Ice-out can be expected by April 25, and the
best fishing is in late spring and summer. There are a lot of
camps located on the pond's rocky and wooded shores.

Stricklin Ridge

SCALE OF MILES

0

Miles

Map 9

Cathance Lake

Cooper and No. 14 Townships
Washington County, Maine Atlas Map 36, E-4

Area: 2,905 acres. *Maximum depth:* 75 feet.
Fishes: Salmon, brook trout, smallmouth bass, yellow perch, smelt, alewife, eel, white sucker, pickerel.

Cathance Lake is one of the more popular Washington County landlocked salmon lakes. A pretty spot, with its highly irregular shoreline, this lake is located adjacent to Route 191 about 15 miles north of East Machias. The western shoreline, which follows Route 191, is lined with camps, but most of the lake's shoreline is undeveloped. The boat access site is at a small store on Route 191. While the lake has a lot of cold, well-oxygenated water, its population of salmon is erratic -- there are some good years, some bad. The lake's tributaries do produce some good brook trout, and trout in the one to two pound class are taken each winter. Cathance is a good place to go fishing for pickerel. The fishing at Cathance remains good from ice-out through September. The average ice-out date is April 29.

Caucomgomoc Lake

T6 R15, T6 R14, T7 R15, T7 R14
Piscataquis County, Maine Atlas Map 55, E-2

Area: 5,081 acres. *Maximum depth:* 79 feet.
Fishes: Salmon, brook trout, lake trout, white perch, yellow perch, hornpout, whitefish, white sucker, longnose sucker.

Caucomgomoc Lake offers superlative scenery from surrounding evergreen-clad hills. With only about four camps located on its shores, this remote pond can be reached over good quality paper company roads. Some very large salmon are taken from this lake, with trolling concentrated at the deep hole off Hubbard Point. Ice-out can be expected by May 15, and June is the best fishing month. For a change of pace, try crossing the lake and fishing the fast water of Caucomgomoc Stream for landlocks and trout. The lake also offers some jumbo-sized white perch.

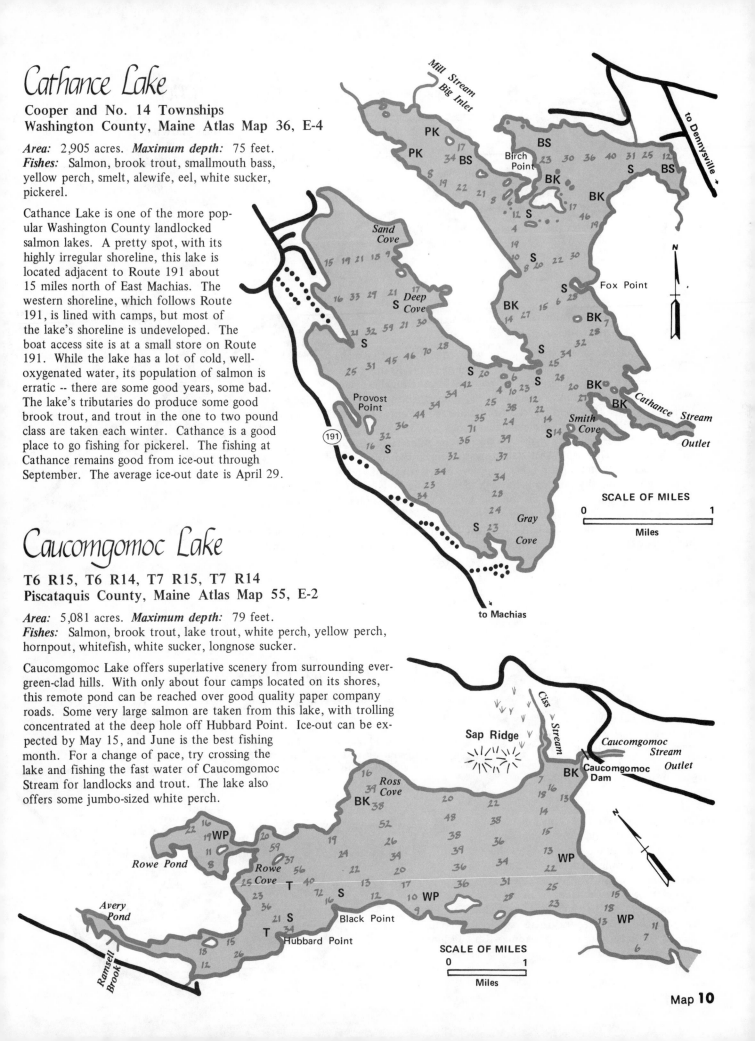

Map **10**

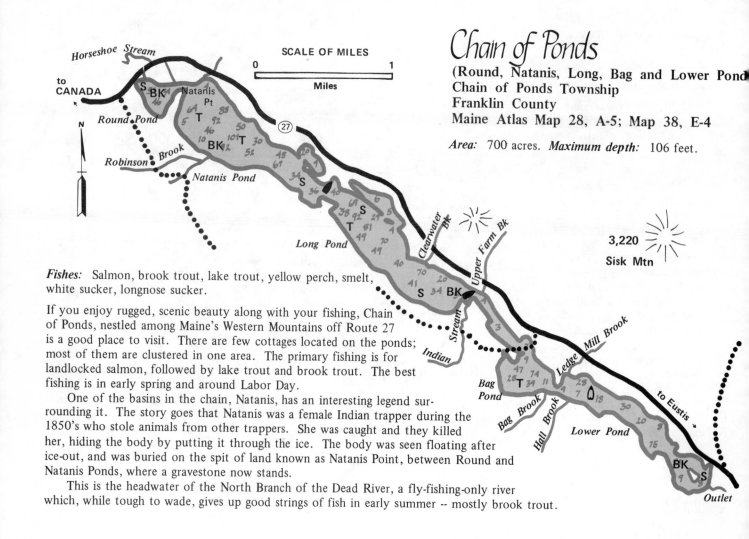

Chain of Ponds

(Round, Natanis, Long, Bag and Lower Pond)
Chain of Ponds Township
Franklin County
Maine Atlas Map 28, A-5; Map 38, E-4

Area: 700 acres. *Maximum depth:* 106 feet.

3,220
Sisk Mtn

Fishes: Salmon, brook trout, lake trout, yellow perch, smelt, white sucker, longnose sucker.

If you enjoy rugged, scenic beauty along with your fishing, Chain of Ponds, nestled among Maine's Western Mountains off Route 27 is a good place to visit. There are few cottages located on the ponds; most of them are clustered in one area. The primary fishing is for landlocked salmon, followed by lake trout and brook trout. The best fishing is in early spring and around Labor Day.

One of the basins in the chain, Natanis, has an interesting legend surrounding it. The story goes that Natanis was a female Indian trapper during the 1850's who stole animals from other trappers. She was caught and they killed her, hiding the body by putting it through the ice. The body was seen floating after ice-out, and was buried on the spit of land known as Natanis Point, between Round and Natanis Ponds, where a gravestone now stands.

This is the headwater of the North Branch of the Dead River, a fly-fishing-only river which, while tough to wade, gives up good strings of fish in early summer -- mostly brook trout.

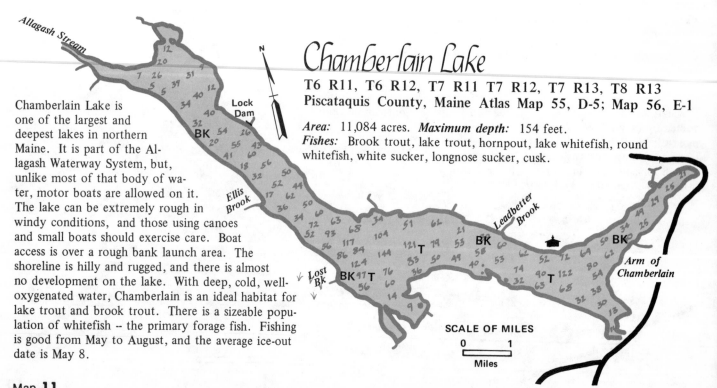

Chamberlain Lake

T6 R11, T6 R12, T7 R11 T7 R12, T7 R13, T8 R13
Piscataquis County, Maine Atlas Map 55, D-5; Map 56, E-1

Area: 11,084 acres. *Maximum depth:* 154 feet.
Fishes: Brook trout, lake trout, hornpout, lake whitefish, round whitefish, white sucker, longnose sucker, cusk.

Chamberlain Lake is one of the largest and deepest lakes in northern Maine. It is part of the Allagash Waterway System, but, unlike most of that body of water, motor boats are allowed on it. The lake can be extremely rough in windy conditions, and those using canoes and small boats should exercise care. Boat access is over a rough bank launch area. The shoreline is hilly and rugged, and there is almost no development on the lake. With deep, cold, well-oxygenated water, Chamberlain is an ideal habitat for lake trout and brook trout. There is a sizeable population of whitefish -- the primary forage fish. Fishing is good from May to August, and the average ice-out date is May 8.

Map 11

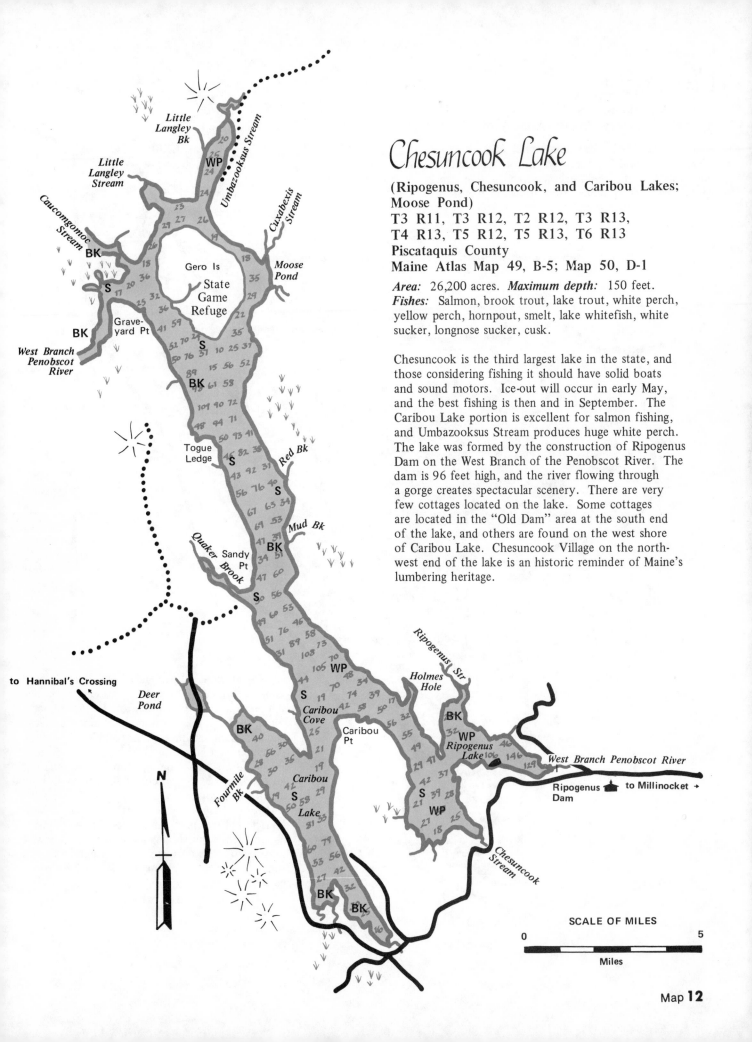

Chesuncook Lake

(Ripogenus, Chesuncook, and Caribou Lakes;
Moose Pond)
T3 R11, T3 R12, T2 R12, T3 R13,
T4 R13, T5 R12, T5 R13, T6 R13
Piscataquis County
Maine Atlas Map 49, B-5; Map 50, D-1

Area: 26,200 acres. *Maximum depth:* 150 feet.
Fishes: Salmon, brook trout, lake trout, white perch,
yellow perch, hornpout, smelt, lake whitefish, white
sucker, longnose sucker, cusk.

Chesuncook is the third largest lake in the state, and
those considering fishing it should have solid boats
and sound motors. Ice-out will occur in early May,
and the best fishing is then and in September. The
Caribou Lake portion is excellent for salmon fishing,
and Umbazooksus Stream produces huge white perch.
The lake was formed by the construction of Ripogenus
Dam on the West Branch of the Penobscot River. The
dam is 96 feet high, and the river flowing through
a gorge creates spectacular scenery. There are very
few cottages located on the lake. Some cottages
are located in the "Old Dam" area at the south end
of the lake, and others are found on the west shore
of Caribou Lake. Chesuncook Village on the northwest end of the lake is an historic reminder of Maine's
lumbering heritage.

SCALE OF MILES

0   5

Miles

Map **12**

China Lake

China, Vassalboro
Kennebec County, Maine Atlas Map 13, A-3

Area: 3,832 acres. *Maximum depth:* 85 feet.
Fishes: Salmon, lake trout, brown trout, smallmouth bass, largemouth bass, white perch, yellow perch, pickerel, smelt, eel, hornpout,
white sucker, pumpkinseed sunfish, redbreast sunfish.

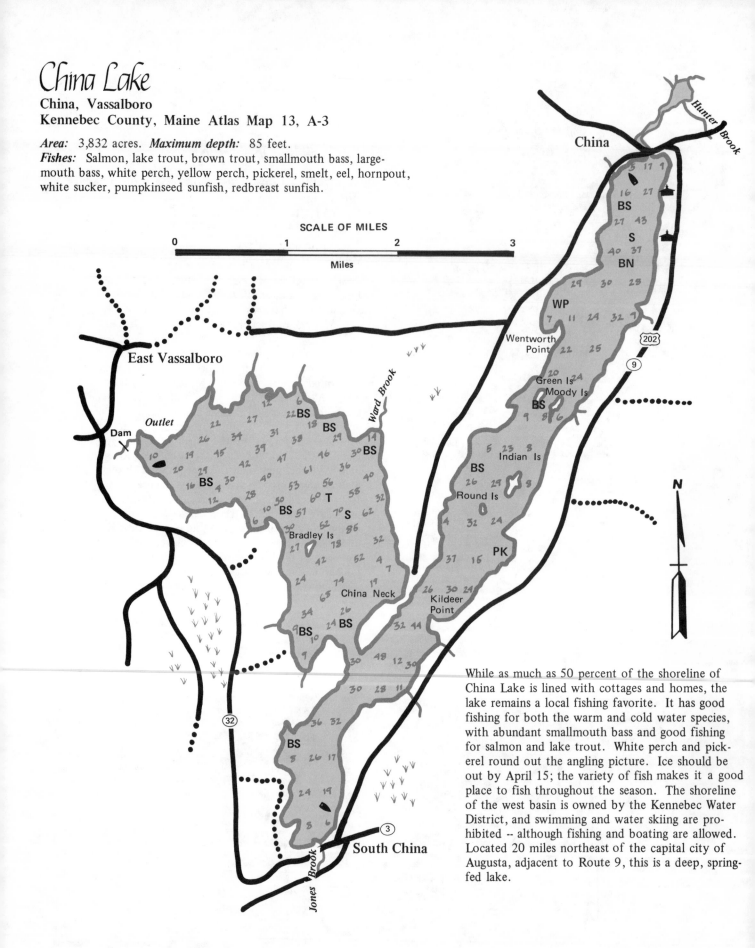

SCALE OF MILES

0   1   2   3

Miles

While as much as 50 percent of the shoreline of
China Lake is lined with cottages and homes, the
lake remains a local fishing favorite. It has good
fishing for both the warm and cold water species,
with abundant smallmouth bass and good fishing
for salmon and lake trout. White perch and pickerel round out the angling picture. Ice should be
out by April 15; the variety of fish makes it a good
place to fish throughout the season. The shoreline
of the west basin is owned by the Kennebec Water
District, and swimming and water skiing are prohibited -- although fishing and boating are allowed.
Located 20 miles northeast of the capital city of
Augusta, adjacent to Route 9, this is a deep, spring-
fed lake.

Map 13

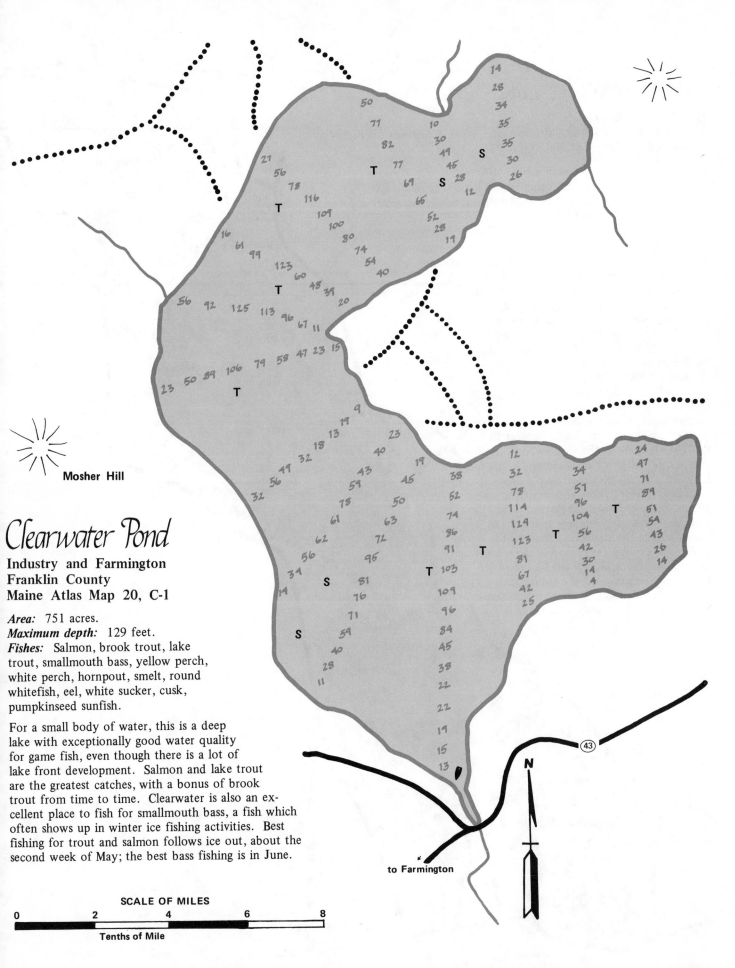

Clearwater Pond

Industry and Farmington
Franklin County
Maine Atlas Map 20, C-1

Area: 751 acres.
Maximum depth: 129 feet.
Fishes: Salmon, brook trout, lake
trout, smallmouth bass, yellow perch,
white perch, hornpout, smelt, round
whitefish, eel, white sucker, cusk,
pumpkinseed sunfish.

For a small body of water, this is a deep
lake with exceptionally good water quality
for game fish, even though there is a lot of
lake front development. Salmon and lake trout
are the greatest catches, with a bonus of brook
trout from time to time. Clearwater is also an excellent place to fish for smallmouth bass, a fish which
often shows up in winter ice fishing activities. Best
fishing for trout and salmon follows ice out, about the
second week of May; the best bass fishing is in June.

Mosher Hill

to Farmington

N

SCALE OF MILES

0   2   4   6   8

Tenths of Mile

Map **14**

Cobbosseecontee Lake

(Cobbossee Lake)
Manchester, Litchfield, Monmouth, West Gardiner, Winthrop
Kennebec County, Maine Atlas Map 12, C-4

Area: 4,950 acres. *Maximum depth:* 100 feet.
Fishes: Salmon, brook trout, smallmouth bass, largemouth bass, white perch, yellow perch, pickerel, hornpout, smelt, eel, white sucker, pumpkinseed sunfish, redbreast sunfish.

When national outdoor magazines publish articles about Maine's best largemouth bass waters, Cobbosseecontee Lake is always near the head of the list. But, while attention is focused on bass, many local residents have learned to use downriggers to locate surprising populations of brook trout and some landlocked salmon in the deep water sections of the lake. As an added bonus, large schools of white perch often feed on the surface at dawn and dusk, making for exciting topwater fishing. One of the reasons for a diversity of fish life in the lake is a wide variety of habitat, from deepwater shoals to extensive swamp areas. In mid-summer, you can expect to find algae blooms in the shallow portions of this rich lake, but the mid-summer fishing for bass and pickerel remains strong in drop-off areas around ledgy shore and about the numerous islands. Cobbosseecontee is a heavily used lake with many summer cottages and homes ringing the shoreline. Even so, the angler who gets up early, even in the prime summer months, will have the lake mostly to himself and may find the fishing action better than he expected. The average date for ice-out on Cobbosseecontee Lake is April 17.

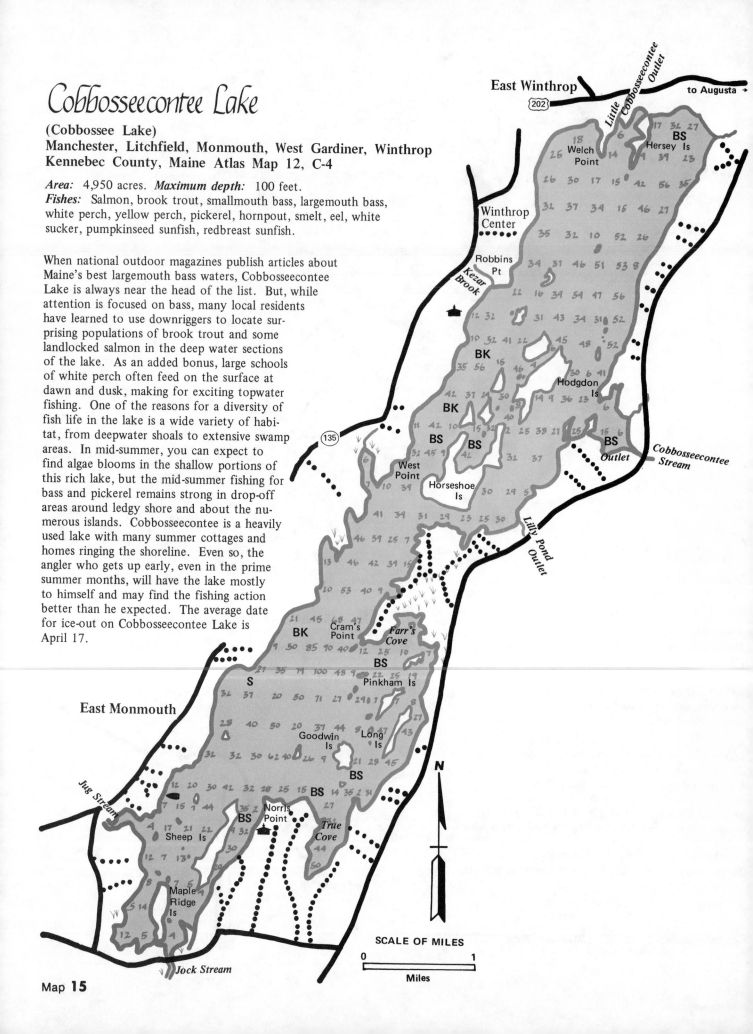

Map 15

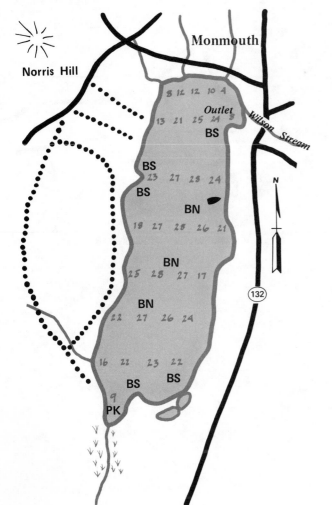

Cochnewagon Pond

Monmouth
Kennebec County, Maine Atlas Map 12, D-2

Area: 385 acres. *Maximum depth:* 28 feet.

Fishes: Brown trout, smallmouth bass, largemouth bass, white perch, yellow perch, pickerel, smelt, hornpout, eel, white sucker, pumpkinseed sunfish, yellowbelly sunfish.

Brown trout are the prime attraction at Cochnewagon. The fishing tends to be spotty, but trollers often catch large white perch, and this keeps interest up. Fishing for both species of bass can be excellent here, and some very big largemouths are present. October is a good time to fish for bass here, and you can be assured of little competition then. The terrain is hilly, with a lot of the shoreline developed with farms and residences. Ice should clear by April 20.

SCALE OF MILES

0   5

Tenths of Mile

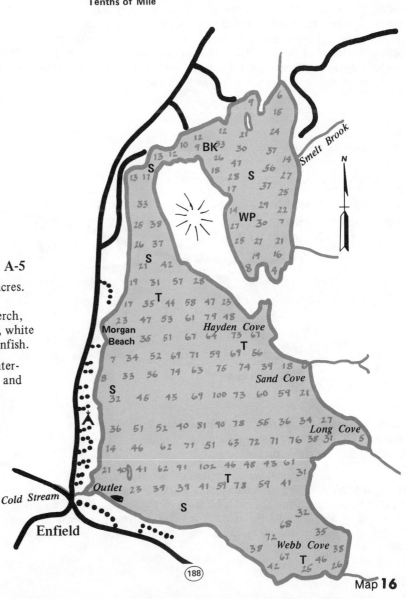

Cold Stream Pond

Enfield, Lincoln, Lowell
Penobscot County, Maine Atlas Map 33, A-5

Area: North basin 704 acres, south basin 2,924 acres.
Maximum depth: 104 feet.

Fishes: Salmon, brook trout, lake trout, white perch, yellow perch, chain pickerel, hornpout, smelt, eel, white sucker, cusk, pumpkinseed sunfish, yellowbelly sunfish.

Despite being a heavily used lake with a lot of water-skiing and swimming near cottages along the west and north shores, fishing is good at Cold Stream Pond for salmon and lake trout. Some very big togue are taken here every year. White perch and pickerel are abundant. Ice-out averages April 25, and the month of May offers the best fishing.

SCALE OF MILES

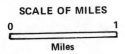

0   1

Miles

Map **16**

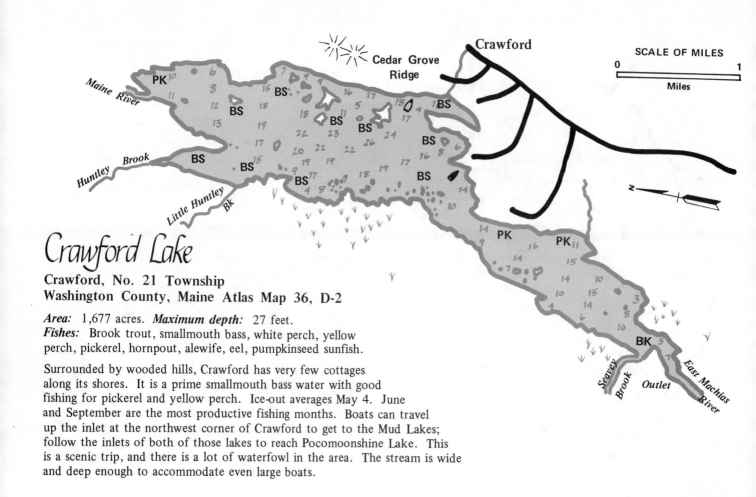

Crawford Lake

Crawford, No. 21 Township
Washington County, Maine Atlas Map 36, D-2

Area: 1,677 acres. *Maximum depth:* 27 feet.
Fishes: Brook trout, smallmouth bass, white perch, yellow
perch, pickerel, hornpout, alewife, eel, pumpkinseed sunfish.

Surrounded by wooded hills, Crawford has very few cottages
along its shores. It is a prime smallmouth bass water with good
fishing for pickerel and yellow perch. Ice-out averages May 4. June
and September are the most productive fishing months. Boats can travel
up the inlet at the northwest corner of Crawford to get to the Mud Lakes;
follow the inlets of both of those lakes to reach Pocomoonshine Lake. This
is a scenic trip, and there is a lot of waterfowl in the area. The stream is wide
and deep enough to accommodate even large boats.

Cross Lake

T16 R5, T17 R5
Aroostook County
Maine Atlas Map 68, D-2

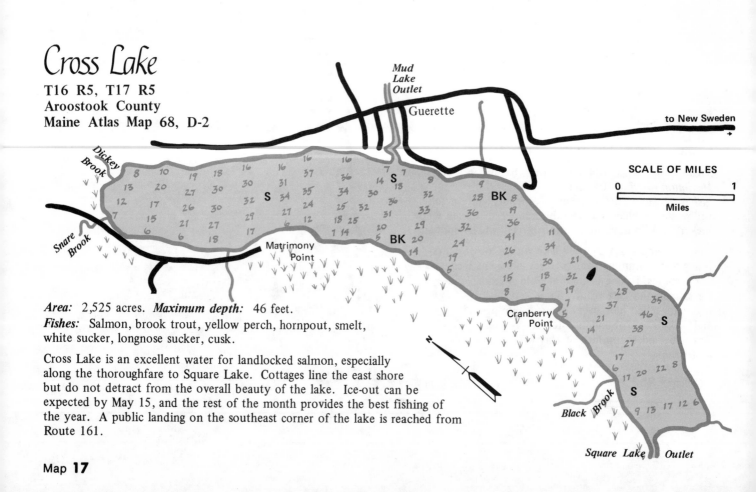

Area: 2,525 acres. *Maximum depth:* 46 feet.
Fishes: Salmon, brook trout, yellow perch, hornpout, smelt,
white sucker, longnose sucker, cusk.

Cross Lake is an excellent water for landlocked salmon, especially
along the thoroughfare to Square Lake. Cottages line the east shore
but do not detract from the overall beauty of the lake. Ice-out can be
expected by May 15, and the rest of the month provides the best fishing of
the year. A public landing on the southeast corner of the lake is reached from
Route 161.

Map 17

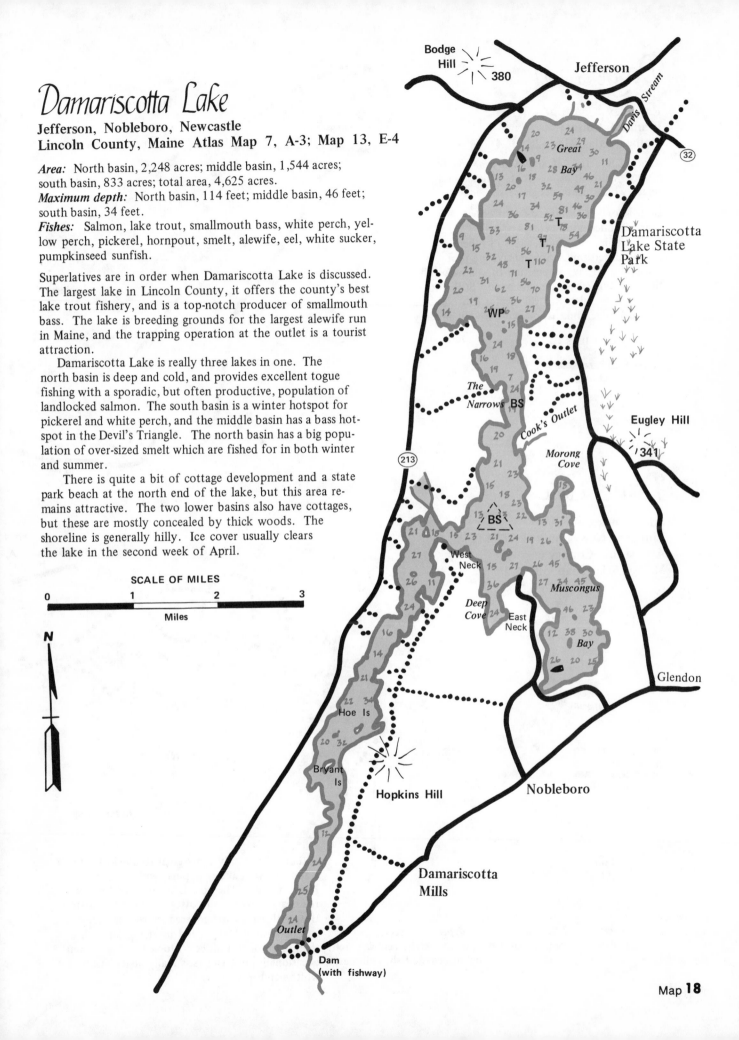

Damariscotta Lake

Jefferson, Nobleboro, Newcastle
Lincoln County, Maine Atlas Map 7, A-3; Map 13, E-4

Area: North basin, 2,248 acres; middle basin, 1,544 acres; south basin, 833 acres; total area, 4,625 acres.
Maximum depth: North basin, 114 feet; middle basin, 46 feet; south basin, 34 feet.
Fishes: Salmon, lake trout, smallmouth bass, white perch, yellow perch, pickerel, hornpout, smelt, alewife, eel, white sucker, pumpkinseed sunfish.

Superlatives are in order when Damariscotta Lake is discussed. The largest lake in Lincoln County, it offers the county's best lake trout fishery, and is a top-notch producer of smallmouth bass. The lake is breeding grounds for the largest alewife run in Maine, and the trapping operation at the outlet is a tourist attraction.

Damariscotta Lake is really three lakes in one. The north basin is deep and cold, and provides excellent togue fishing with a sporadic, but often productive, population of landlocked salmon. The south basin is a winter hotspot for pickerel and white perch, and the middle basin has a bass hotspot in the Devil's Triangle. The north basin has a big population of over-sized smelt which are fished for in both winter and summer.

There is quite a bit of cottage development and a state park beach at the north end of the lake, but this area remains attractive. The two lower basins also have cottages, but these are mostly concealed by thick woods. The shoreline is generally hilly. Ice cover usually clears the lake in the second week of April.

SCALE OF MILES

```
0          1          2          3
```
Miles

N

Map **18**

Dodge Pond

Rangeley
Franklin County
Maine Atlas Map 28, E-4

Area: 230 acres. *Maximum depth:* 51 feet.
Fishes: Salmon, brook trout, yellow perch, smelt, white sucker, longnose sucker.

Dodge Pond is an up-and-down fishery. Some years produce good catches of brook trout, others good catches of salmon, and still others not many fish of either kind. Apparently, the problem is caused by a heavy population of yellow perch, which thrive in this rather shallow pond. Still, the water quality is excellent for cold water fish. The best time to fish Dodge Pond is following ice-out in early May.

SCALE OF MILES

0   3

Tenths of Mile

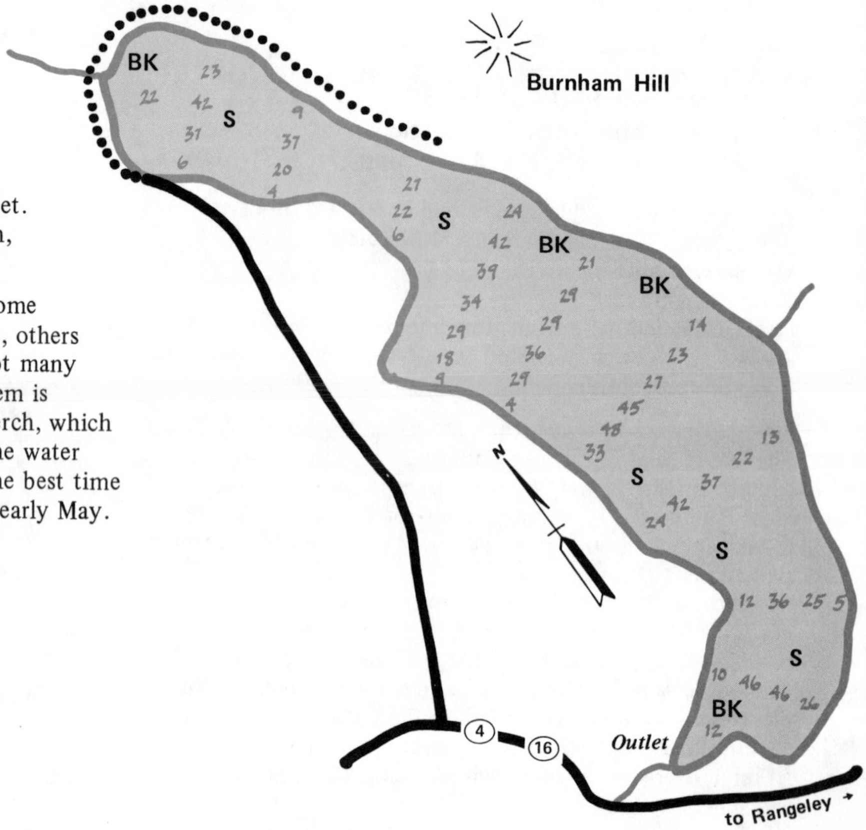

Burnham Hill

to Rangeley

Outlet

Drews Lake

(Meduxnekeag Lake)
Linneus, New Limerick, Oakfield
Aroostook County
Maine Atlas Map 53, A-1

to U.S. Route 2A,
Houlton

Baxter Brook

Bear Bk

Higgins Bk

Meduxnekeag Mill Stream

Bates Ridge

SCALE OF MILES

0   5

Tenths of Mile

Morrison Brook

Hunt Ridge

Area: 1,057 acres. *Maximum depth:* 49 feet.
Fishes: Salmon, brook trout, white perch, yellow perch, smelt, eel, white sucker, pumpkinseed sunfish, redbreast sunfish.

Although it is only a marginal landlocked salmon water, Drews Lake is popular with people in the Houlton area. The lake is surrounded by paved roads and year-round cottages, but still is attractive, with hardwood-covered shorelines. Ice-out will be around May 5, and most regulars fish it then or through the ice. Brook trout are taken occasionally, but Drews is really at its best as a white perch producer.

Map **19**

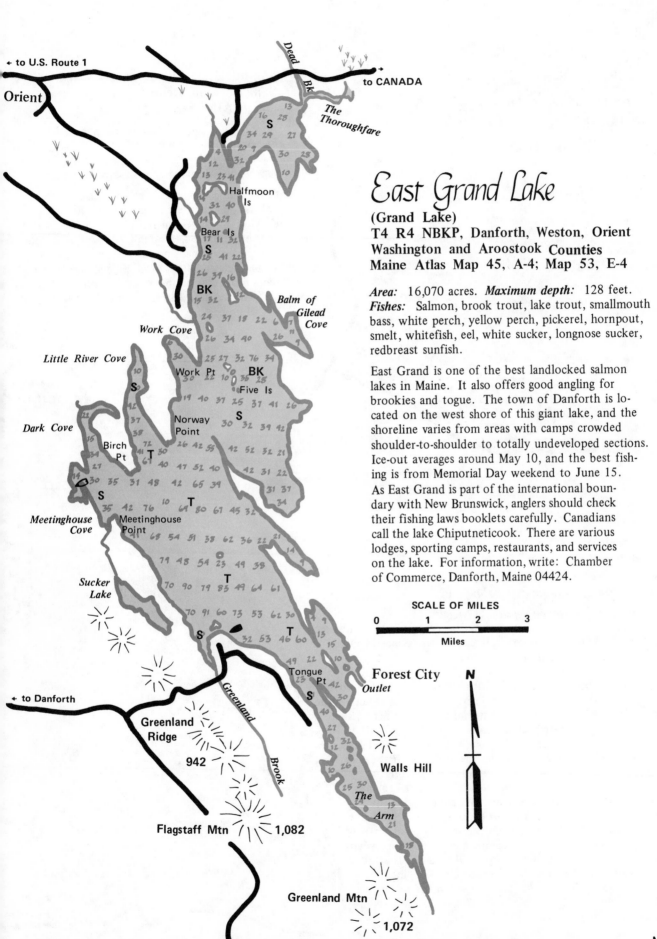

← to U.S. Route 1

Orient

Dead Bk

to CANADA

The Thoroughfare

Halfmoon Is

Bear Is

BK

Balm of Gilead Cove

Work Cove

Little River Cove

Work Pt

Five Is

Norway Point

Dark Cove

Birch Pt

Meetinghouse Cove

Meetinghouse Point

Sucker Lake

← to Danforth

Tongue Pt

Forest City
Outlet

Greenland Brook

Greenland Ridge

942

Flagstaff Mtn 1,082

Walls Hill

The Arm

N

Greenland Mtn

1,072

East Grand Lake

(Grand Lake)
T4 R4 NBKP, Danforth, Weston, Orient
Washington and Aroostook Counties
Maine Atlas Map 45, A-4; Map 53, E-4

Area: 16,070 acres. *Maximum depth:* 128 feet.
Fishes: Salmon, brook trout, lake trout, smallmouth
bass, white perch, yellow perch, pickerel, hornpout,
smelt, whitefish, eel, white sucker, longnose sucker,
redbreast sunfish.

East Grand is one of the best landlocked salmon
lakes in Maine. It also offers good angling for
brookies and togue. The town of Danforth is located on the west shore of this giant lake, and the
shoreline varies from areas with camps crowded
shoulder-to-shoulder to totally undeveloped sections.
Ice-out averages around May 10, and the best fishing is from Memorial Day weekend to June 15.
As East Grand is part of the international boun-
dary with New Brunswick, anglers should check
their fishing laws booklets carefully. Canadians
call the lake Chiputneticook. There are various
lodges, sporting camps, restaurants, and services
on the lake. For information, write: Chamber
of Commerce, Danforth, Maine 04424.

SCALE OF MILES

0   1   2   3

Miles

Map 20

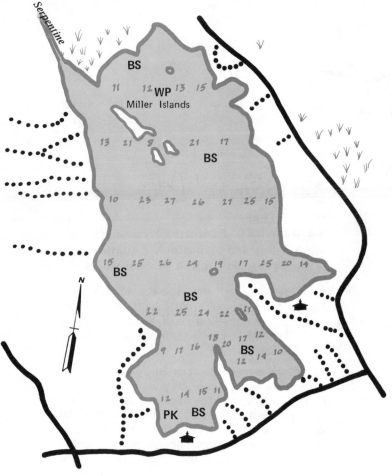

East Pond

(East Lake)
Smithfield, Oakland
Somerset and Kennebec Counties
Maine Atlas Map 20, D-5

Area: 1,705 acres. *Maximum depth:* 27 feet.
Fishes: Smallmouth bass, largemouth bass, white perch, yellow perch, pickerel, hornpout, eel, white sucker, pumpkinseed sunfish, brown trout.

Good fishing for both large and smallmouth black bass is found at East Pond, part of the Belgrade chain of lakes. The perch fishing can be excellent, and recent efforts to establish brown trout could add another dimension to the fishing here. Ice should be cleared by April 20, and June is the most productive month. The shoreline is hilly and wooded, and cottages cover about a third of the lake front.

SCALE OF MILES

0   1

Miles

Echo Lake

(Crotched Pond)
Fayette, Mt. Vernon, Readfield
Kennebec County, Maine Atlas Map 12, A-2

Area: 1,061 acres. *Maximum depth:* 117 feet.
Fishes: Salmon, lake trout, smallmouth bass, largemouth bass, white perch, yellow perch, chain pickerel, hornpout, smelt, eel, white sucker, cusk, pumpkinseed sunfish, redbreast sunfish.

To find Echo Lake, head down Route 41 from Readfield or Mt. Vernon. You are there when you come to the chimney -- a tall brick structure, the only remains of an old mill on the short stream connecting Echo Lake and Taylor Pond. A fine state boat launch site is located here. There is a fair amount of development on this lake, but its shores are heavily wooded and it remains attractive. The inlet is one of the first places to clear of ice in the spring, and it is often fished on opening day (April 1). Ice usually clears by the second week of April. The best fishing is in May and June for salmon and lake trout, and in the second and third weeks of June for the smallmouth bass which inhabit the rocky shorelines. There is a good chance you may spot a nesting osprey along this lake, and loons are common in early spring. What with many boys' and girls' summer camps on this lake, it is a busy place in mid-summer. There is a heavy smelt run up the inlet; while smelting is not allowed in the stream itself, boats anchored in the lake at night make good catches. Echo Lake is also a good place to ice fish at night for cusk.

Map **21**

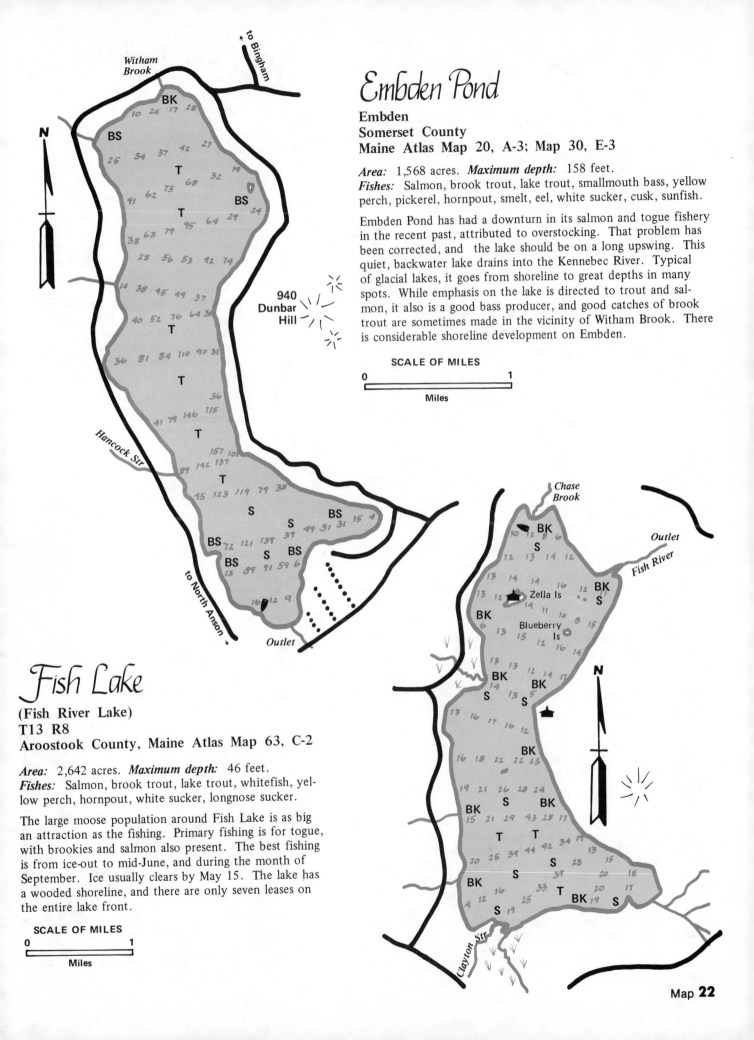

Embden Pond

Embden
Somerset County
Maine Atlas Map 20, A-3; Map 30, E-3

Area: 1,568 acres. *Maximum depth:* 158 feet.
Fishes: Salmon, brook trout, lake trout, smallmouth bass, yellow perch, pickerel, hornpout, smelt, eel, white sucker, cusk, sunfish.

Embden Pond has had a downturn in its salmon and togue fishery in the recent past, attributed to overstocking. That problem has been corrected, and the lake should be on a long upswing. This quiet, backwater lake drains into the Kennebec River. Typical of glacial lakes, it goes from shoreline to great depths in many spots. While emphasis on the lake is directed to trout and salmon, it also is a good bass producer, and good catches of brook trout are sometimes made in the vicinity of Witham Brook. There is considerable shoreline development on Embden.

SCALE OF MILES

0   1

Miles

Fish Lake

(Fish River Lake)
T13 R8
Aroostook County, Maine Atlas Map 63, C-2

Area: 2,642 acres. *Maximum depth:* 46 feet.
Fishes: Salmon, brook trout, lake trout, whitefish, yellow perch, hornpout, white sucker, longnose sucker.

The large moose population around Fish Lake is as big an attraction as the fishing. Primary fishing is for togue, with brookies and salmon also present. The best fishing is from ice-out to mid-June, and during the month of September. Ice usually clears by May 15. The lake has a wooded shoreline, and there are only seven leases on the entire lake front.

SCALE OF MILES

0   1

Miles

Map **22**

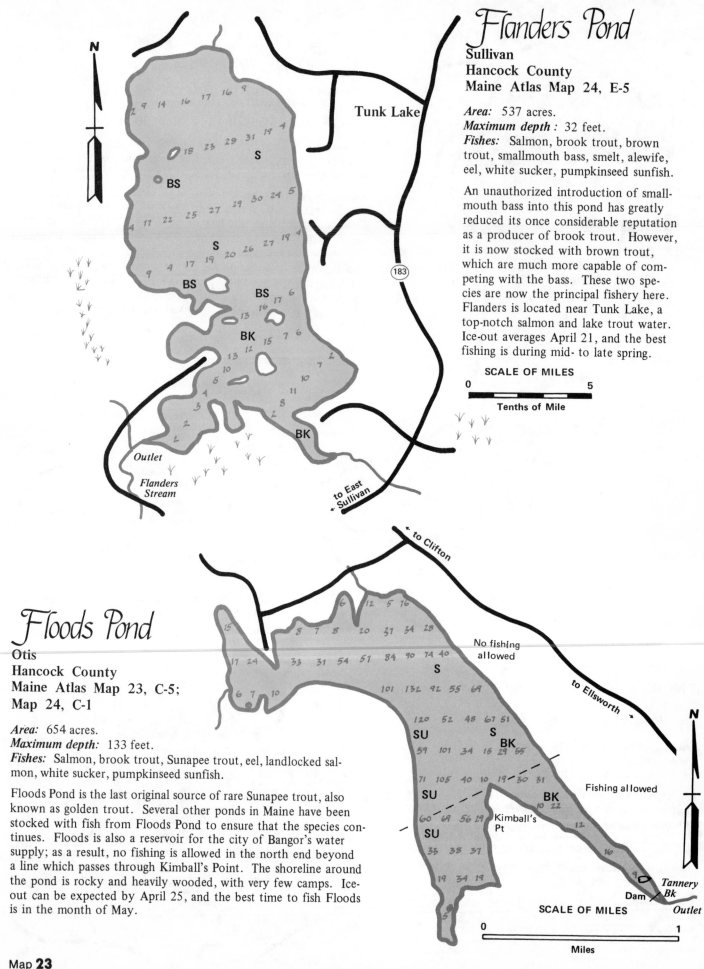

Flanders Pond

Sullivan
Hancock County
Maine Atlas Map 24, E-5

Area: 537 acres.
Maximum depth : 32 feet.
Fishes: Salmon, brook trout, brown trout, smallmouth bass, smelt, alewife, eel, white sucker, pumpkinseed sunfish.

An unauthorized introduction of smallmouth bass into this pond has greatly reduced its once considerable reputation as a producer of brook trout. However, it is now stocked with brown trout, which are much more capable of competing with the bass. These two species are now the principal fishery here. Flanders is located near Tunk Lake, a top-notch salmon and lake trout water. Ice-out averages April 21, and the best fishing is during mid- to late spring.

SCALE OF MILES

0   5

Tenths of Mile

Tunk Lake

183

to East
Sullivan

Outlet
Flanders
Stream

Floods Pond

Otis
Hancock County
Maine Atlas Map 23, C-5;
Map 24, C-1

Area: 654 acres.
Maximum depth: 133 feet.
Fishes: Salmon, brook trout, Sunapee trout, eel, landlocked salmon, white sucker, pumpkinseed sunfish.

Floods Pond is the last original source of rare Sunapee trout, also known as golden trout. Several other ponds in Maine have been stocked with fish from Floods Pond to ensure that the species continues. Floods is also a reservoir for the city of Bangor's water supply; as a result, no fishing is allowed in the north end beyond a line which passes through Kimball's Point. The shoreline around the pond is rocky and heavily wooded, with very few camps. Ice-out can be expected by April 25, and the best time to fish Floods is in the month of May.

to Clifton

No fishing
allowed

to Ellsworth

Fishing allowed

Kimball's
Pt

Tannery
Bk
Dam
Outlet

SCALE OF MILES

0   1

Miles

Map **23**

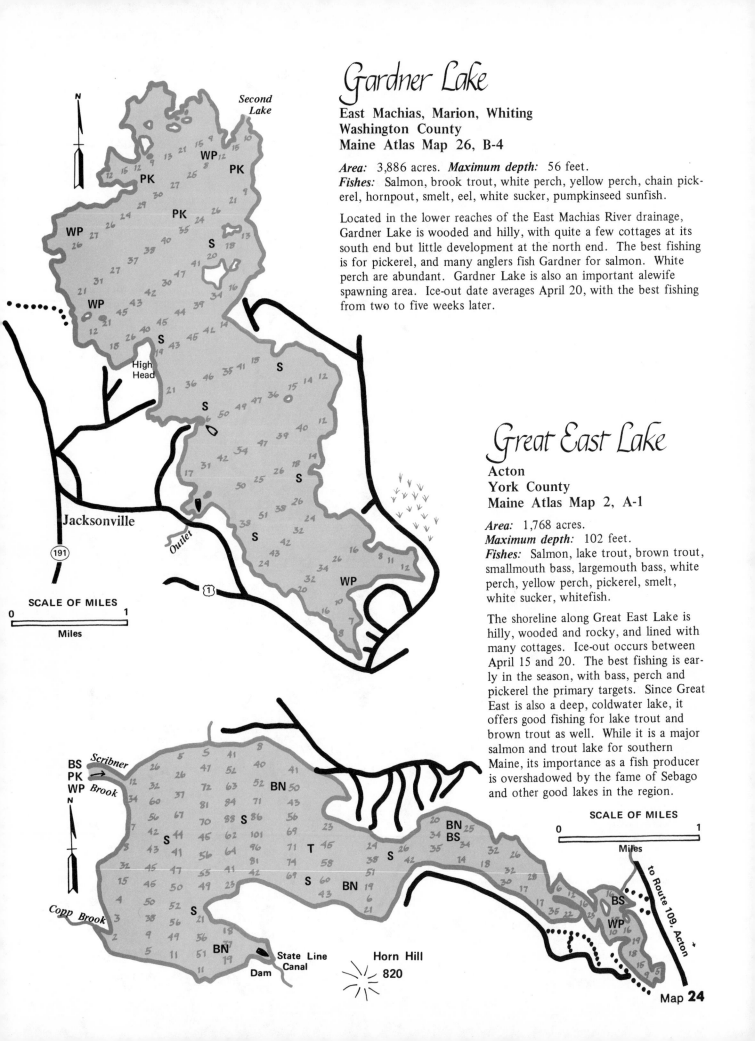

Gardner Lake

East Machias, Marion, Whiting
Washington County
Maine Atlas Map 26, B-4

Area: 3,886 acres. *Maximum depth:* 56 feet.
Fishes: Salmon, brook trout, white perch, yellow perch, chain pickerel, hornpout, smelt, eel, white sucker, pumpkinseed sunfish.

Located in the lower reaches of the East Machias River drainage, Gardner Lake is wooded and hilly, with quite a few cottages at its south end but little development at the north end. The best fishing is for pickerel, and many anglers fish Gardner for salmon. White perch are abundant. Gardner Lake is also an important alewife spawning area. Ice-out date averages April 20, with the best fishing from two to five weeks later.

Great East Lake

Acton
York County
Maine Atlas Map 2, A-1

Area: 1,768 acres.
Maximum depth: 102 feet.
Fishes: Salmon, lake trout, brown trout, smallmouth bass, largemouth bass, white perch, yellow perch, pickerel, smelt, white sucker, whitefish.

The shoreline along Great East Lake is hilly, wooded and rocky, and lined with many cottages. Ice-out occurs between April 15 and 20. The best fishing is early in the season, with bass, perch and pickerel the primary targets. Since Great East is also a deep, coldwater lake, it offers good fishing for lake trout and brown trout as well. While it is a major salmon and trout lake for southern Maine, its importance as a fish producer is overshadowed by the fame of Sebago and other good lakes in the region.

Map **24**

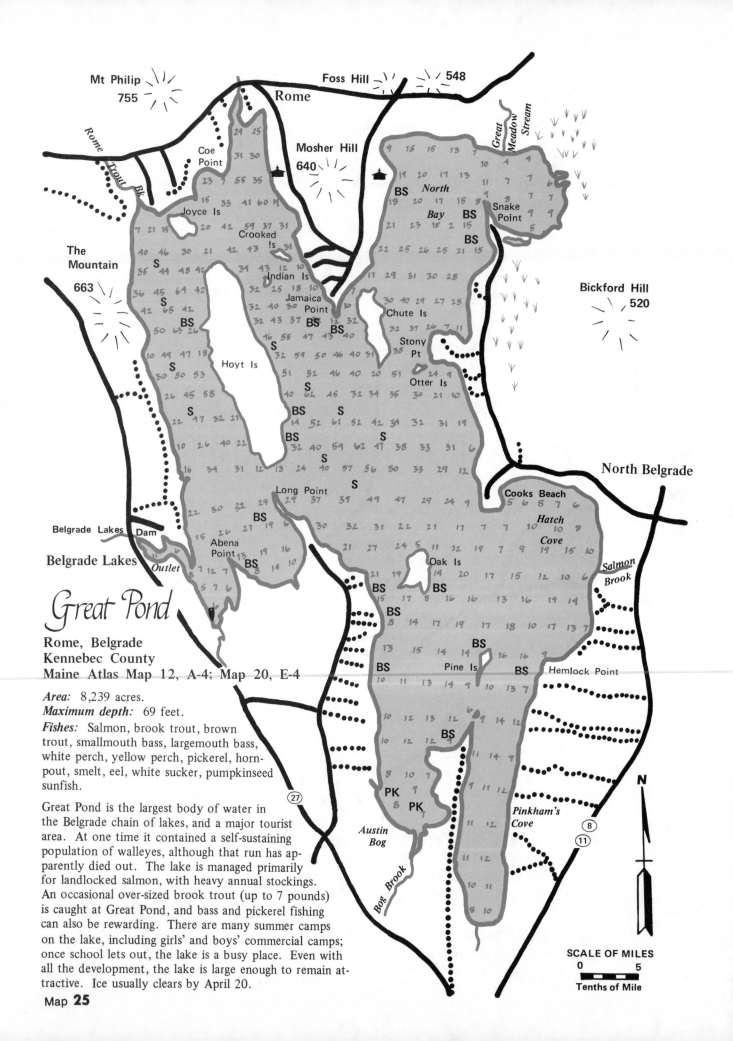

Mt Philip 755

Foss Hill 548

Rome

Mosher Hill 640

Rome Trout Bk

Coe Point

Joyce Is

Crooked Is

Indian Is

Jamaica Point

The Mountain 663

Hoyt Is

BS

BS

BS

BS

BS

BS

BS

Long Point

Abena Point

Belgrade Lakes Dam

Belgrade Lakes

Outlet

North Bay

Snake Point

BS

BS

Chute Is

Stony Pt

Otter Is

Bickford Hill 520

Cooks Beach

Hatch Cove

Oak Is

BS

BS

BS

BS

BS

Pine Is

Hemlock Point

BS

North Belgrade

Salmon Brook

Great Meadow Stream

PK

PK

Austin Bog

Bog Brook

Pinkham's Cove

Great Pond

Rome, Belgrade
Kennebec County
Maine Atlas Map 12, A-4; Map 20, E-4

Area: 8,239 acres.
Maximum depth: 69 feet.
Fishes: Salmon, brook trout, brown
trout, smallmouth bass, largemouth bass,
white perch, yellow perch, pickerel, hornpout, smelt, eel, white sucker, pumpkinseed
sunfish.

Great Pond is the largest body of water in
the Belgrade chain of lakes, and a major tourist
area. At one time it contained a self-sustaining
population of walleyes, although that run has apparently died out. The lake is managed primarily
for landlocked salmon, with heavy annual stockings.
An occasional over-sized brook trout (up to 7 pounds)
is caught at Great Pond, and bass and pickerel fishing
can also be rewarding. There are many summer camps
on the lake, including girls' and boys' commercial camps;
once school lets out, the lake is a busy place. Even with
all the development, the lake is large enough to remain attractive. Ice usually clears by April 20.

Map 25

N

SCALE OF MILES
0   5
Tenths of Mile

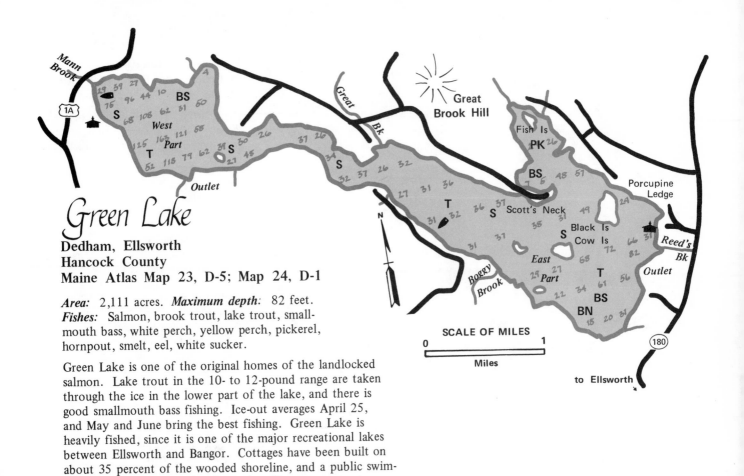

Green Lake

Dedham, Ellsworth
Hancock County
Maine Atlas Map 23, D-5; Map 24, D-1

Area: 2,111 acres. *Maximum depth:* 82 feet.
Fishes: Salmon, brook trout, lake trout, small-mouth bass, white perch, yellow perch, pickerel, hornpout, smelt, eel, white sucker.

Green Lake is one of the original homes of the landlocked salmon. Lake trout in the 10- to 12-pound range are taken through the ice in the lower part of the lake, and there is good smallmouth bass fishing. Ice-out averages April 25, and May and June bring the best fishing. Green Lake is heavily fished, since it is one of the major recreational lakes between Ellsworth and Bangor. Cottages have been built on about 35 percent of the wooded shoreline, and a public swimming beach (fee charged) is located at the extreme western end of the lake.

Hancock Pond

Denmark, Sebago Lake
Oxford and Cumberland Counties
Maine Atlas Map 4, B-3

Area: 858 acres. *Maximum depth:* 59 feet.
Fishes: Brown trout, smallmouth bass, largemouth bass, chain pickerel, yellow perch, hornpout, smelt.

Brown trout are the top attraction at Hancock Pond, and the best fishing for them is in the spring, with ice-out sometime in late April. Hancock is basically a shallow pond. The shoreline is flat and only moderately developed. As the weather warms and the brown trout fishing drops off, Hancock offers good fishing for both largemouth and smallmouth bass. Hancock is a winter favorite among smelt anglers.

SCALE OF MILES
0   1
Miles

1,030
Allen Mtn

Map **26**

Hatcase Pond

Dedham, Eddington
Hancock and Penobscot Counties
Maine Atlas Map 23, C-5

Area: 168 acres. *Maximum depth:* 77 feet.
Fishes: Salmon, brook trout, smallmouth bass, white perch, pickerel, smelt, eel, white sucker, sunfish.

Hatcase Pond is part of the City of Bangor's water supply. As a result, the extreme northern end near the pumping station is closed to fishing. While there is no public launch site, there is a launching site for carry-in canoes. There is no ice fishing on the pond; the trout limit has been reduced to two fish daily, with a 12-inch minimum, in order to create a trophy trout water. June is the best month to fish for trout. Smallmouth bass fishing is considered excellent at Hatcase during mid-spring, when the fish are on their spawning beds. The shoreline is rocky and heavily wooded, with only a few cottages. Ice-out occurs by April 25.

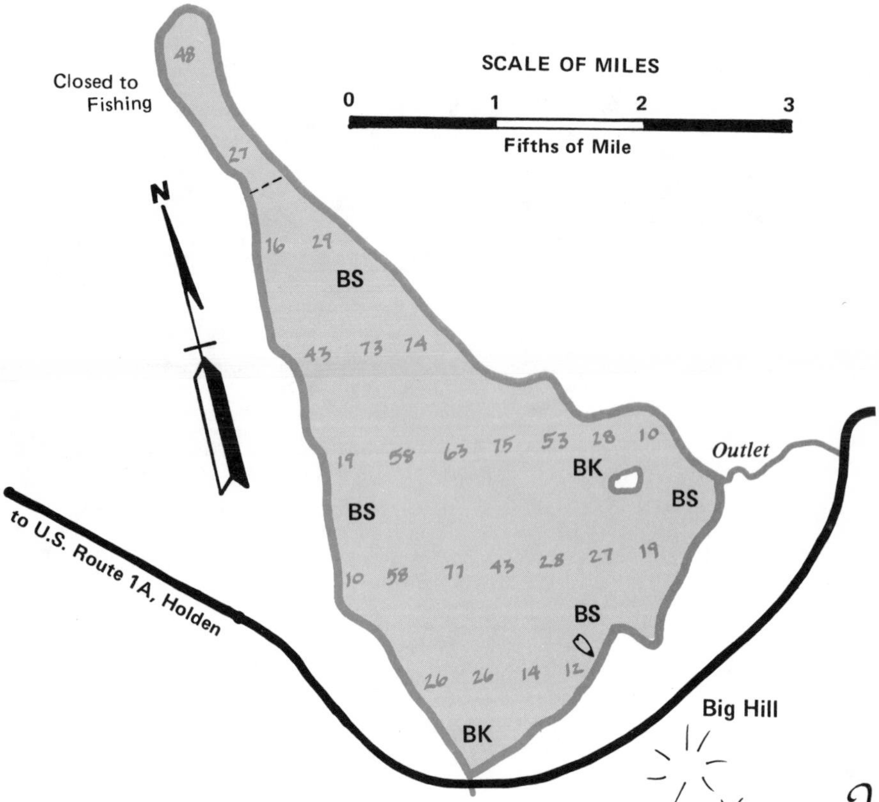

SCALE OF MILES
Fifths of Mile

Closed to Fishing

to U.S. Route 1A, Holden

Outlet

Big Hill

Hermon Pond

Hermon
Penobscot County
Maine Atlas Map 22, B-5

Area: 461 acres. *Maximum depth:* 17 feet.
Fishes: Smallmouth bass, white perch, yellow perch, pickerel, hornpout, eel, white sucker, pumpkinseed sunfish.

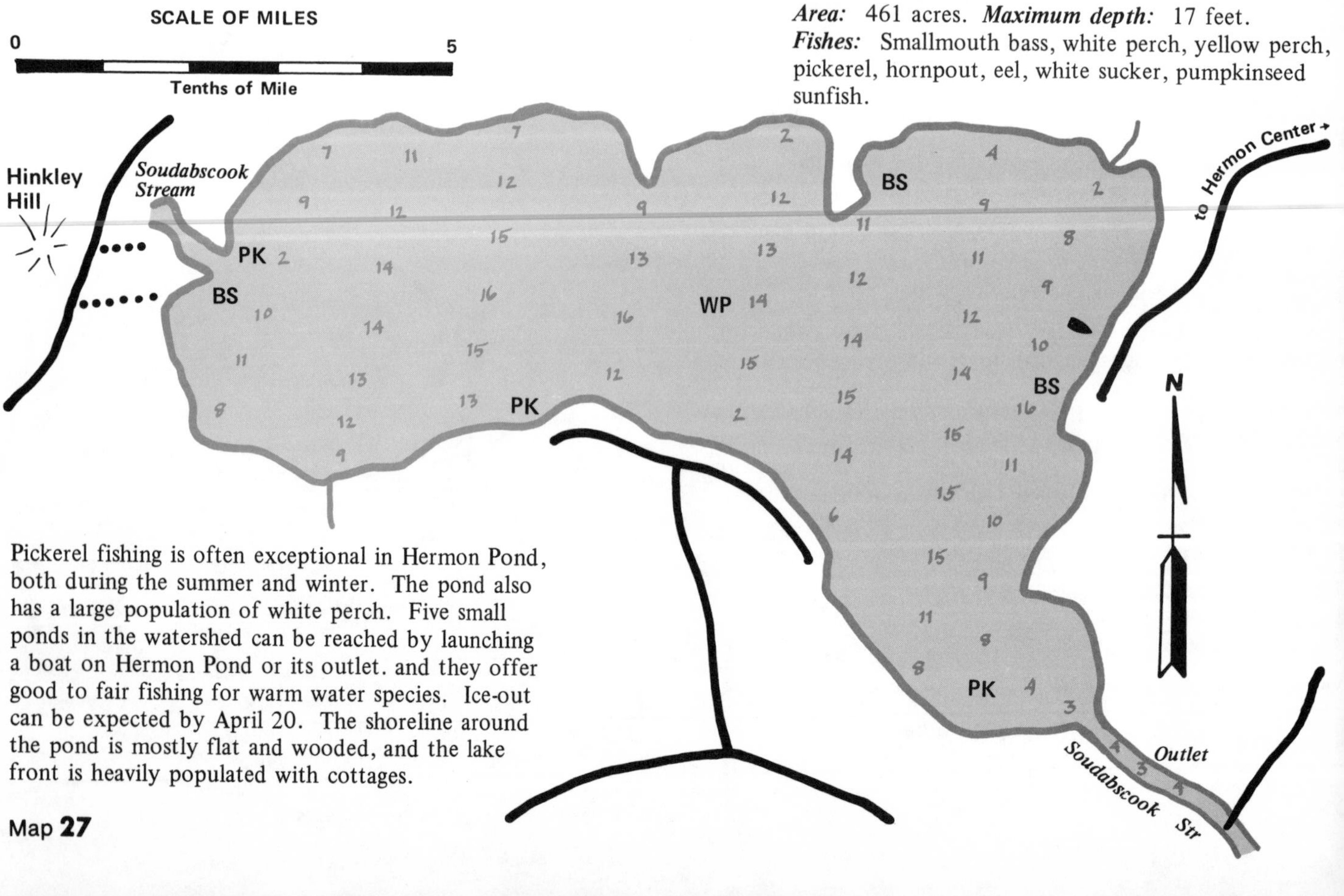

SCALE OF MILES
Tenths of Mile

Hinkley Hill

Soudabscook Stream

to Hermon Center →

Outlet

Soudabscook Str

Pickerel fishing is often exceptional in Hermon Pond, both during the summer and winter. The pond also has a large population of white perch. Five small ponds in the watershed can be reached by launching a boat on Hermon Pond or its outlet. and they offer good to fair fishing for warm water species. Ice-out can be expected by April 20. The shoreline around the pond is mostly flat and wooded, and the lake front is heavily populated with cottages.

Map 27

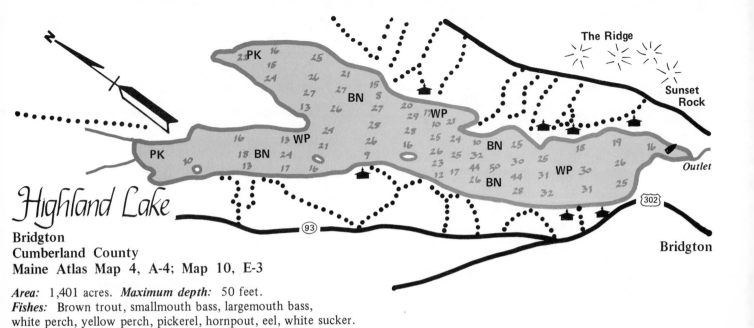

Highland Lake

Bridgton
Cumberland County
Maine Atlas Map 4, A-4; Map 10, E-3

Area: 1,401 acres. *Maximum depth:* 50 feet.
Fishes: Brown trout, smallmouth bass, largemouth bass,
white perch, yellow perch, pickerel, hornpout, eel, white sucker.

Highland Lake is 4½ miles long, with hilly and wooded surrounding country. There are 241 lots along the shoreline, most of them
with cottages. Highland Lake is a popular summer resort area, and
about 50 cottages are available for rent. Ice-out can be expected
by May 1, and the best fishing -- for white perch, followed by
bass and brown trout -- is in July and August. For information,
write: Lakes Environmental Association, Brigdton, Maine 04009.

SCALE OF MILES

0   1

Miles

Hopkins Pond

Mariaville, Clifton
Hancock and Penobscot Counties
Maine Atlas Map 24, B-1

Area: 442 acres. *Maximum depth:* 65 feet.
Fishes: Salmon, brook trout, lake trout, smelt, white sucker,
pumpkinseed sunfish.

Hopkins is a popular fishing pond, and in the past was noted for
the size of its brook trout. However, the trout tend to be smaller
now -- the pond has become more accessible with a carry-in launch
site on the east side, near the outlet. A small population of lake
trout inhabits the lake's deep area, and a few good fish are taken
each year. Good numbers of landlocked salmon are maintained
through stocking. The best fishing is from ice-out, about April
25, through mid-spring. The shoreline is hilly, rocky and wooded.
About 20 percent of the shoreline is settled with camps.

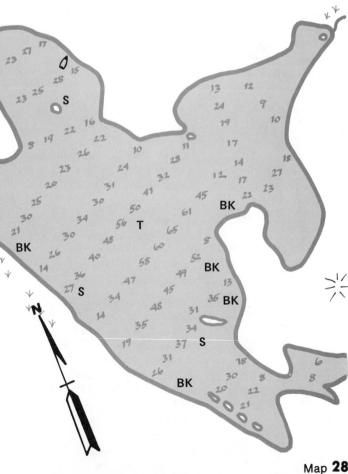

SCALE OF MILES

0   3

Tenths of Mile

Map **28**

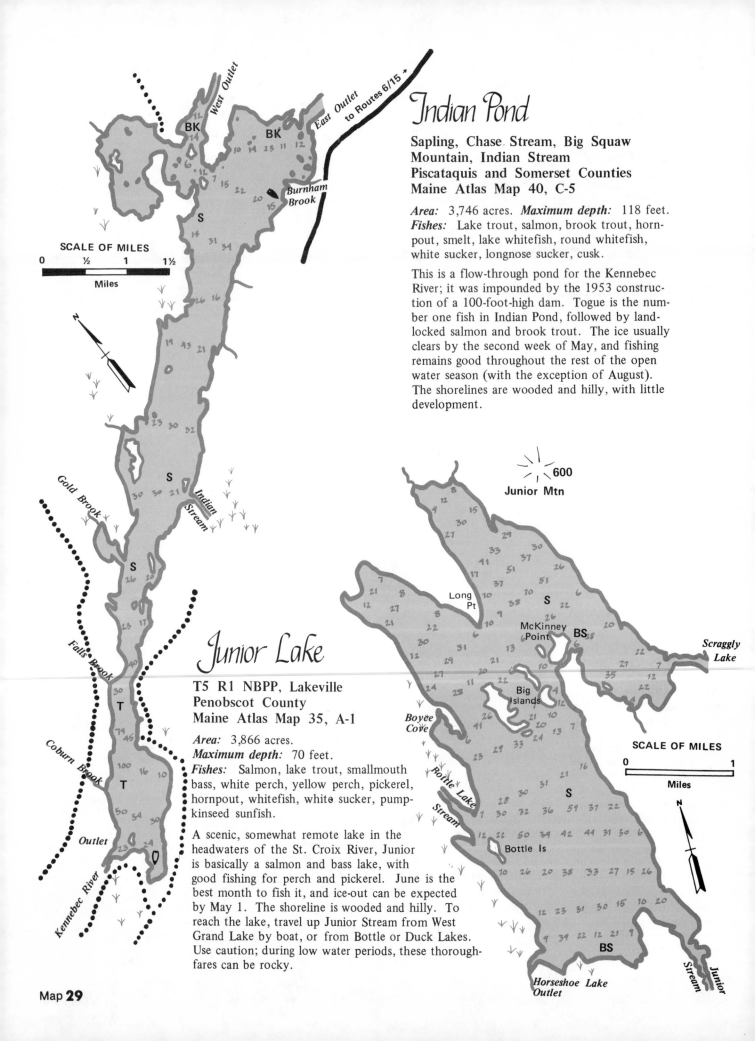

Indian Pond

Sapling, Chase Stream, Big Squaw Mountain, Indian Stream
Piscataquis and Somerset Counties
Maine Atlas Map 40, C-5

Area: 3,746 acres. *Maximum depth:* 118 feet.
Fishes: Lake trout, salmon, brook trout, hornpout, smelt, lake whitefish, round whitefish, white sucker, longnose sucker, cusk.

This is a flow-through pond for the Kennebec River; it was impounded by the 1953 construction of a 100-foot-high dam. Togue is the number one fish in Indian Pond, followed by landlocked salmon and brook trout. The ice usually clears by the second week of May, and fishing remains good throughout the rest of the open water season (with the exception of August). The shorelines are wooded and hilly, with little development.

Junior Lake

T5 R1 NBPP, Lakeville
Penobscot County
Maine Atlas Map 35, A-1

Area: 3,866 acres.
Maximum depth: 70 feet.
Fishes: Salmon, lake trout, smallmouth bass, white perch, yellow perch, pickerel, hornpout, whitefish, white sucker, pumpkinseed sunfish.

A scenic, somewhat remote lake in the headwaters of the St. Croix River, Junior is basically a salmon and bass lake, with good fishing for perch and pickerel. June is the best month to fish it, and ice-out can be expected by May 1. The shoreline is wooded and hilly. To reach the lake, travel up Junior Stream from West Grand Lake by boat, or from Bottle or Duck Lakes. Use caution; during low water periods, these thoroughfares can be rocky.

Map **29**

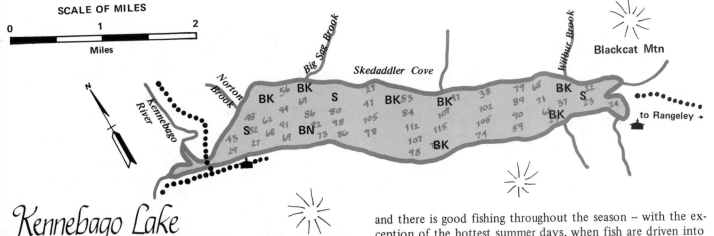

Kennebago Lake

Davis, Stetsontown Twp
Franklin County, Maine Atlas Map 28, C-4

Area: 1,700 acres. *Maximum depth:* 116 feet.
Fishes: Salmon, brook trout, brown trout, smelt.

Kennebago is unusual among lakes of its size -- only fly fishing is permitted, and no rough fish are present. Brook trout, brown trout and salmon all inhabit the same areas of Kennebago Lake, and there is good fishing throughout the season -- with the exception of the hottest summer days, when fish are driven into the depths. Long famous for its quality trout and salmon fishery, including Kennebago River (which flows into Cupsuptic Lake), Kennebago offers finest salmon fishing in September. Ice-out can be expected by May 15. The lake is surrounded by wooded hills, and, except for two sets of sporting camps at opposite ends of the lake, there is little shoreline development. Access is over private paper company roads.

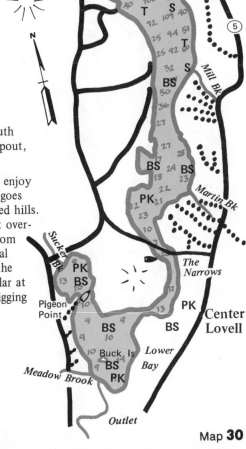

Kezar Lake

Lovell
Oxford County, Maine Atlas Map 10, D-2

Area: 2,510 acres. *Maximum depth:* 155 feet.
Fishes: Salmon, brook trout, brown trout, lake trout, smallmouth bass, largemouth bass, white perch, yellow perch, pickerel, hornpout, smelt, whitefish, eel, white sucker.

By alternating between warm and coldwater species, anglers can enjoy good fishing on Kezar Lake from May through September. Ice goes out in late April on this long, narrow lake surrounded by wooded hills. The shorelines have some cottage development, but Kezar is not over-populated. The large number of salmon in Kezar Lake result from natural production in Great and Mill Brooks and also from annual stockings. Lake trout is the second favorite fish at Kezar, and the smallmouth bass fishery is good. Fishing for smelt is also popular at Kezar -- they are taken both in summer and winter by anglers jigging deep with small pieces of cut bait or worms.

SCALE OF MILES

0   1

Miles

Map **30**

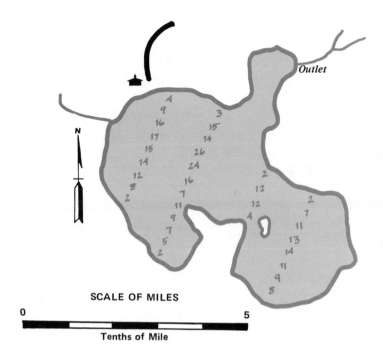

Kidney Pond

T3 R10
Piscataquis County, Maine Atlas Map 50, D-4

Area: 96 acres. *Maximum depth:* 33 feet.
Fishes: Brook trout.

Kidney Pond is one of a number of good trout ponds located within Baxter State Park; while small, it is listed here because it has a set of sporting camps located on its shores. Kidney Pond Camps existed prior to the establishment of the park. The road to the pond is private, and fishermen who are not guests at the sporting camps need permission from the proprietor to use the access facilities. Other than small minnows, the brook trout is the only fish found in Kidney Pond. The Baxter State Park limit of five trout per day applies to Kidney Pond, and this is a fly fishing only water. Kidney Pond is a beautiful location, with ice-out about May 1. The best fishing is in late May, early June, and the month of September.

SCALE OF MILES

0   5

Tenths of Mile

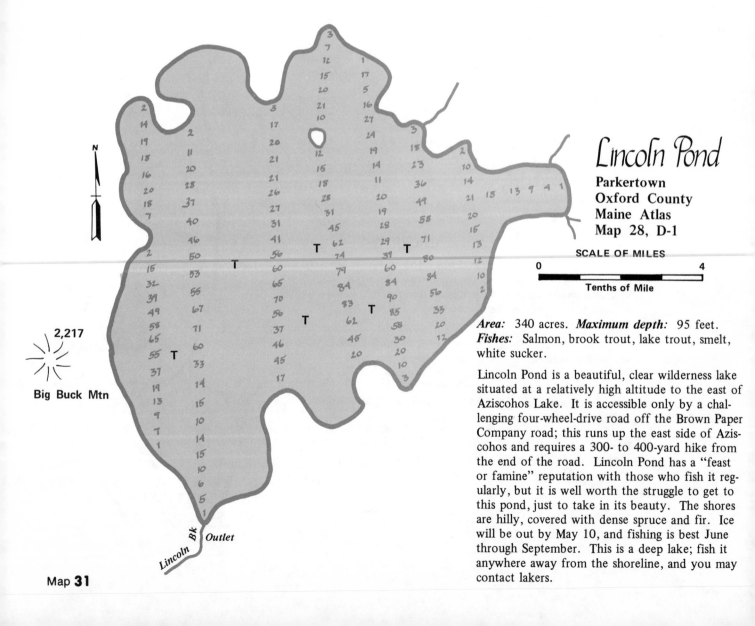

Lincoln Pond

Parkertown
Oxford County
Maine Atlas
Map 28, D-1

SCALE OF MILES

0   4

Tenths of Mile

Area: 340 acres. *Maximum depth:* 95 feet.
Fishes: Salmon, brook trout, lake trout, smelt, white sucker.

Lincoln Pond is a beautiful, clear wilderness lake situated at a relatively high altitude to the east of Aziscohos Lake. It is accessible only by a challenging four-wheel-drive road off the Brown Paper Company road; this runs up the east side of Aziscohos and requires a 300- to 400-yard hike from the end of the road. Lincoln Pond has a "feast or famine" reputation with those who fish it regularly, but it is well worth the struggle to get to this pond, just to take in its beauty. The shores are hilly, covered with dense spruce and fir. Ice will be out by May 10, and fishing is best June through September. This is a deep lake; fish it anywhere away from the shoreline, and you may contact lakers.

2,217

Big Buck Mtn

Map **31**

Little Jim Pond

Jim Pond, King and Bartlett Townships
Franklin and Somerset Counties
Maine Atlas Map 29, A-2

Area: 64 acres.
Maximum depth: 37 feet.
Fishes: Brook trout, lake trout.

Little Jim Pond is a classic Maine trout pond located north of Flagstaff Lake, with access via a dirt road connecting to Route 27 near Eustis. We include it here as an example of the diversity of fishing experience available in Maine. This is a fly-fishing-only pond; neither bait nor trolling is allowed, and flies must be cast. Trout action can be hot if a fly hatch is on. An occasional lake trout is taken on sunken streamers, and brook trout up to four pounds are reported. The boat launch here is rough, and trailered boats would have to be carried 100 yards to the water. Ice-out occurs in late May, and the best fishing is from then through the end of June.

SCALE OF MILES

0   ¼   ½

Miles

Little Kennebago Lake

Stetsontown Township
Franklin County, Maine Atlas Map 28, C-3

Area: 190 acres. *Maximum depth:* 56 feet.
Fishes: Salmon, brook trout, smelt.

Little Kennebago Lake is a remote brook trout pond with difficult access. While there is a road on its east shore, the road is chained off to the public. Usual access, other than coming up Kennebago Stream from big Kennebago Lake, is from Route 27. Just past Eustis there is a dirt road to the left, marked as the road to Tim Pond. By following this road until it comes to Kennebago River (where there is a Forest Service picnic ground), you can launch a canoe or small boat into the river and paddle upstream to the south end of Little Kennebago. This is a fly-fishing-only water, with no motors allowed. The brook trout are small, 8 to 10 inches, but there are lots of them. Ice-out can be expected by the second week of May. Fish can be found anywhere in the pond, particularly during evening mayfly and caddis fly hatches.

SCALE OF MILES

0   3

Tenths of Mile

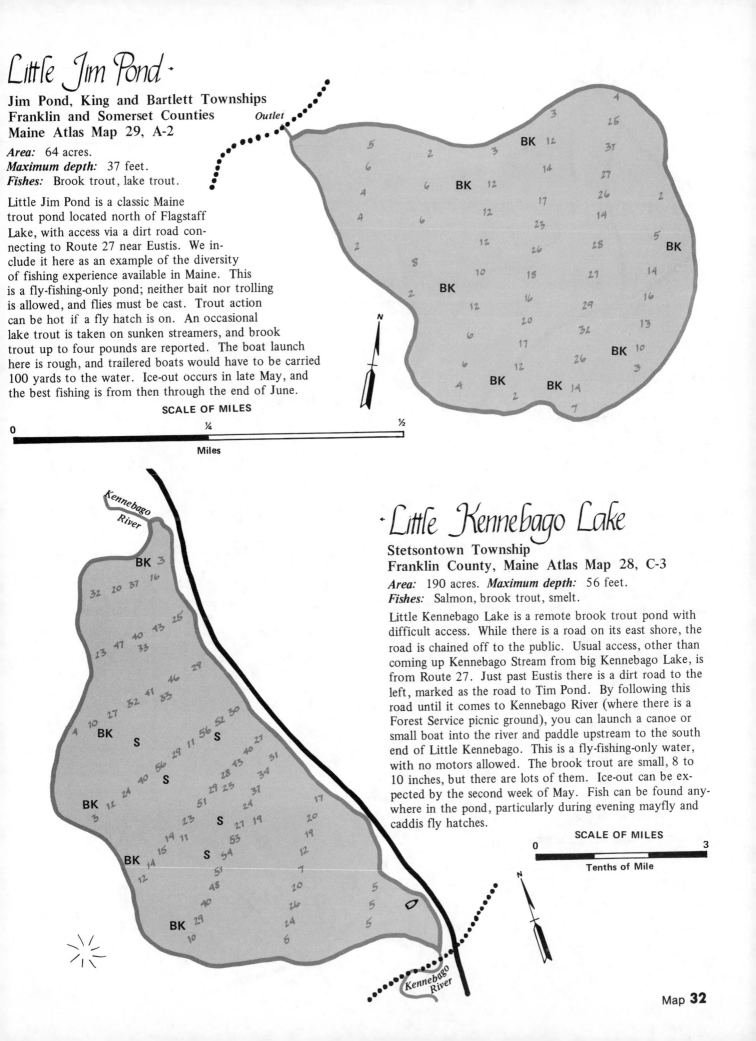

Map **32**

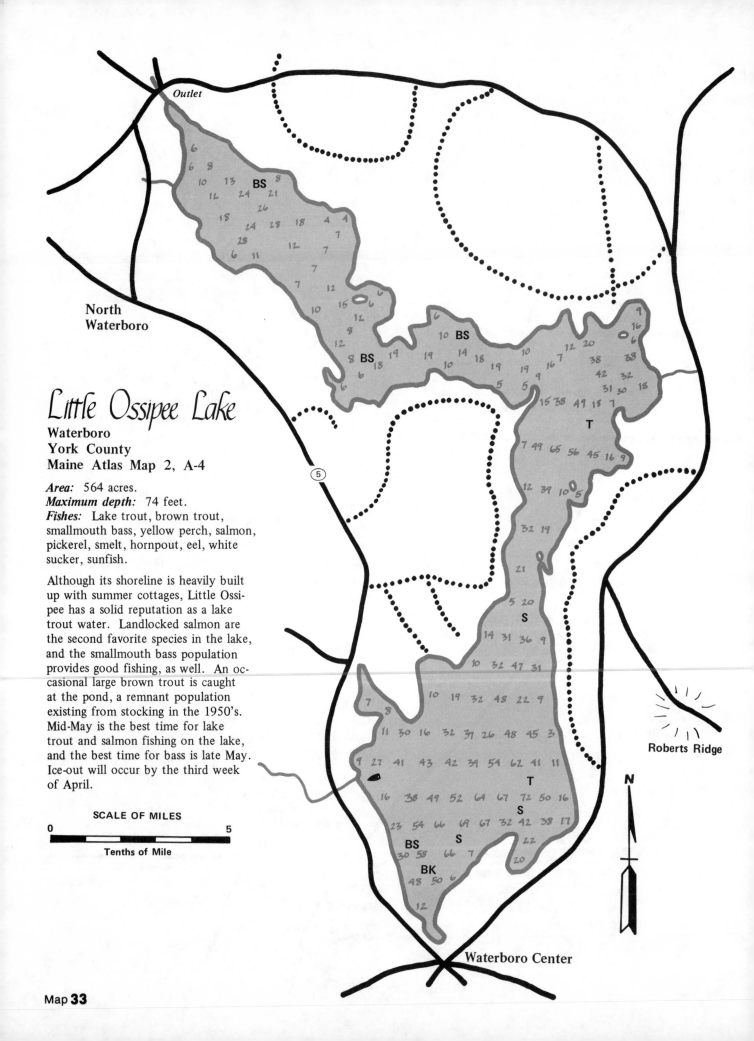

Outlet

North
Waterboro

Little Ossipee Lake

Waterboro
York County
Maine Atlas Map 2, A-4

Area: 564 acres.
Maximum depth: 74 feet.
Fishes: Lake trout, brown trout,
smallmouth bass, yellow perch, salmon,
pickerel, smelt, hornpout, eel, white
sucker, sunfish.

Although its shoreline is heavily built
up with summer cottages, Little Ossipee has a solid reputation as a lake
trout water. Landlocked salmon are
the second favorite species in the lake,
and the smallmouth bass population
provides good fishing, as well. An occasional large brown trout is caught
at the pond, a remnant population
existing from stocking in the 1950's.
Mid-May is the best time for lake
trout and salmon fishing on the lake,
and the best time for bass is late May.
Ice-out will occur by the third week
of April.

SCALE OF MILES

0   5

Tenths of Mile

Roberts Ridge

N

Waterboro Center

Map **33**

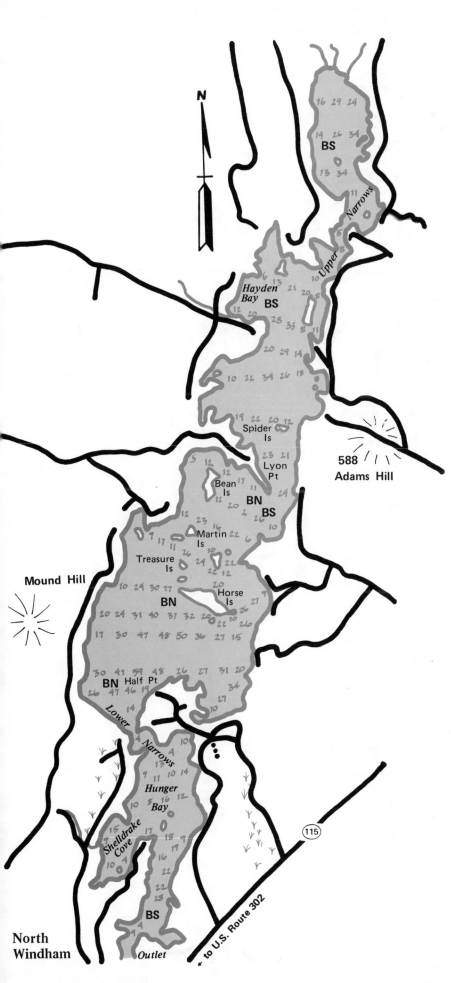

Little Sebago Lake

Gray, Windham
Cumberland County
Maine Atlas Map 5, C-2

Area: 1,898 acres.
Maximum depth: 52 feet.
Fishes: Brown trout, smallmouth bass, largemouth bass, white perch, yellow perch, chain pickerel, hornpout, white sucker, pumpkinseed sunfish, yellowbelly sunfish.

A highly irregular shoreline and shallow water make Little Sebago primarily a bass lake, but its deepwater sections also harbor good-sized brown trout. The shoreline is flat and heavily studded with cottages and homes, but the bass fishing is still good enough to draw fishermen to the lake. Ice-out can be expected by the fourth week in April. The best fishing occurs from mid-May through June for brown trout, and in early mornings and evenings during August for bass.

SCALE OF MILES

0   1

Miles

Map **34**

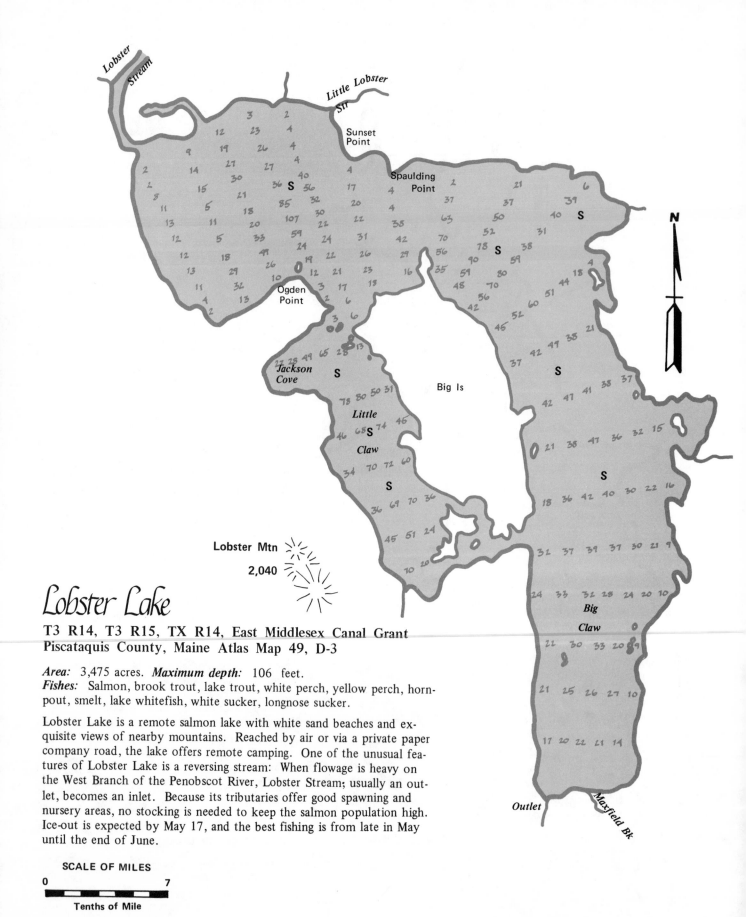

Lobster Lake

T3 R14, T3 R15, TX R14, East Middlesex Canal Grant
Piscataquis County, Maine Atlas Map 49, D-3

Area: 3,475 acres. *Maximum depth:* 106 feet.
Fishes: Salmon, brook trout, lake trout, white perch, yellow perch, horn-pout, smelt, lake whitefish, white sucker, longnose sucker.

Lobster Lake is a remote salmon lake with white sand beaches and exquisite views of nearby mountains. Reached by air or via a private paper company road, the lake offers remote camping. One of the unusual features of Lobster Lake is a reversing stream: When flowage is heavy on the West Branch of the Penobscot River, Lobster Stream; usually an outlet, becomes an inlet. Because its tributaries offer good spawning and nursery areas, no stocking is needed to keep the salmon population high. Ice-out is expected by May 17, and the best fishing is from late in May until the end of June.

SCALE OF MILES

0   7

Tenths of Mile

Map **35**

Long Pond

Rome, Belgrade, Mt. Vernon
Kennebec County, Maine Atlas Map 12, A-4; Map 20, E-3

Area: 2,714 acres. *Maximum depth:* 106 feet.
Fishes: Salmon, brook trout, smallmouth bass, largemouth bass, white perch, yellow perch, pickerel, hornpout, smelt, eel, white sucker.

Long Pond, one of the Belgrade chain of lakes, is heavily fished early in the season for landlocked salmon, but continues to be one of the best landlocked salmon lakes in the state. Surrounded by wooded hills, it is a picturesque lake, with long stretches of shoreline free of any type of development. The inlet area at Belgrade Lakes (a town) is one of the first areas in the region to clear of ice, and is heavily fished for both landlocks and spawning white perch. Long Pond, really two lakes joined by a thoroughfare, should be ice-free by the third week of April. Both the upper and lower basins provide ample habitat for both cold and warmwater species. The weedy and shallow end of the lower basin is best for largemouth bass and pickerel. The rocky shorelines and islands are good for smallmouths and white perch. Salmon fishing is concentrated around the deepest portions of the lake. For information write: Belgrade Lakes Region, Inc., Dept. B, Belgrade, Maine 04917.

SCALE OF MILES

0   5

Tenths of Mile

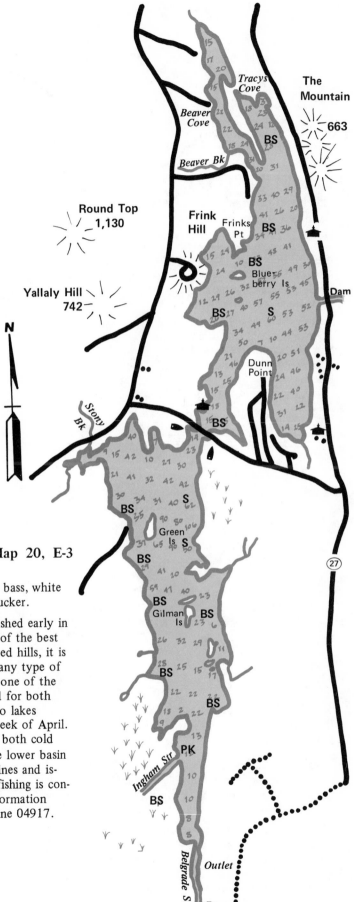

Map **36**

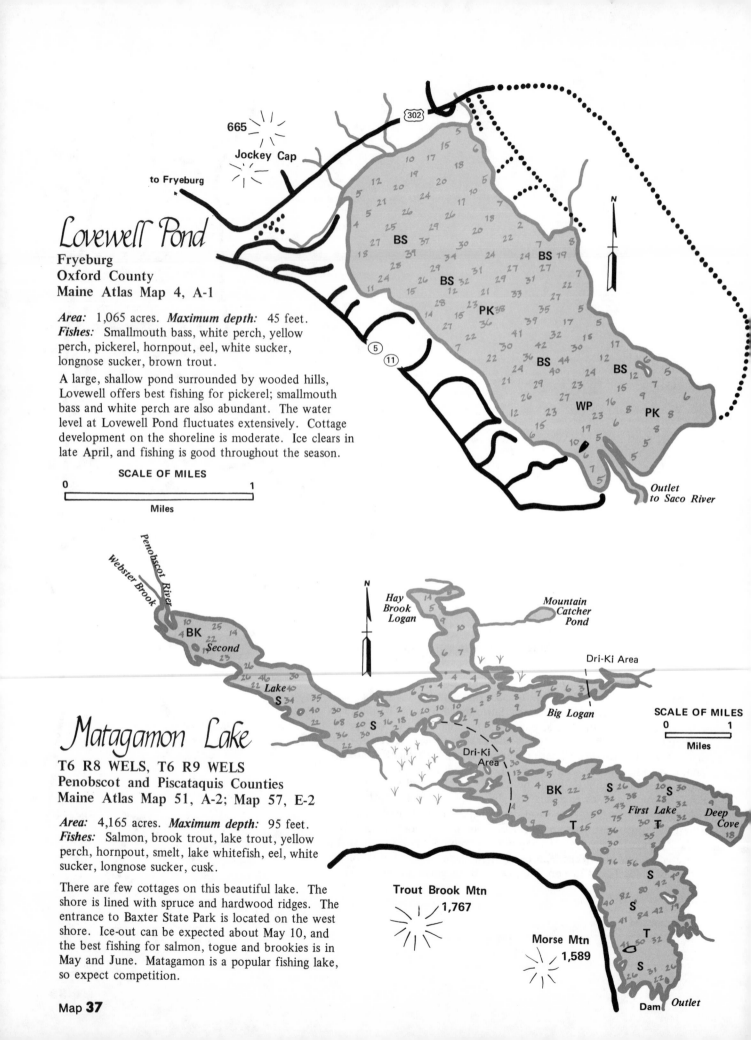

Lovewell Pond

Fryeburg
Oxford County
Maine Atlas Map 4, A-1

Area: 1,065 acres. *Maximum depth:* 45 feet.
Fishes: Smallmouth bass, white perch, yellow perch, pickerel, hornpout, eel, white sucker, longnose sucker, brown trout.

A large, shallow pond surrounded by wooded hills, Lovewell offers best fishing for pickerel; smallmouth bass and white perch are also abundant. The water level at Lovewell Pond fluctuates extensively. Cottage development on the shoreline is moderate. Ice clears in late April, and fishing is good throughout the season.

SCALE OF MILES

0   1

Miles

665

Jockey Cap

to Fryeburg

302

5
11

Outlet
to Saco River

Matagamon Lake

T6 R8 WELS, T6 R9 WELS
Penobscot and Piscataquis Counties
Maine Atlas Map 51, A-2; Map 57, E-2

Area: 4,165 acres. *Maximum depth:* 95 feet.
Fishes: Salmon, brook trout, lake trout, yellow perch, hornpout, smelt, lake whitefish, eel, white sucker, longnose sucker, cusk.

There are few cottages on this beautiful lake. The shore is lined with spruce and hardwood ridges. The entrance to Baxter State Park is located on the west shore. Ice-out can be expected about May 10, and the best fishing for salmon, togue and brookies is in May and June. Matagamon is a popular fishing lake, so expect competition.

Penobscot River
Webster Brook

Second Lake

Hay Brook Logan

Mountain Catcher Pond

Dri-Ki Area

Big Logan

Dri-Ki Area

SCALE OF MILES

0   1

Miles

First Lake

Deep Cove

Trout Brook Mtn
1,767

Morse Mtn
1,589

Dam   Outlet

Map **37**

Maranacook Lake

Readfield and Winthrop
Kennebec County, Maine Atlas Map 12, B-3

Area: 1,673 acres. *Maximum depth:* 118 feet.
Fishes: Brown trout, lake trout, landlocked salmon, smallmouth bass, largemouth bass, white perch, yellow perch, pickerel, hornpout, smelt, eel, white sucker, pumpkinseed sunfish, redbreast sunfish.

The angler looking for variety will like Maranacook Lake, for quite a number of species are found in its waters. Brown trout and togue hold the most interest for Maranacook regulars. But the lake's most productive fishing is probably for bass, perch and pickerel, species which are often overlooked by residents. Maranacook also yields salmon and smelt. While there is heavy cottage and year-round development on Maranacook, it remains an attractive lake; wooded slopes lead down to the shore in most areas. Ice goes out sometime between April 20 and 25. The second two weeks in June are a good time to fish this lake, as is September.

SCALE OF MILES

0   1

Miles

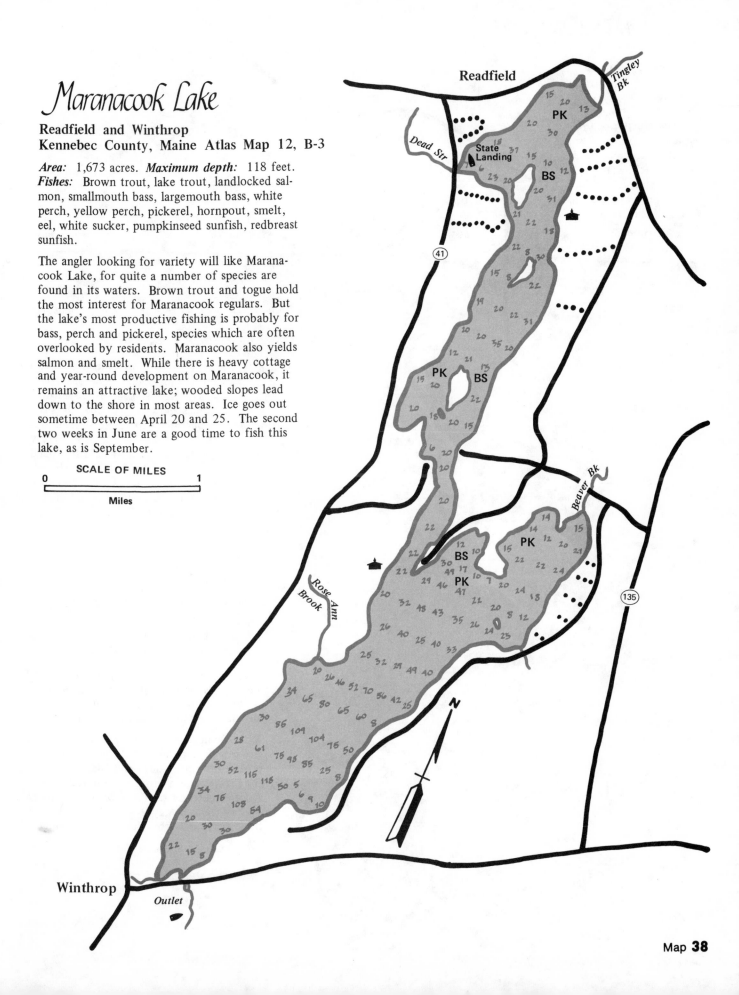

Map **38**

Mattanawcook Pond

Lincoln
Penobscot County
Maine Atlas Map 44, E-1

Area: 832 acres.
Maximum depth: 20 feet.
Fishes: Brook trout, small-mouth bass, white perch, yellow perch, chain pickerel, hornpout, eel, white sucker, pumpkinseed sunfish, redbreast sunfish.

SCALE OF MILES

0   5

Tenths of Mile

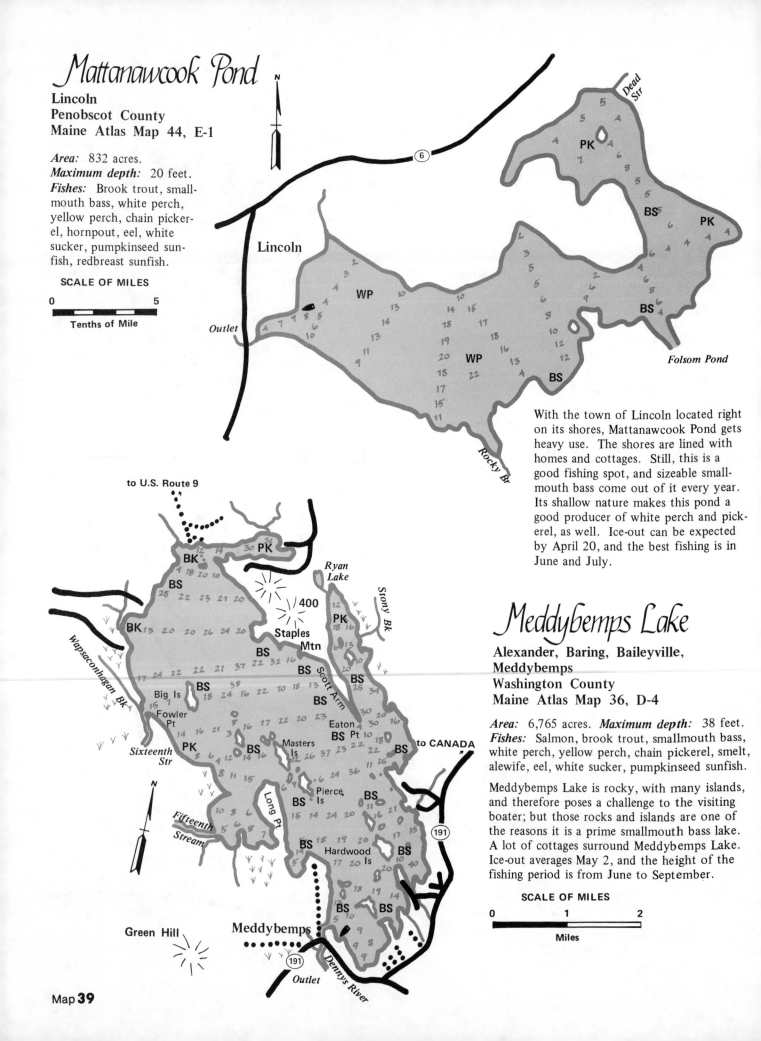

With the town of Lincoln located right on its shores, Mattanawcook Pond gets heavy use. The shores are lined with homes and cottages. Still, this is a good fishing spot, and sizeable small-mouth bass come out of it every year. Its shallow nature makes this pond a good producer of white perch and pickerel, as well. Ice-out can be expected by April 20, and the best fishing is in June and July.

Meddybemps Lake

Alexander, Baring, Baileyville, Meddybemps
Washington County
Maine Atlas Map 36, D-4

Area: 6,765 acres. *Maximum depth:* 38 feet.
Fishes: Salmon, brook trout, smallmouth bass, white perch, yellow perch, chain pickerel, smelt, alewife, eel, white sucker, pumpkinseed sunfish.

Meddybemps Lake is rocky, with many islands, and therefore poses a challenge to the visiting boater; but those rocks and islands are one of the reasons it is a prime smallmouth bass lake. A lot of cottages surround Meddybemps Lake. Ice-out averages May 2, and the height of the fishing period is from June to September.

SCALE OF MILES

0   1   2

Miles

Map **39**

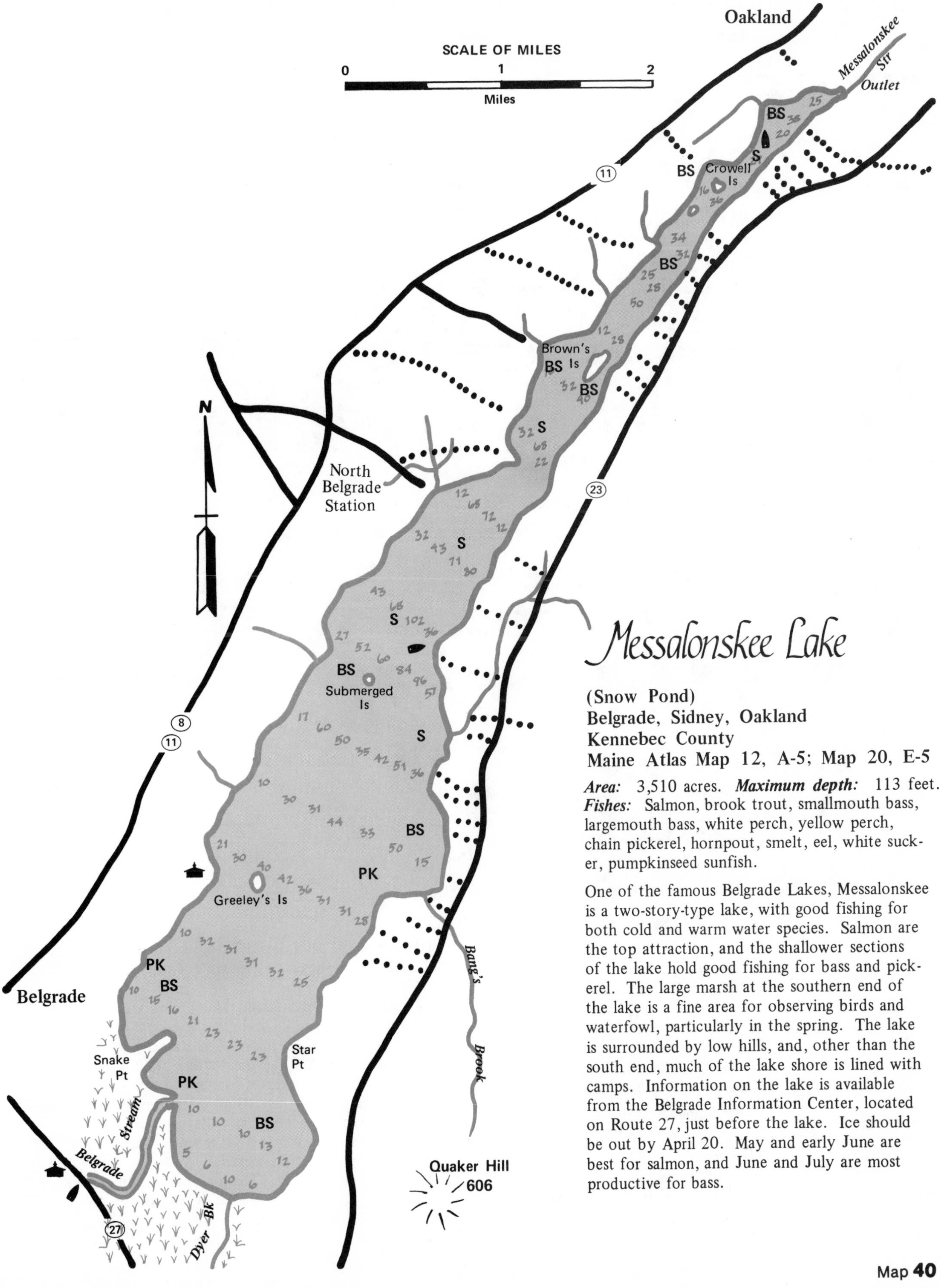

Oakland

SCALE OF MILES

0   1   2

Miles

Messalonskee Str
Outlet

BS
25
38
20

BS   Crowell
        Is   S

16
36

34
31

BS

25
28
50

12
18

Brown's
Is
BS

32
40   BS

North
Belgrade
Station

32   S
68
22

12
68   72
       12

32
43   S
71   30

43
68
27   S 102
51   36
60
BS   84
Submerged 96
Is   57

17
60
50   S
35 42
42 51
36

10
30
31
44   33
        50
21
30   15
40 42
36 31   BS
31
28   PK

Greeley's Is

10
32 31
31
31 31 25

PK
BS
10
15
16
21
23
23   Star
23   23 Pt

Snake
Pt
PK

10
10   13
10   12
5
6
10 6

Belgrade

Belgrade
Stream

Dyer Bk

(27)

(8)
(11)

(11)

(23)

N

Bang's
Brook

Quaker Hill
606

Messalonskee Lake

(Snow Pond)
Belgrade, Sidney, Oakland
Kennebec County
Maine Atlas Map 12, A-5; Map 20, E-5

Area: 3,510 acres. *Maximum depth:* 113 feet.
Fishes: Salmon, brook trout, smallmouth bass,
largemouth bass, white perch, yellow perch,
chain pickerel, hornpout, smelt, eel, white sucker, pumpkinseed sunfish.

One of the famous Belgrade Lakes, Messalonskee
is a two-story-type lake, with good fishing for
both cold and warm water species. Salmon are
the top attraction, and the shallower sections
of the lake hold good fishing for bass and pickerel. The large marsh at the southern end of
the lake is a fine area for observing birds and
waterfowl, particularly in the spring. The lake
is surrounded by low hills, and, other than the
south end, much of the lake shore is lined with
camps. Information on the lake is available
from the Belgrade Information Center, located
on Route 27, just before the lake. Ice should
be out by April 20. May and early June are
best for salmon, and June and July are most
productive for bass.

Map **40**

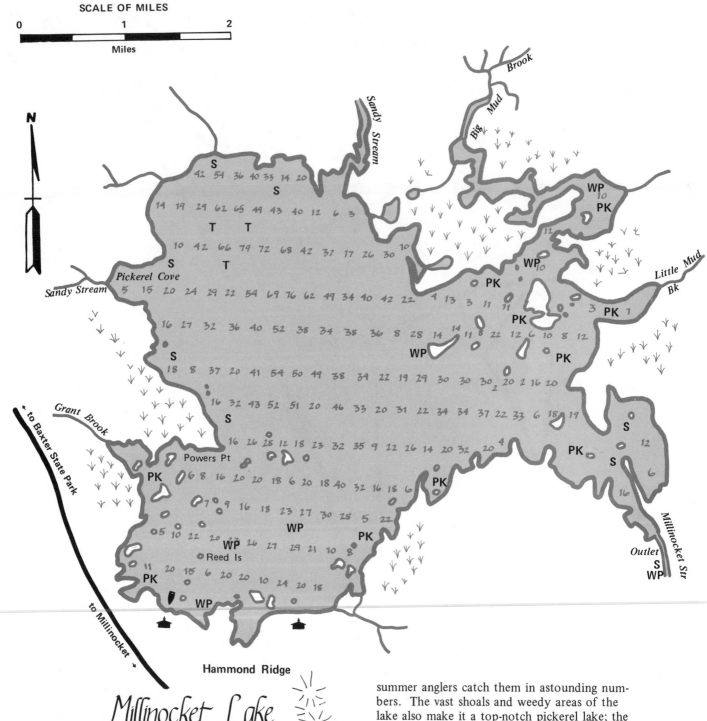

SCALE OF MILES

0   1   2

Miles

N

Brook

Sandy Stream

Big Mud

S
42 54 36 40 33 14 20
S
14 19 29 62 65 49 43 40 12 6 3
T T
10 42 66 79 72 68 42 37 17 26 30 10
S
T
Pickerel Cove
5 15 20 24 29 22 54 69 76 62 49 34 40 42 22
Sandy Stream
16 27 32 36 40 52 38 34 38 36 8 28 14 14
S
18 8 37 20 41 54 50 49 38 34 22 19 29 30 30 30 20 2 16 20
16 32 43 52 51 20 46 33 20 31 22 34 34 37 22 33 6 18 19
S
16 26 28 12 18 23 32 35 9 22 26 14 20 32 20 4
Powers Pt
Grant Brook
PK
6 8 16 20 20 18 6 20 18 40 32 16 18 6
7 9 16 18 23 27 30 28 5 22
5 10 22 20
WP
WP 26 27 29 21 10 8
Reed Is
11 20 15 6 20 20 10 24 20 18
PK
WP

to Baxter State Park

to Millinocket

Hammond Ridge

WP 10
PK
12
WP 10
PK
WP
PK
4 13 3 11 11
PK
11 8 22 12 6 10 8 12
WP
PK
Little Mud
Bk
3 PK 1
S
PK 12
S
6
16
Millinocket Str
Outlet
S
WP
PK
WP

Millinocket Lake

T1 R8, T2 R8, T1 R9, T2 R9
Penobscot and Piscataquis Counties
Maine Atlas Map 43, A-2; Map 51, E-2

Area: 8,960 acres. *Maximum depth:* 86 feet.
Fishes: Salmon, brook trout, white perch, yellow perch, pickerel, hornpout, smelt, eel, white sucker, longnose sucker, cusk, pumpkinseed sunfish, yellowbelly sunfish.

While landlocked salmon are probably the most sought-after game fish at Millinocket Lake, the lake has an overabundance of white perch, and summer anglers catch them in astounding numbers. The vast shoals and weedy areas of the lake also make it a top-notch pickerel lake; the best pickerel fishing is in the Mud Brook area. Work has been done to improve the lake's togue fishery, and lake trout in the 9- to 14-pound class have been taken. A dam at the outlet of the lake creates Millinocket Stream, where pools offer good fly casting for salmon and brook trout. Ice will be out by early May, and the best fishing for salmon is from ice-out until July. July and August are especially good for pickerel and perch. The lake has a rocky shoreline. Cottages are clustered in the Pump House area, along the south shore, near the outlet and near Sandy Stream.

Map **41**

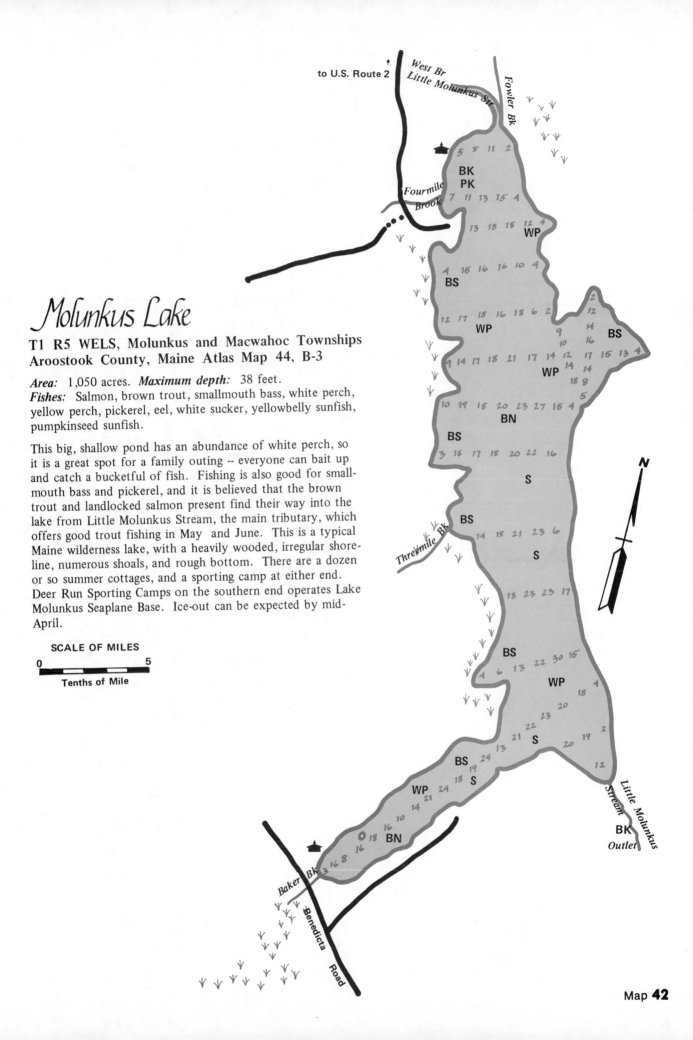

Molunkus Lake

T1 R5 WELS, Molunkus and Macwahoc Townships
Aroostook County, Maine Atlas Map 44, B-3

Area: 1,050 acres. *Maximum depth:* 38 feet.
Fishes: Salmon, brown trout, smallmouth bass, white perch, yellow perch, pickerel, eel, white sucker, yellowbelly sunfish, pumpkinseed sunfish.

This big, shallow pond has an abundance of white perch, so it is a great spot for a family outing -- everyone can bait up and catch a bucketful of fish. Fishing is also good for smallmouth bass and pickerel, and it is believed that the brown trout and landlocked salmon present find their way into the lake from Little Molunkus Stream, the main tributary, which offers good trout fishing in May and June. This is a typical Maine wilderness lake, with a heavily wooded, irregular shoreline, numerous shoals, and rough bottom. There are a dozen or so summer cottages, and a sporting camp at either end. Deer Run Sporting Camps on the southern end operates Lake Molunkus Seaplane Base. Ice-out can be expected by mid-April.

SCALE OF MILES

0 — 5

Tenths of Mile

to U.S. Route 2

West Br Little Molunkus Str

Fowler Bk

Fourmile Brook

BK PK

5 8 11 2
7 13 13 15 4
13 13 15 12 4
WP
4 15 16 16 10 4
BS
12 17 18 16 18 6 2
WP
9 14 17 18 21 17 14 12
WP
18 8
10 19 18 20 23 27 15 4
BN
BS
3 16 17 18 20 22 16

2
12
9 14
10 16
14 17 15 13 4
BS
14 14
5

S

Threemile Bk

BS
14 18 21 23 6

S

18 23 23 17

BS
4 6 13 22 30 15
WP
18 4
23 20
22 13
21 22 S 20 19 2
BS 24 20 12
19
WP 15 S
21 24
14

O 18 BN
16 16
3 16 8 16

Baker Bk

Benedicta Road

N

Little Molunkus Stream

BK
Outlet

Map **42**

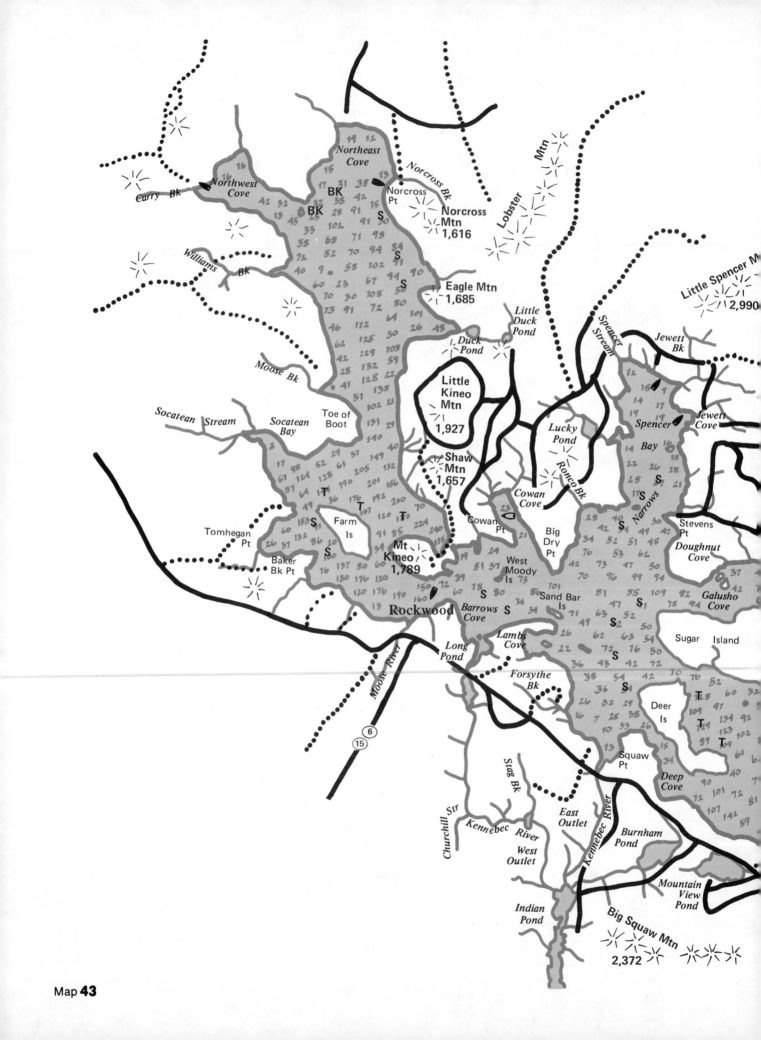

Map **43**

Moosehead Lake

Greenville, Beaver Cove Plantation, Lily Bay Township, Spencer Bay Township, Days Academy Grant, Kineo Township, Northeast Carry Township, Seboomook Township, Big W and Little W Townships, West Middlesex Canal Grant, Tomhegan Township, Rockwood Strip, Taunton and Raynham Academy Grant, Sandbar Tract, Misery Gore, Sapling Township, Big Squaw and Little Squaw Townships, Harfords Point Township, Cove Point Township
Piscataquis County
Maine Atlas Map 40, A-5; Map 41, B-2
Map 48, E-5; Map 49, E-1

Area: 74,890 acres. *Maximum depth:* 246 feet.
Fishes: Salmon, brook trout, lake trout, hornpout, smelt, lake whitefish, round whitefish, eel, white sucker, longnose sucker, cusk, sunfish.

Maine's largest lake has been a famous fishing and vacation resort for more than a century. Thirty miles long and 20 miles wide, it drains an area of 1,266 square miles. With a sparse population and no industry, the Moosehead region offers waters among the best in the state for salmon, brook trout, and lake trout. Many tributaries provide ample fish spawning areas as well as angling opportunities. Moosehead is the headwater of the Kennebec River, the second largest in the state. The East and West Outlet dams are good locations to fish for brookies and landlocks.

Greenville is the lake's largest town, located on the extreme southern tip. This fair-sized community offers all the services a fisherman or vacationer could want, including float plane service. The other major town on Moosehead is Rockwood, located halfway up the lake's western shore. Rockwood is a fishing and hunting town, with many accommodations and guides available for visitors. The Moose River, entering the lake at Rockwood, is a prime fishing location, as are the waters around spectacular Mt. Kineo, opposite Rockwood.

A prime attraction of the lake's east shore is Lily Bay State Park, which offers camping, swimming, picnicking, and boat launching. For more information on the Moosehead Lake region, write to: Greenville Chamber of Commerce, Greenville, Maine 04441. The *Moosehead Lake Map & Guide,* available from DeLorme Publishing Company, shows the Moosehead region in full color and high detail, with text about recreation and history of the area.

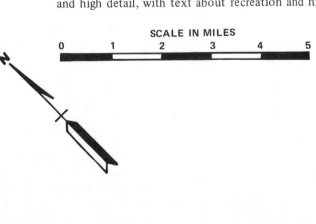

SCALE IN MILES

0   1   2   3   4   5

Map **44**

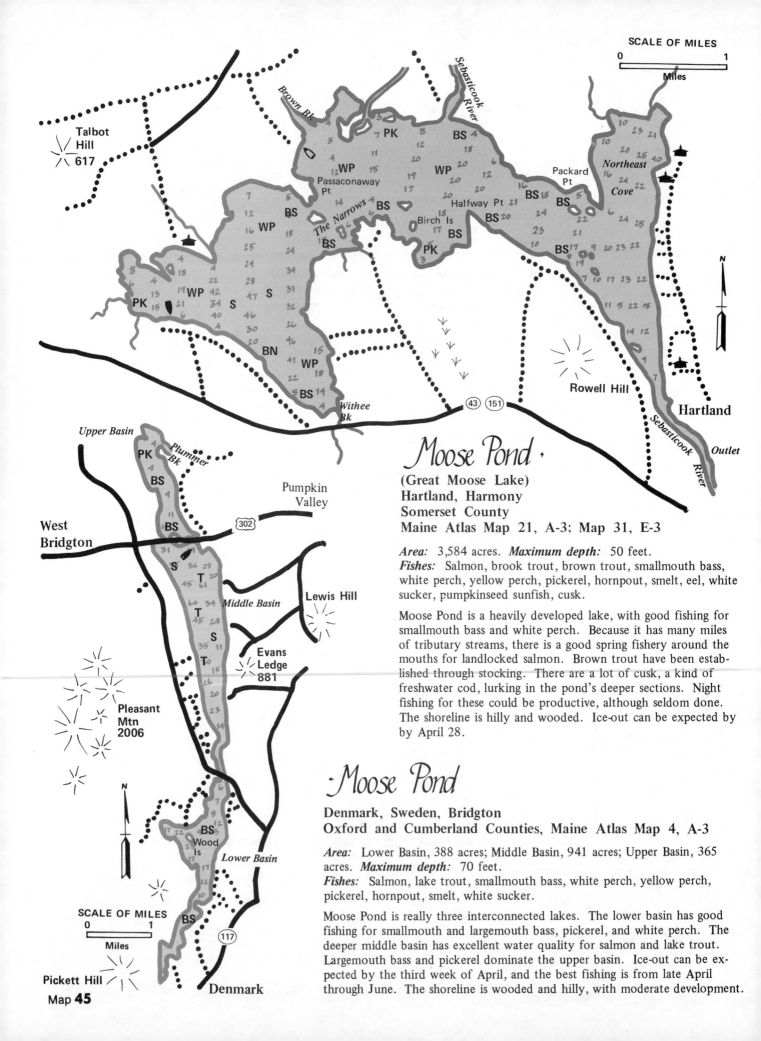

Moose Pond ·

(Great Moose Lake)
Hartland, Harmony
Somerset County
Maine Atlas Map 21, A-3; Map 31, E-3

Area: 3,584 acres. *Maximum depth:* 50 feet.
Fishes: Salmon, brook trout, brown trout, smallmouth bass, white perch, yellow perch, pickerel, hornpout, smelt, eel, white sucker, pumpkinseed sunfish, cusk.

Moose Pond is a heavily developed lake, with good fishing for smallmouth bass and white perch. Because it has many miles of tributary streams, there is a good spring fishery around the mouths for landlocked salmon. Brown trout have been established through stocking. There are a lot of cusk, a kind of freshwater cod, lurking in the pond's deeper sections. Night fishing for these could be productive, although seldom done. The shoreline is hilly and wooded. Ice-out can be expected by by April 28.

Moose Pond

Denmark, Sweden, Bridgton
Oxford and Cumberland Counties, Maine Atlas Map 4, A-3

Area: Lower Basin, 388 acres; Middle Basin, 941 acres; Upper Basin, 365 acres. *Maximum depth:* 70 feet.
Fishes: Salmon, lake trout, smallmouth bass, white perch, yellow perch, pickerel, hornpout, smelt, white sucker.

Moose Pond is really three interconnected lakes. The lower basin has good fishing for smallmouth and largemouth bass, pickerel, and white perch. The deeper middle basin has excellent water quality for salmon and lake trout. Largemouth bass and pickerel dominate the upper basin. Ice-out can be expected by the third week of April, and the best fishing is from late April through June. The shoreline is wooded and hilly, with moderate development.

Map 45

Musquacook Lakes

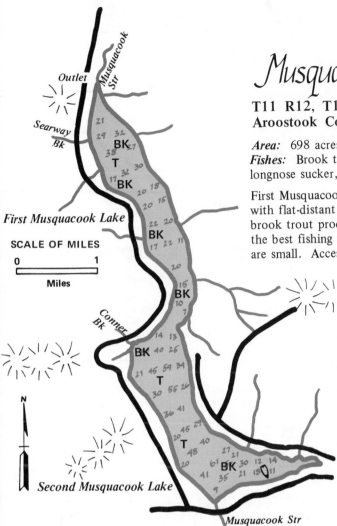

T11 R12, T12 R12
Aroostook County, Maine Atlas Map 62, D-2

Area: 698 acres. *Maximum depth :* 48 feet.
Fishes: Brook trout, lake trout, whitefish, round whitefish, white sucker, longnose sucker, cusk.

First Musquacook is a wilderness area lake surrounded by fir, spruce, and cedar, with flat-distant hills. While it is considered marginal water, it is still a good brook trout producer. Ice-out should take place by May 15, and that is when the best fishing will occur. Lake trout fishing can be good in July, but the fish are small. Access is over North Maine Woods roads.

T11 R11
Aroostook County, Maine Atlas Map 62, E-2

Area: 813 acres. *Maximum depth:* 62 feet.
Fishes: Brook trout, lake trout, lake whitefish, round whitefish, white sucker, longnose sucker, cusk.

Second Musquacook gets a good amount of angling pressure because it is easily accessible by a good North Maine Woods gravel road from the Six-Mile Gate from Ashland. The primary fish is lake trout. There are no cottages on the lake, and the shoreline is hilly, with spruce-fir cover. Ice-out should occur by May 15, and the fishing should be good until July. There are good campsites at this lake.

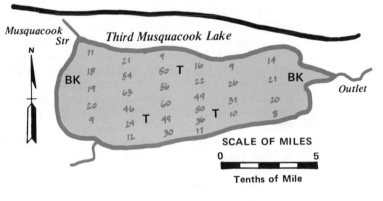

T11 R11
Aroostook County, Maine Atlas Map 62, E-3

Area: 397 acres. *Maximum depth:* 64 feet.
Fishes: Brook trout, lake trout, lake whitefish, white sucker, cusk.

Access to Third Musquacook is difficult, requiring a one-mile walk, rewarded by excellent lake trout fishing and little competition from other fishermen. The lake is surrounded by hardwood ridges. Ice-out should occur by May 15, and the good fishing lasts until August.

T11 R11, T10 R11
Aroostook and Piscataquis Counties
Maine Atlas Map 56, A-3

Area: 749 acres. *Maximum depth:* 40 feet.
Fishes: Brook trout, hornpout, lake whitefish, white sucker.

Fourth Musquacook is a marginal trout water which can produce very well at ice-out (May 15). The surrounding land is flat and swampy, and the trees are black spruce with some fir. Access is over North Maine Woods logging roads.

Map **46**

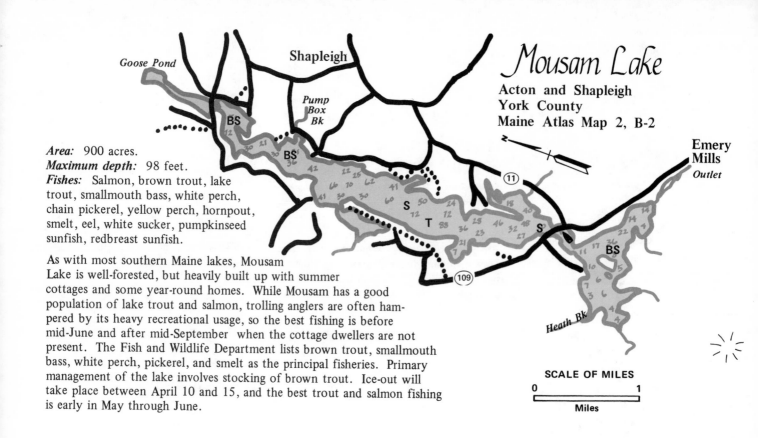

Mousam Lake

Acton and Shapleigh
York County
Maine Atlas Map 2, B-2

Area: 900 acres.
Maximum depth: 98 feet.
Fishes: Salmon, brown trout, lake trout, smallmouth bass, white perch, chain pickerel, yellow perch, hornpout, smelt, eel, white sucker, pumpkinseed sunfish, redbreast sunfish.

As with most southern Maine lakes, Mousam Lake is well-forested, but heavily built up with summer cottages and some year-round homes. While Mousam has a good population of lake trout and salmon, trolling anglers are often hampered by its heavy recreational usage, so the best fishing is before mid-June and after mid-September when the cottage dwellers are not present. The Fish and Wildlife Department lists brown trout, smallmouth bass, white perch, pickerel, and smelt as the principal fisheries. Primary management of the lake involves stocking of brown trout. Ice-out will take place between April 10 and 15, and the best trout and salmon fishing is early in May through June.

SCALE OF MILES

0   1

Miles

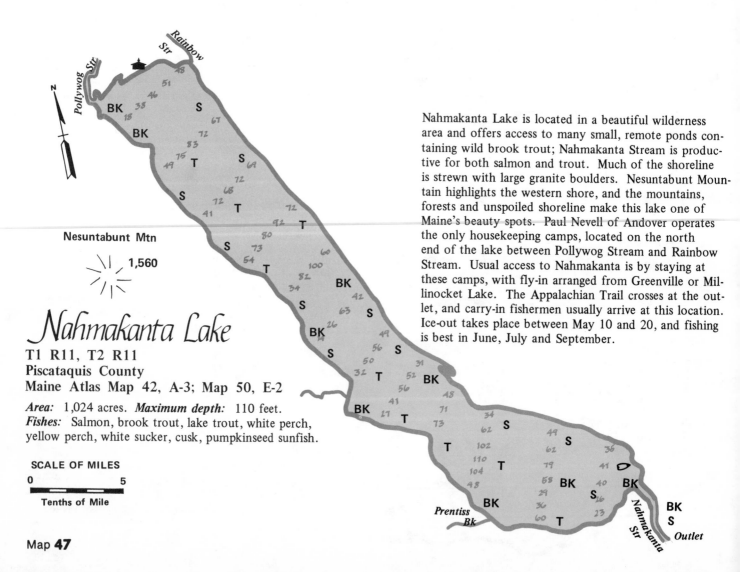

Nahmakanta Lake is located in a beautiful wilderness area and offers access to many small, remote ponds containing wild brook trout; Nahmakanta Stream is productive for both salmon and trout. Much of the shoreline is strewn with large granite boulders. Nesuntabunt Mountain highlights the western shore, and the mountains, forests and unspoiled shoreline make this lake one of Maine's beauty spots. Paul Nevell of Andover operates the only housekeeping camps, located on the north end of the lake between Pollywog Stream and Rainbow Stream. Usual access to Nahmakanta is by staying at these camps, with fly-in arranged from Greenville or Millinocket Lake. The Appalachian Trail crosses at the outlet, and carry-in fishermen usually arrive at this location. Ice-out takes place between May 10 and 20, and fishing is best in June, July and September.

Nesuntabunt Mtn

1,560

Nahmakanta Lake

T1 R11, T2 R11
Piscataquis County
Maine Atlas Map 42, A-3; Map 50, E-2

Area: 1,024 acres. **Maximum depth:** 110 feet.
Fishes: Salmon, brook trout, lake trout, white perch, yellow perch, white sucker, cusk, pumpkinseed sunfish.

SCALE OF MILES

0   5

Tenths of Mile

Map **47**

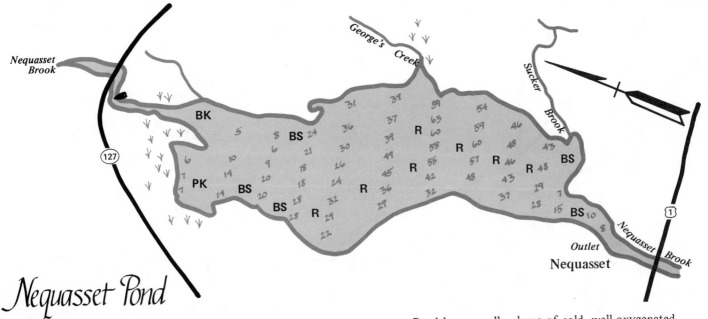

Nequasset Pond

Woolwich
Sagadahoc County, Maine Atlas Map 6, B-5

Area: 430 acres. *Maximum depth:* 63 feet.
Fishes: Rainbow trout, salmon brook trout, smallmouth bass, largemouth bass, white perch, yellow perch, pickerel, hornpout, smelt, alewife, eel, white sucker, pumpkinseed sunfish, redbreast sunfish.

Nequasset Pond has a small volume of cold, well-oxygenated water for coldwater fish. Rainbow trout have been stocked here in recent years, and appear to be doing well. Nequasset is the source of a commercial fishery for alewives. Ice should be out by the third week of April.

SCALE OF MILES

0   1

Miles

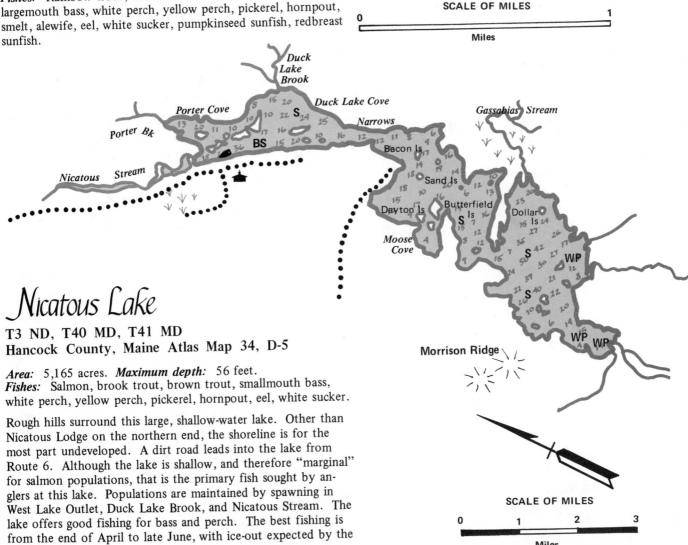

Nicatous Lake

T3 ND, T40 MD, T41 MD
Hancock County, Maine Atlas Map 34, D-5

Area: 5,165 acres. *Maximum depth:* 56 feet.
Fishes: Salmon, brook trout, brown trout, smallmouth bass, white perch, yellow perch, pickerel, hornpout, eel, white sucker.

Rough hills surround this large, shallow-water lake. Other than Nicatous Lodge on the northern end, the shoreline is for the most part undeveloped. A dirt road leads into the lake from Route 6. Although the lake is shallow, and therefore "marginal" for salmon populations, that is the primary fish sought by anglers at this lake. Populations are maintained by spawning in West Lake Outlet, Duck Lake Brook, and Nicatous Stream. The lake offers good fishing for bass and perch. The best fishing is from the end of April to late June, with ice-out expected by the middle of April.

SCALE OF MILES

0   1   2   3

Miles

Map **48**

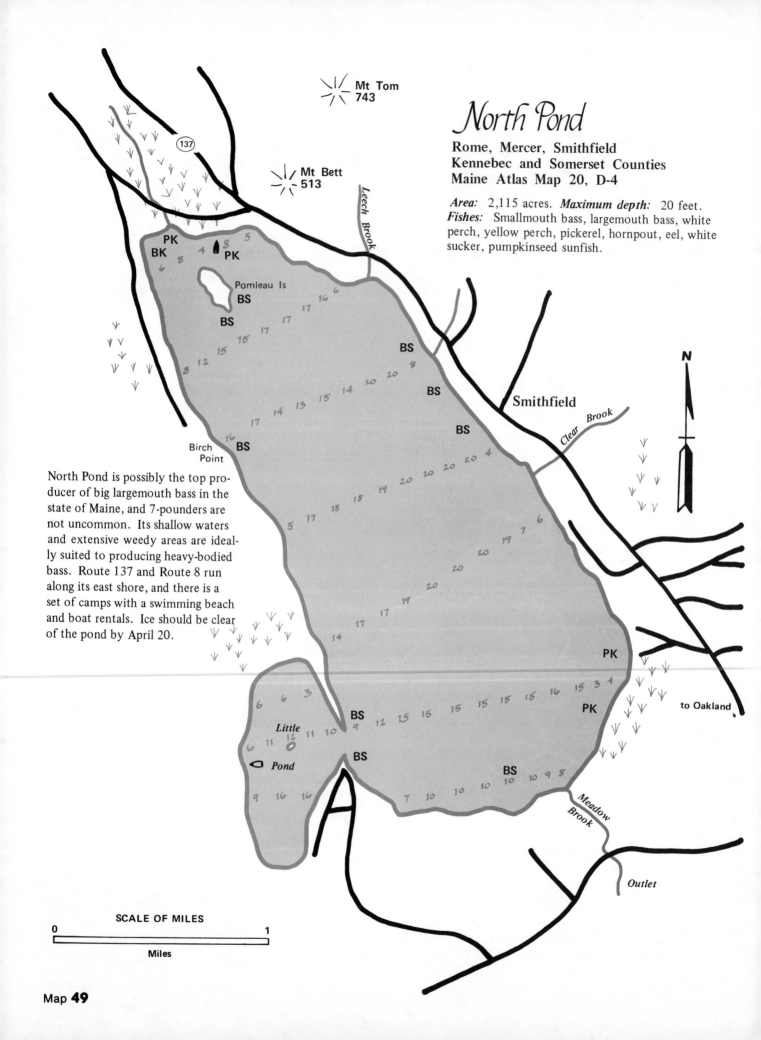

North Pond

Rome, Mercer, Smithfield
Kennebec and Somerset Counties
Maine Atlas Map 20, D-4

Area: 2,115 acres. *Maximum depth:* 20 feet.
Fishes: Smallmouth bass, largemouth bass, white perch, yellow perch, pickerel, hornpout, eel, white sucker, pumpkinseed sunfish.

Mt Tom
743

Mt Bett
513

Leech Brook

Pomleau Is

Smithfield

Clear Brook

Birch Point

Little Pond

to Oakland

Meadow Brook

Outlet

North Pond is possibly the top producer of big largemouth bass in the state of Maine, and 7-pounders are not uncommon. Its shallow waters and extensive weedy areas are ideally suited to producing heavy-bodied bass. Route 137 and Route 8 run along its east shore, and there is a set of camps with a swimming beach and boat rentals. Ice should be clear of the pond by April 20.

SCALE OF MILES

0   1

Miles

Map **49**

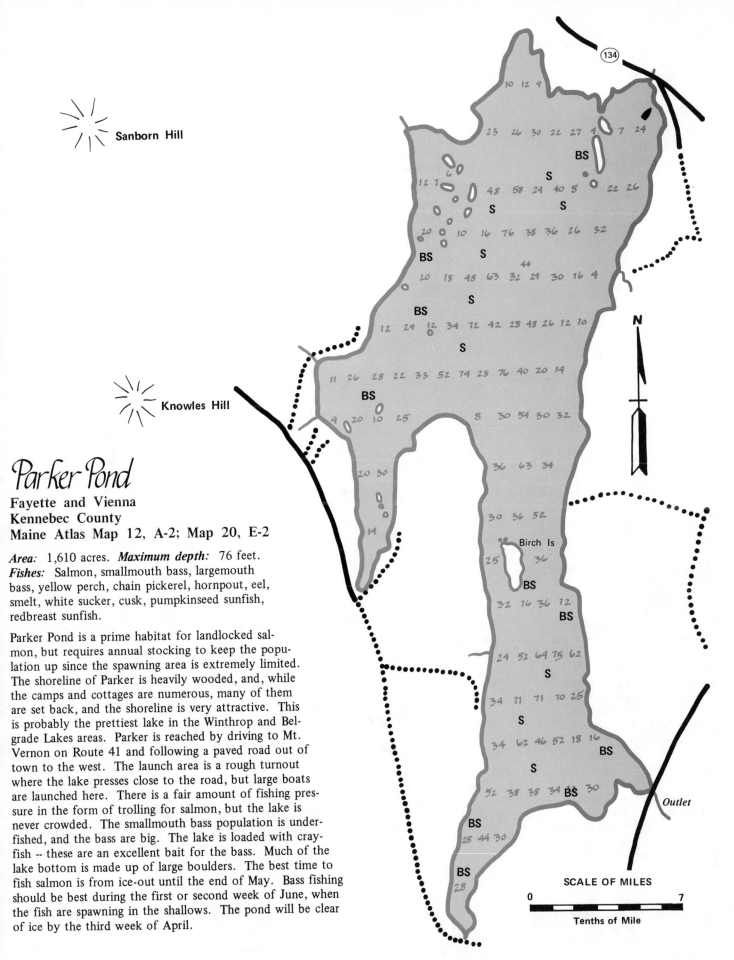

Sanborn Hill

Knowles Hill

Parker Pond

Fayette and Vienna
Kennebec County
Maine Atlas Map 12, A-2; Map 20, E-2

Area: 1,610 acres. *Maximum depth:* 76 feet.
Fishes: Salmon, smallmouth bass, largemouth
bass, yellow perch, chain pickerel, hornpout, eel,
smelt, white sucker, cusk, pumpkinseed sunfish,
redbreast sunfish.

Parker Pond is a prime habitat for landlocked salmon, but requires annual stocking to keep the population up since the spawning area is extremely limited.
The shoreline of Parker is heavily wooded, and, while
the camps and cottages are numerous, many of them
are set back, and the shoreline is very attractive. This
is probably the prettiest lake in the Winthrop and Belgrade Lakes areas. Parker is reached by driving to Mt.
Vernon on Route 41 and following a paved road out of
town to the west. The launch area is a rough turnout
where the lake presses close to the road, but large boats
are launched here. There is a fair amount of fishing pressure in the form of trolling for salmon, but the lake is
never crowded. The smallmouth bass population is under-
fished, and the bass are big. The lake is loaded with cray-
fish -- these are an excellent bait for the bass. Much of the
lake bottom is made up of large boulders. The best time to
fish salmon is from ice-out until the end of May. Bass fishing
should be best during the first or second week of June, when
the fish are spawning in the shallows. The pond will be clear
of ice by the third week of April.

Birch Is

SCALE OF MILES

0 ————————————— 7

Tenths of Mile

Outlet

N

Map **50**

Pemadumcook Chain of Lakes

(Ambajejus, Pemadumcook, North Twin, South Twin, Elbow Lakes
T3 Indian Purchase, T4 Indian Purchase, T1 R9 WELS, T1 R10
Penobscot and Piscataquis Counties
Maine Atlas Map 42, A-5; Map 43, A-1, B-1

Area: 18,300 acres. *Maximum depth:* 101 feet.
Fishes: Salmon, brook trout, lake trout, white perch, yellow perch, pickerel, hornpout, smelt, whitefish, eel, white sucker, longnose sucker, cusk, pumpkinseed sunfish, yellowbelly sunfish.

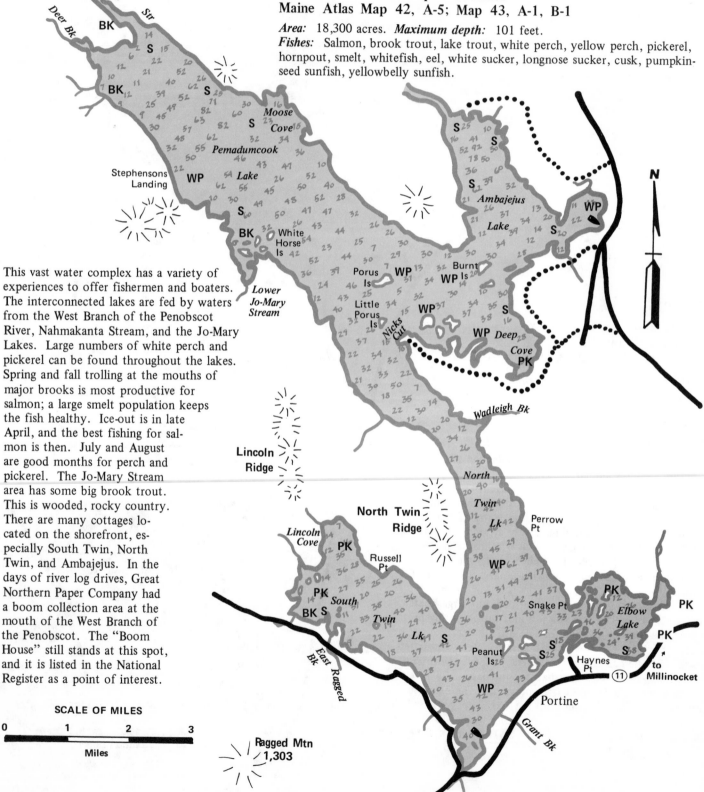

This vast water complex has a variety of experiences to offer fishermen and boaters. The interconnected lakes are fed by waters from the West Branch of the Penobscot River, Nahmakanta Stream, and the Jo-Mary Lakes. Large numbers of white perch and pickerel can be found throughout the lakes. Spring and fall trolling at the mouths of major brooks is most productive for salmon; a large smelt population keeps the fish healthy. Ice-out is in late April, and the best fishing for salmon is then. July and August are good months for perch and pickerel. The Jo-Mary Stream area has some big brook trout. This is wooded, rocky country. There are many cottages located on the shorefront, especially South Twin, North Twin, and Ambajejus. In the days of river log drives, Great Northern Paper Company had a boom collection area at the mouth of the West Branch of the Penobscot. The "Boom House" still stands at this spot, and it is listed in the National Register as a point of interest.

SCALE OF MILES

0   1   2   3

Miles

Map 51

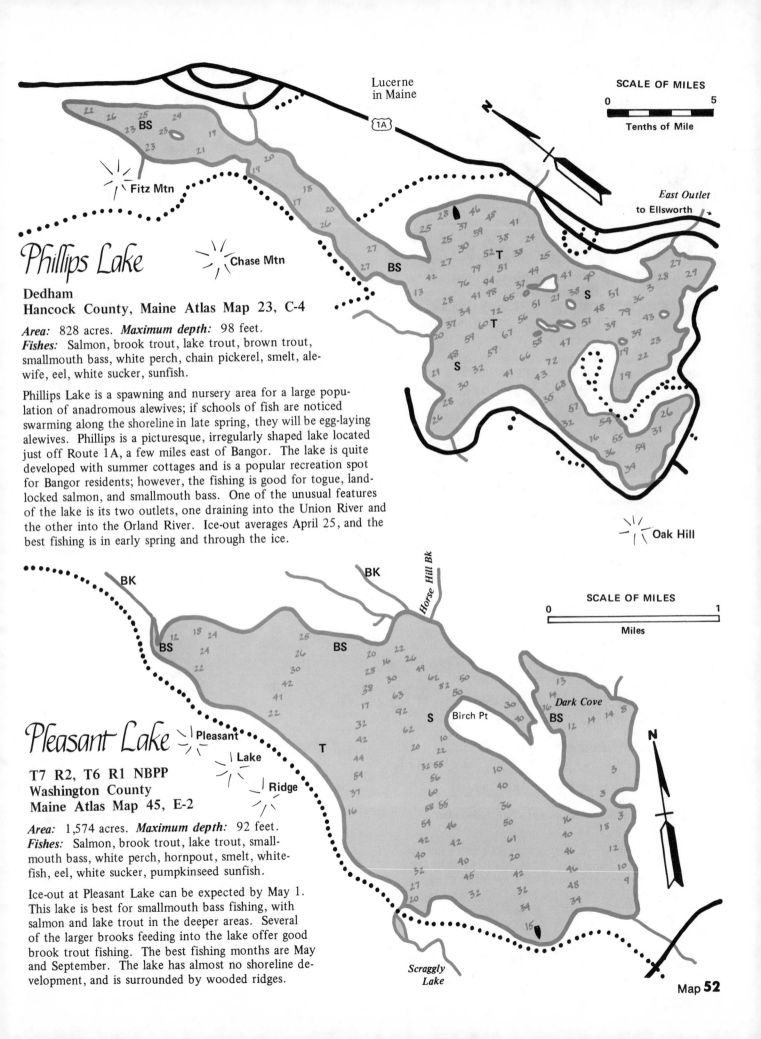

SCALE OF MILES
0   5
Tenths of Mile

Lucerne in Maine

1A

East Outlet
to Ellsworth →

Phillips Lake

Dedham
Hancock County, Maine Atlas Map 23, C-4

Area: 828 acres. *Maximum depth:* 98 feet.
Fishes: Salmon, brook trout, lake trout, brown trout, smallmouth bass, white perch, chain pickerel, smelt, alewife, eel, white sucker, sunfish.

Phillips Lake is a spawning and nursery area for a large population of anadromous alewives; if schools of fish are noticed swarming along the shoreline in late spring, they will be egg-laying alewives. Phillips is a picturesque, irregularly shaped lake located just off Route 1A, a few miles east of Bangor. The lake is quite developed with summer cottages and is a popular recreation spot for Bangor residents; however, the fishing is good for togue, landlocked salmon, and smallmouth bass. One of the unusual features of the lake is its two outlets, one draining into the Union River and the other into the Orland River. Ice-out averages April 25, and the best fishing is in early spring and through the ice.

Fitz Mtn

Chase Mtn

Oak Hill

BK   BK

Horse Hill Bk

SCALE OF MILES
0   1
Miles

Dark Cove

Birch Pt

Pleasant Lake

Pleasant
Lake
Ridge

T7 R2, T6 R1 NBPP
Washington County
Maine Atlas Map 45, E-2

Area: 1,574 acres. *Maximum depth:* 92 feet.
Fishes: Salmon, brook trout, lake trout, smallmouth bass, white perch, hornpout, smelt, whitefish, eel, white sucker, pumpkinseed sunfish.

Ice-out at Pleasant Lake can be expected by May 1. This lake is best for smallmouth bass fishing, with salmon and lake trout in the deeper areas. Several of the larger brooks feeding into the lake offer good brook trout fishing. The best fishing months are May and September. The lake has almost no shoreline development, and is surrounded by wooded ridges.

Scraggly
Lake

N

Map **52**

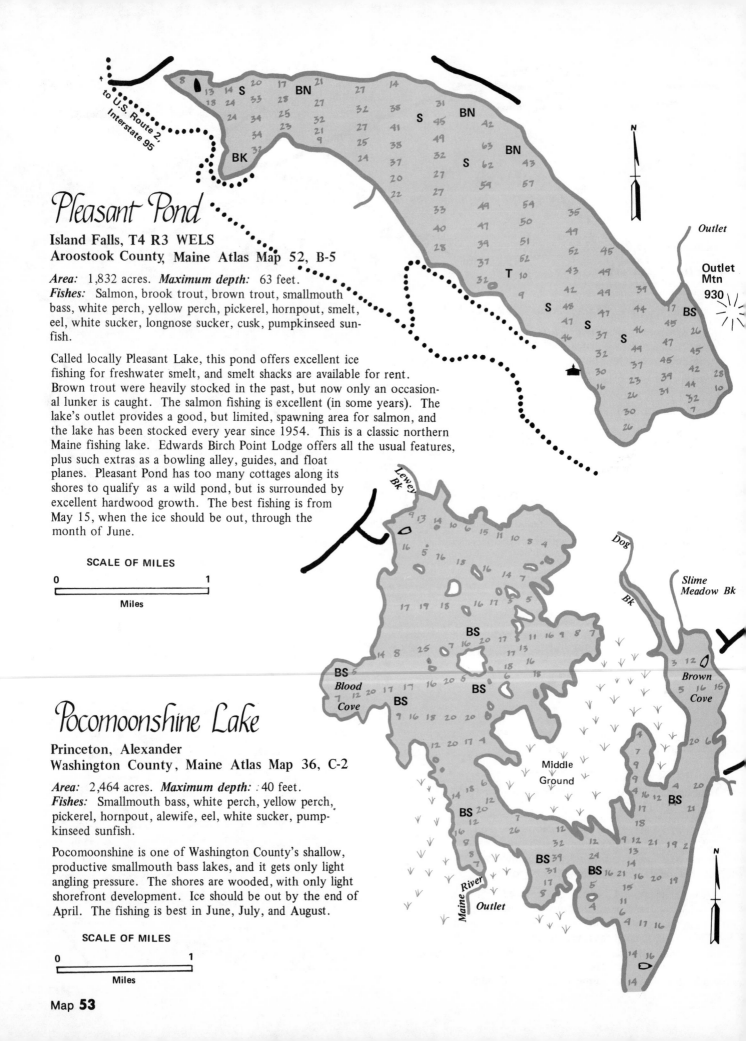

Pleasant Pond

Island Falls, T4 R3 WELS
Aroostook County, Maine Atlas Map 52, B-5

Area: 1,832 acres. *Maximum depth:* 63 feet.
Fishes: Salmon, brook trout, brown trout, smallmouth bass, white perch, yellow perch, pickerel, hornpout, smelt, eel, white sucker, longnose sucker, cusk, pumpkinseed sunfish.

Called locally Pleasant Lake, this pond offers excellent ice fishing for freshwater smelt, and smelt shacks are available for rent. Brown trout were heavily stocked in the past, but now only an occasional lunker is caught. The salmon fishing is excellent (in some years). The lake's outlet provides a good, but limited, spawning area for salmon, and the lake has been stocked every year since 1954. This is a classic northern Maine fishing lake. Edwards Birch Point Lodge offers all the usual features, plus such extras as a bowling alley, guides, and float planes. Pleasant Pond has too many cottages along its shores to qualify as a wild pond, but is surrounded by excellent hardwood growth. The best fishing is from May 15, when the ice should be out, through the month of June.

SCALE OF MILES

0 ————————————— 1

Miles

Pocomoonshine Lake

Princeton, Alexander
Washington County, Maine Atlas Map 36, C-2

Area: 2,464 acres. *Maximum depth:* 40 feet.
Fishes: Smallmouth bass, white perch, yellow perch, pickerel, hornpout, alewife, eel, white sucker, pumpkinseed sunfish.

Pocomoonshine is one of Washington County's shallow, productive smallmouth bass lakes, and it gets only light angling pressure. The shores are wooded, with only light shorefront development. Ice should be out by the end of April. The fishing is best in June, July, and August.

SCALE OF MILES

0 ————————————— 1

Miles

Map **53**

Some anglers think of Porter Lake as primarily a brook trout water, although the Fish and Wildlife Department says the principal fishery here is for lake trout, white perch, yellow perch, pickerel, and smelt. Although it has been stocked with rainbow trout in the past, Porter Lake is not considered to have good water quality for cold-water fish. The best fishing occurs during the smelt run in early spring when game fish congregate around the brook at the extreme southern end of the pond. There is a lot of cottage development along the shoreline. Ice-out will take place by the second week of May.

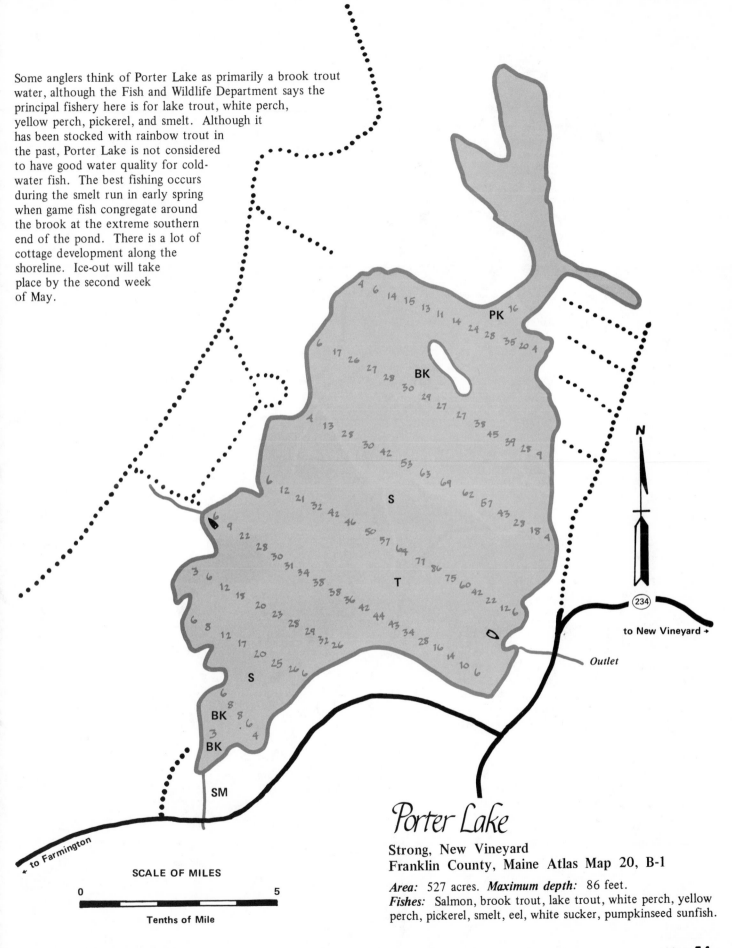

N

(234)

to New Vineyard →

Outlet

← to Farmington

SCALE OF MILES

0   5

Tenths of Mile

Porter Lake

Strong, New Vineyard
Franklin County, Maine Atlas Map 20, B-1

Area: 527 acres. *Maximum depth:* 86 feet.
Fishes: Salmon, brook trout, lake trout, white perch, yellow perch, pickerel, smelt, eel, white sucker, pumpkinseed sunfish.

Map **54**

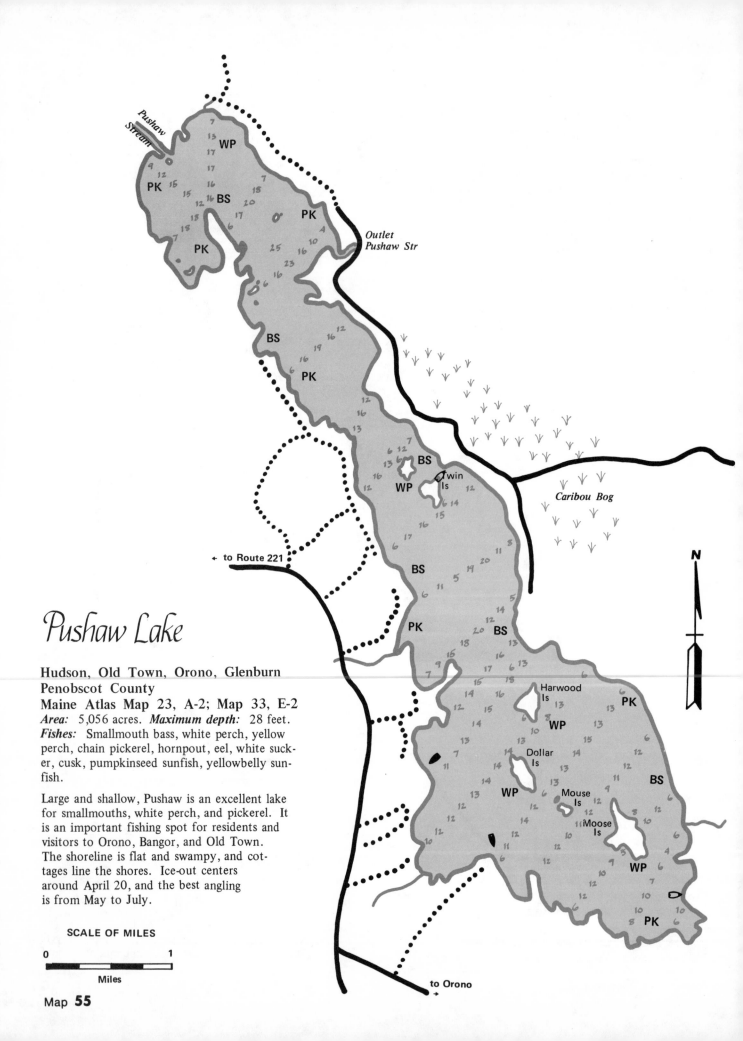

Pushaw Lake

Hudson, Old Town, Orono, Glenburn
Penobscot County
Maine Atlas Map 23, A-2; Map 33, E-2
Area: 5,056 acres. *Maximum depth:* 28 feet.
Fishes: Smallmouth bass, white perch, yellow
perch, chain pickerel, hornpout, eel, white suck-
er, cusk, pumpkinseed sunfish, yellowbelly sun-
fish.

Large and shallow, Pushaw is an excellent lake
for smallmouths, white perch, and pickerel. It
is an important fishing spot for residents and
visitors to Orono, Bangor, and Old Town.
The shoreline is flat and swampy, and cottages line the shores. Ice-out centers
around April 20, and the best angling
is from May to July.

SCALE OF MILES

0   1

Miles

Map **55**

Pushaw
Stream

WP

PK

PK

BS

PK

Outlet
Pushaw Str

BS

PK

← to Route 221

BS

WP

Twin
Is

Caribou Bog

BS

PK

N

Harwood
Is

PK

WP

Dollar
Is

BS

WP

Mouse
Is

Moose
Is

WP

PK

to Orono

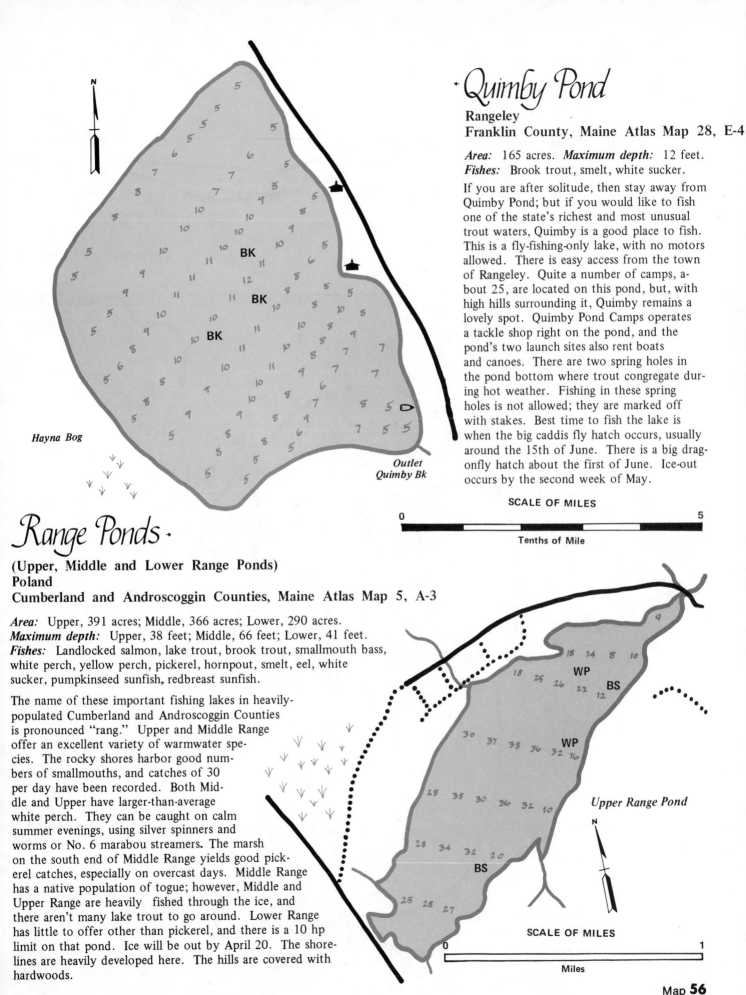

Quimby Pond

Rangeley
Franklin County, Maine Atlas Map 28, E-4

Area: 165 acres. *Maximum depth:* 12 feet.
Fishes: Brook trout, smelt, white sucker.

If you are after solitude, then stay away from Quimby Pond; but if you would like to fish one of the state's richest and most unusual trout waters, Quimby is a good place to fish. This is a fly-fishing-only lake, with no motors allowed. There is easy access from the town of Rangeley. Quite a number of camps, a-bout 25, are located on this pond, but, with high hills surrounding it, Quimby remains a lovely spot. Quimby Pond Camps operates a tackle shop right on the pond, and the pond's two launch sites also rent boats and canoes. There are two spring holes in the pond bottom where trout congregate during hot weather. Fishing in these spring holes is not allowed; they are marked off with stakes. Best time to fish the lake is when the big caddis fly hatch occurs, usually around the 15th of June. There is a big drag-onfly hatch about the first of June. Ice-out occurs by the second week of May.

SCALE OF MILES

0   5

Tenths of Mile

Hayna Bog

Outlet Quimby Bk

Range Ponds

(Upper, Middle and Lower Range Ponds)
Poland
Cumberland and Androscoggin Counties, Maine Atlas Map 5, A-3

Area: Upper, 391 acres; Middle, 366 acres; Lower, 290 acres.
Maximum depth: Upper, 38 feet; Middle, 66 feet; Lower, 41 feet.
Fishes: Landlocked salmon, lake trout, brook trout, smallmouth bass, white perch, yellow perch, pickerel, hornpout, smelt, eel, white sucker, pumpkinseed sunfish, redbreast sunfish.

The name of these important fishing lakes in heavily-populated Cumberland and Androscoggin Counties is pronounced "rang." Upper and Middle Range offer an excellent variety of warmwater spe-cies. The rocky shores harbor good num-bers of smallmouths, and catches of 30 per day have been recorded. Both Mid-dle and Upper have larger-than-average white perch. They can be caught on calm summer evenings, using silver spinners and worms or No. 6 marabou streamers. The marsh on the south end of Middle Range yields good pick-erel catches, especially on overcast days. Middle Range has a native population of togue; however, Middle and Upper Range are heavily fished through the ice, and there aren't many lake trout to go around. Lower Range has little to offer other than pickerel, and there is a 10 hp limit on that pond. Ice will be out by April 20. The shore-lines are heavily developed here. The hills are covered with hardwoods.

Upper Range Pond

SCALE OF MILES

0   1

Miles

Map **56**

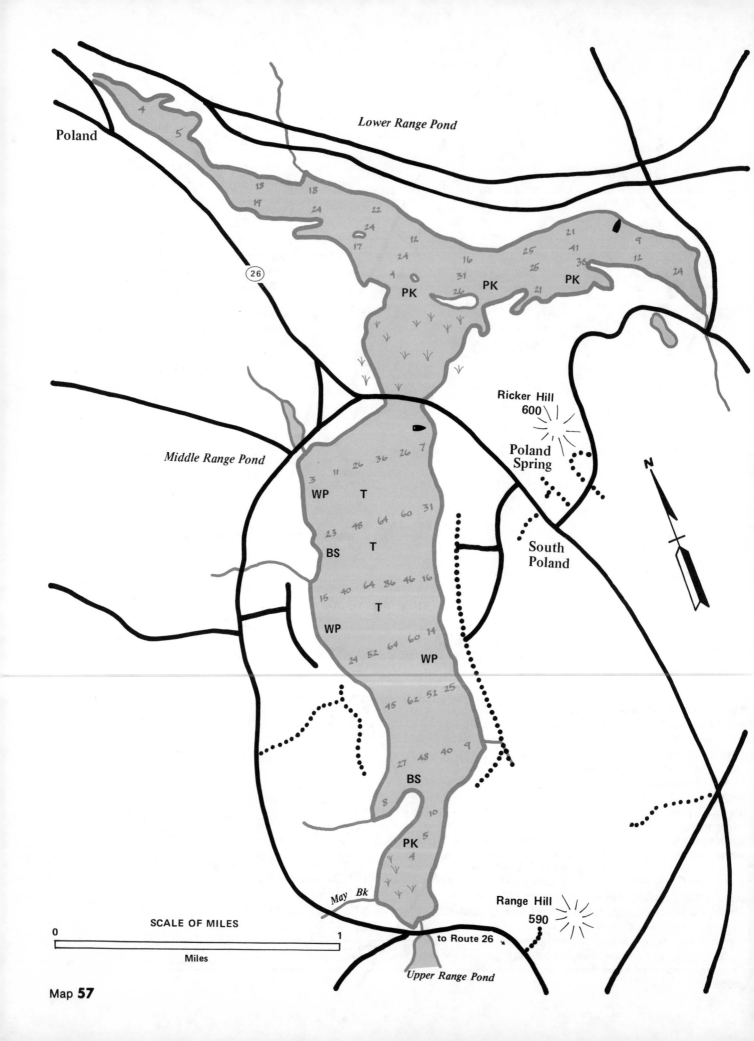

Poland

Lower Range Pond

4
5
13   18
14   24   22
24   12
17   16   21   9
4   24   25   41   12
PK   31   26   36   24
PK   26   PK   21   PK

(26)

Ricker Hill
600

Poland
Spring

Middle Range Pond

7
26   36   26
3   11
WP   T
48   64   60   31
23
BS   T   64   36   46   16
15   40
T
WP   64   60   14
24   52   WP

South
Poland

N

45   62   52   25

27   48   40   9

BS

8

10

PK   5
4

May Bk

Range Hill
590

SCALE OF MILES

0 _____ 1

Miles

to Route 26 →

Upper Range Pond

Map **57**

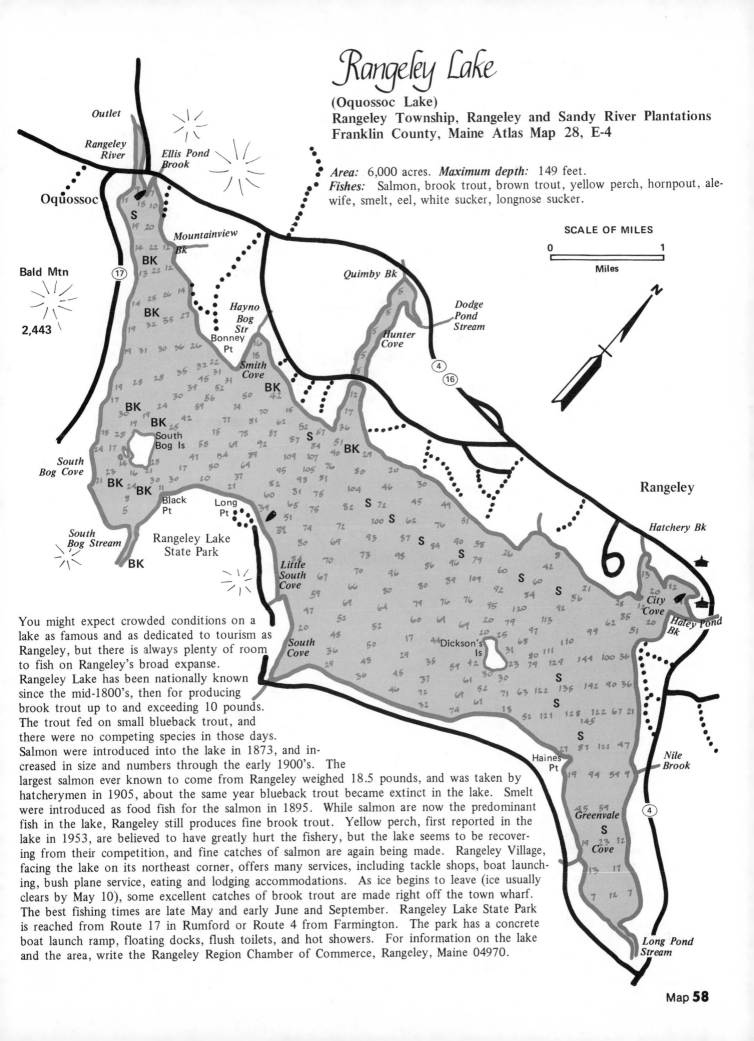

Rangeley Lake

(Oquossoc Lake)
Rangeley Township, Rangeley and Sandy River Plantations
Franklin County, Maine Atlas Map 28, E-4

Area: 6,000 acres. *Maximum depth:* 149 feet.
Fishes: Salmon, brook trout, brown trout, yellow perch, hornpout, alewife, smelt, eel, white sucker, longnose sucker.

SCALE OF MILES

0   1

Miles

You might expect crowded conditions on a lake as famous and as dedicated to tourism as Rangeley, but there is always plenty of room to fish on Rangeley's broad expanse. Rangeley Lake has been nationally known since the mid-1800's, then for producing brook trout up to and exceeding 10 pounds. The trout fed on small blueback trout, and there were no competing species in those days. Salmon were introduced into the lake in 1873, and increased in size and numbers through the early 1900's. The largest salmon ever known to come from Rangeley weighed 18.5 pounds, and was taken by hatcherymen in 1905, about the same year blueback trout became extinct in the lake. Smelt were introduced as food fish for the salmon in 1895. While salmon are now the predominant fish in the lake, Rangeley still produces fine brook trout. Yellow perch, first reported in the lake in 1953, are believed to have greatly hurt the fishery, but the lake seems to be recovering from their competition, and fine catches of salmon are again being made. Rangeley Village, facing the lake on its northeast corner, offers many services, including tackle shops, boat launching, bush plane service, eating and lodging accommodations. As ice begins to leave (ice usually clears by May 10), some excellent catches of brook trout are made right off the town wharf. The best fishing times are late May and early June and September. Rangeley Lake State Park is reached from Route 17 in Rumford or Route 4 from Farmington. The park has a concrete boat launch ramp, floating docks, flush toilets, and hot showers. For information on the lake and the area, write the Rangeley Region Chamber of Commerce, Rangeley, Maine 04970.

Map **58**

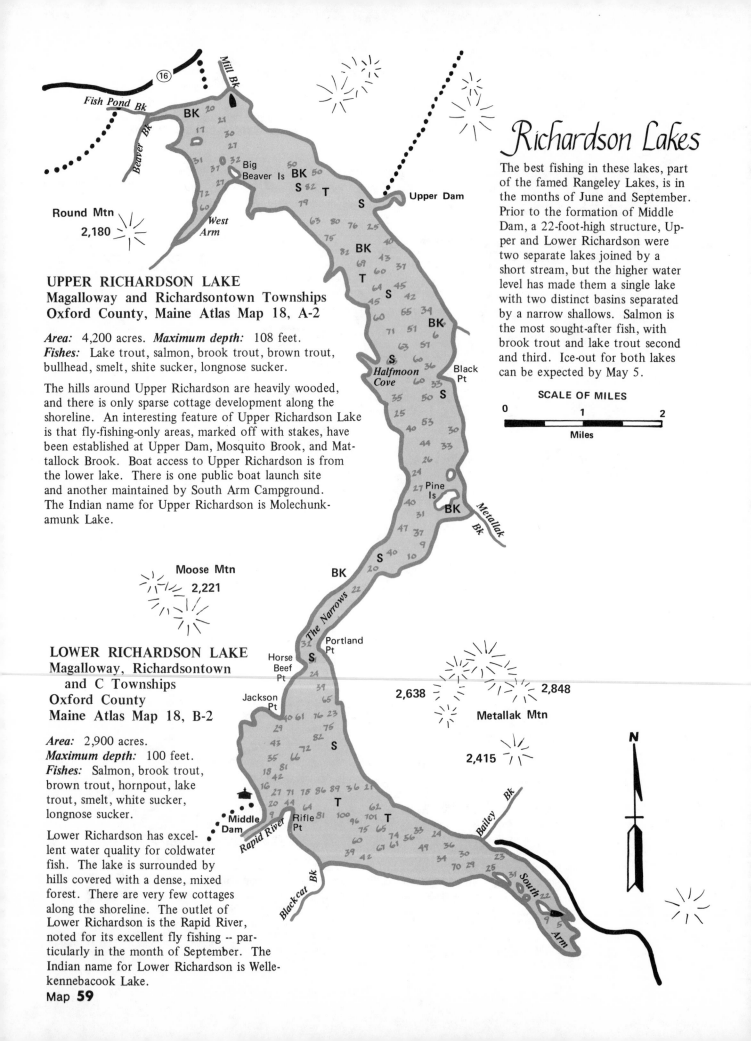

Richardson Lakes

The best fishing in these lakes, part of the famed Rangeley Lakes, is in the months of June and September. Prior to the formation of Middle Dam, a 22-foot-high structure, Upper and Lower Richardson were two separate lakes joined by a short stream, but the higher water level has made them a single lake with two distinct basins separated by a narrow shallows. Salmon is the most sought-after fish, with brook trout and lake trout second and third. Ice-out for both lakes can be expected by May 5.

SCALE OF MILES

Miles

UPPER RICHARDSON LAKE
Magalloway and Richardsontown Townships
Oxford County, Maine Atlas Map 18, A-2

Area: 4,200 acres. *Maximum depth:* 108 feet.
Fishes: Lake trout, salmon, brook trout, brown trout, bullhead, smelt, shite sucker, longnose sucker.

The hills around Upper Richardson are heavily wooded, and there is only sparse cottage development along the shoreline. An interesting feature of Upper Richardson Lake is that fly-fishing-only areas, marked off with stakes, have been established at Upper Dam, Mosquito Brook, and Mattallock Brook. Boat access to Upper Richardson is from the lower lake. There is one public boat launch site and another maintained by South Arm Campground. The Indian name for Upper Richardson is Molechunkamunk Lake.

LOWER RICHARDSON LAKE
Magalloway, Richardsontown
and C Townships
Oxford County
Maine Atlas Map 18, B-2

Area: 2,900 acres.
Maximum depth: 100 feet.
Fishes: Salmon, brook trout, brown trout, hornpout, lake trout, smelt, white sucker, longnose sucker.

Lower Richardson has excellent water quality for coldwater fish. The lake is surrounded by hills covered with a dense, mixed forest. There are very few cottages along the shoreline. The outlet of Lower Richardson is the Rapid River, noted for its excellent fly fishing -- particularly in the month of September. The Indian name for Lower Richardson is Wellekennebacook Lake.

Map **59**

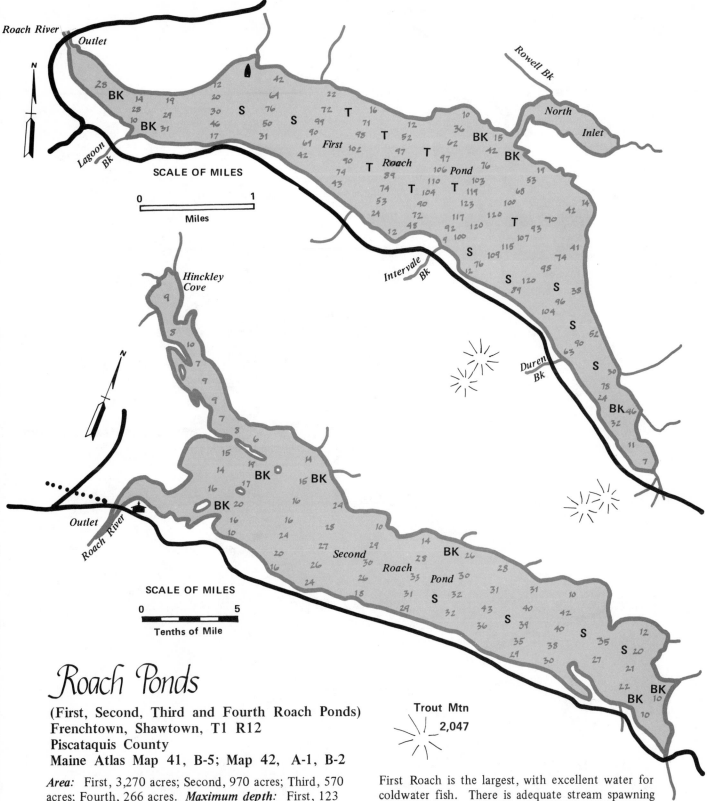

Roach Ponds

(First, Second, Third and Fourth Roach Ponds)
Frenchtown, Shawtown, T1 R12
Piscataquis County
Maine Atlas Map 41, B-5; Map 42, A-1, B-2

Area: First, 3,270 acres; Second, 970 acres; Third, 570 acres; Fourth, 266 acres. *Maximum depth:* First, 123 feet; Second, 46 feet; Third, 26 feet; Fourth, 38 feet. *Fishes:* Salmon, brook trout, lake trout, hornpout, cusk, smelt, lake whitefish, round whitefish, white sucker.

First, Second, Third, and Fourth Roach Ponds form a chain of pretty ponds in a wilderness setting, all with hilly shorelines and background mountains covered with spruce and fir. All four ponds offer good trout and salmon fishing, best in late May through June. Ice-out occurs by May 5.

First Roach is the largest, with excellent water for coldwater fish. There is adequate stream spawning for brook trout and salmon, and shoals for lake trout to spawn. First Roach is a very deep lake.

After recovering from a water level problem, Second Roach is coming back nicely as a salmon and brook trout fishery. With a good smelt population, this water offers better salmon fishing than the two upper ponds. Trout fishing is often good in the rivers above and below this pond.

Trout Mtn
2,047

Map **60**

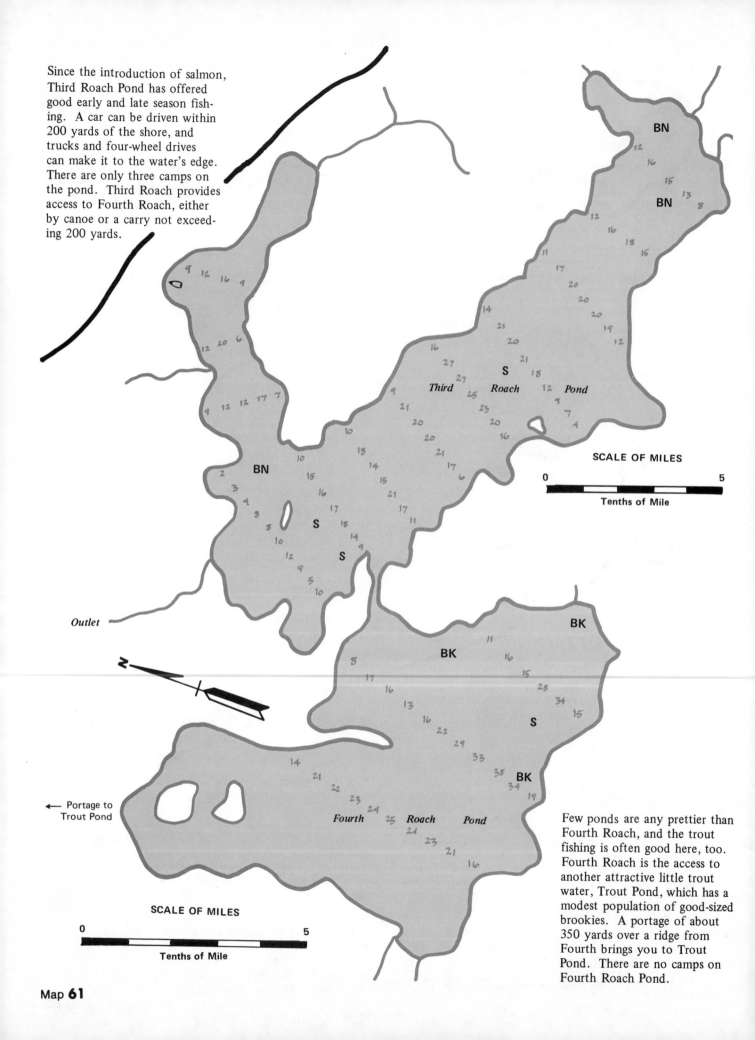

Since the introduction of salmon, Third Roach Pond has offered good early and late season fishing. A car can be driven within 200 yards of the shore, and trucks and four-wheel drives can make it to the water's edge. There are only three camps on the pond. Third Roach provides access to Fourth Roach, either by canoe or a carry not exceeding 200 yards.

BN

BN

BN

Third Roach Pond

S

SCALE OF MILES

0   5

Tenths of Mile

BN

S

S

Outlet

N

← Portage to
Trout Pond

BK

BK

S

BK

Fourth Roach Pond

Few ponds are any prettier than Fourth Roach, and the trout fishing is often good here, too. Fourth Roach is the access to another attractive little trout water, Trout Pond, which has a modest population of good-sized brookies. A portage of about 350 yards over a ridge from Fourth brings you to Trout Pond. There are no camps on Fourth Roach Pond.

SCALE OF MILES

0   5

Tenths of Mile

Map 61

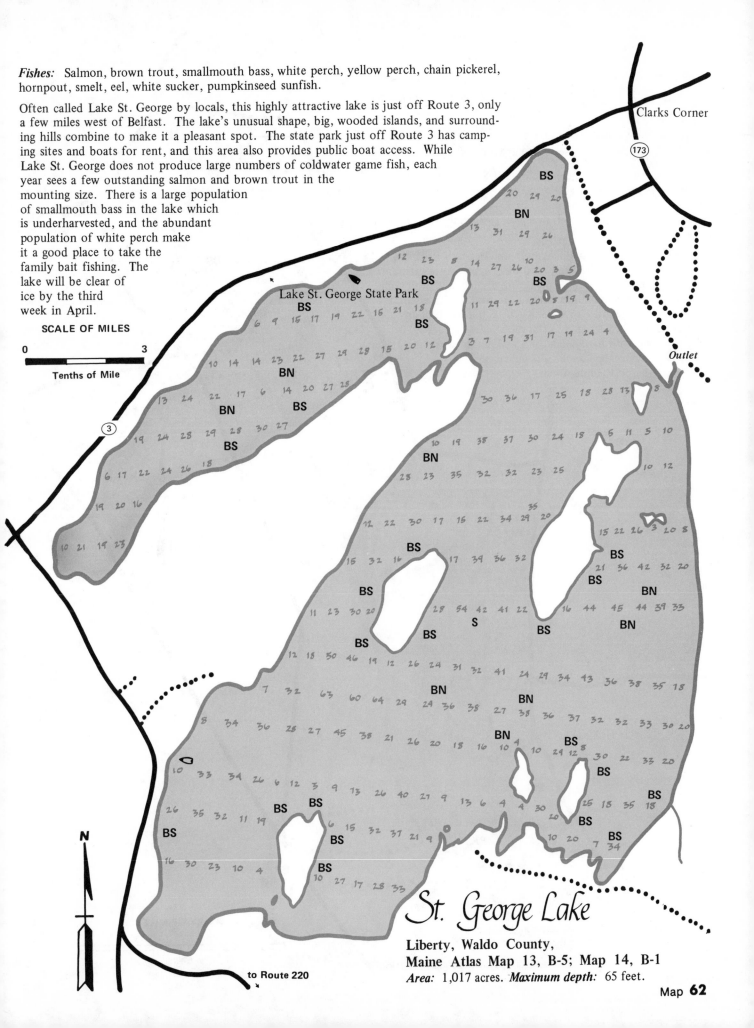

Fishes: Salmon, brown trout, smallmouth bass, white perch, yellow perch, chain pickerel, hornpout, smelt, eel, white sucker, pumpkinseed sunfish.

Often called Lake St. George by locals, this highly attractive lake is just off Route 3, only a few miles west of Belfast. The lake's unusual shape, big, wooded islands, and surrounding hills combine to make it a pleasant spot. The state park just off Route 3 has camping sites and boats for rent, and this area also provides public boat access. While Lake St. George does not produce large numbers of coldwater game fish, each year sees a few outstanding salmon and brown trout in the mounting size. There is a large population of smallmouth bass in the lake which is underharvested, and the abundant population of white perch make it a good place to take the family bait fishing. The lake will be clear of ice by the third week in April.

SCALE OF MILES

0   3

Tenths of Mile

Clarks Corner

173

Lake St. George State Park

Outlet

N

to Route 220

St. George Lake

Liberty, Waldo County,
Maine Atlas Map 13, B-5; Map 14, B-1
Area: 1,017 acres. *Maximum depth:* 65 feet.

Map **62**

Salmon and McGrath Lakes

(Ellis Pond)
Belgrade, Oakland
Kennebec County, Maine Atlas Map 20, E-5

Area: Salmon Lake, 562 acres; McGrath Pond, 486 acres.
Maximum depth: Salmon Lake, 57 feet; McGrath Pond, 27 feet.
Fishes: Brown trout, smallmouth bass, largemouth bass, white perch, yellow perch, pickerel, hornpout, eel, white sucker, pumpkinseed sunfish.

Salmon Lake (also called Ellis Pond) and McGrath Pond are really a single body of water joined by a narrow thoroughfare. Both ponds provide decent brown trout fishing, and Waterville area anglers fish these ponds hard in the winter. Excellent catches of largemouth bass are made here, and both basins hold good-sized white perch. The surrounding land is hilly, forested with hardwoods, and well-dotted with shoreline camps. May, June, September, and ice season are the best fishing times.

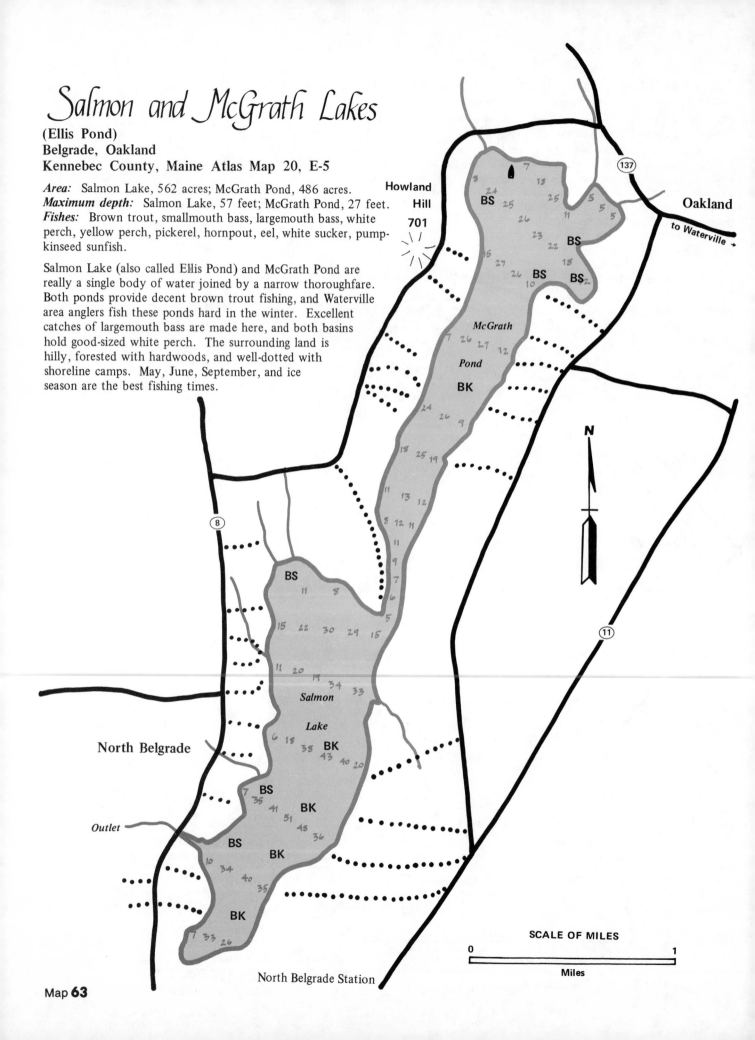

Howland
Hill
701

Oakland

to Waterville →

McGrath
Pond

Salmon
Lake

North Belgrade

Outlet

North Belgrade Station

SCALE OF MILES

0   1

Miles

N

Map **63**

Scraggly Lake

T6 R1, T5 R1
Washington and Penobscot Counties, Maine Atlas Map 35, A-2; Map 45, E-2

Area: 2,758 acres. *Maximum depth:* 42 feet.
Fishes: Salmon, lake trout, smallmouth bass, white perch, yellow perch, chain pickerel, hornpout, whitefish, white sucker.

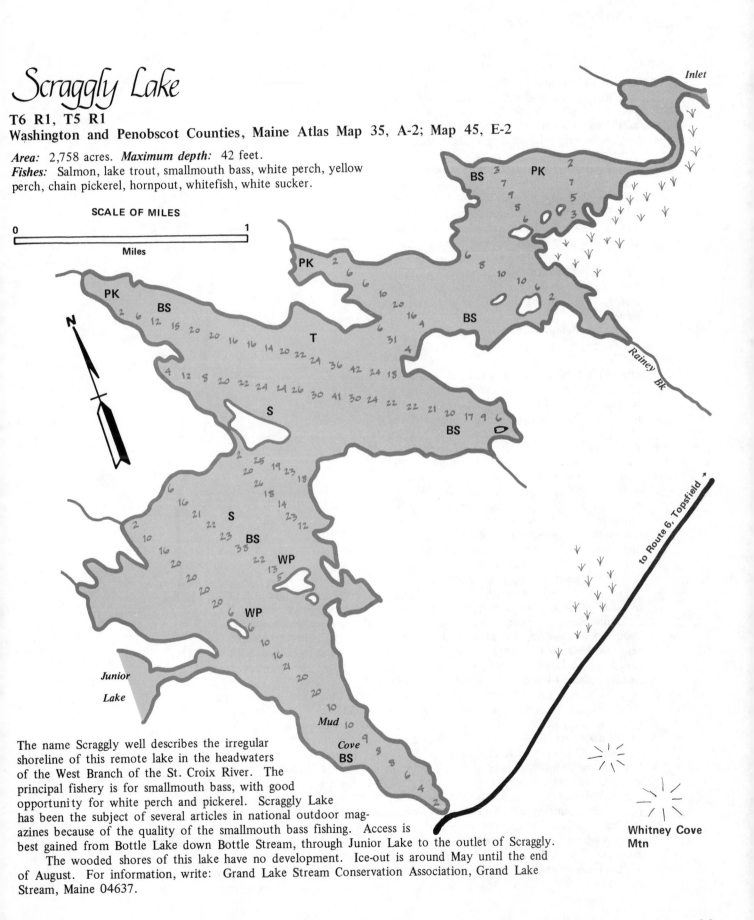

SCALE OF MILES

0 — 1

Miles

Inlet

Rainey Bk

to Route 6, Topsfield

Whitney Cove Mtn

Junior Lake

Mud Cove

The name Scraggly well describes the irregular shoreline of this remote lake in the headwaters of the West Branch of the St. Croix River. The principal fishery is for smallmouth bass, with good opportunity for white perch and pickerel. Scraggly Lake has been the subject of several articles in national outdoor magazines because of the quality of the smallmouth bass fishing. Access is best gained from Bottle Lake down Bottle Stream, through Junior Lake to the outlet of Scraggly.

The wooded shores of this lake have no development. Ice-out is around May until the end of August. For information, write: Grand Lake Stream Conservation Association, Grand Lake Stream, Maine 04637.

Map **64**

Sebago Lake

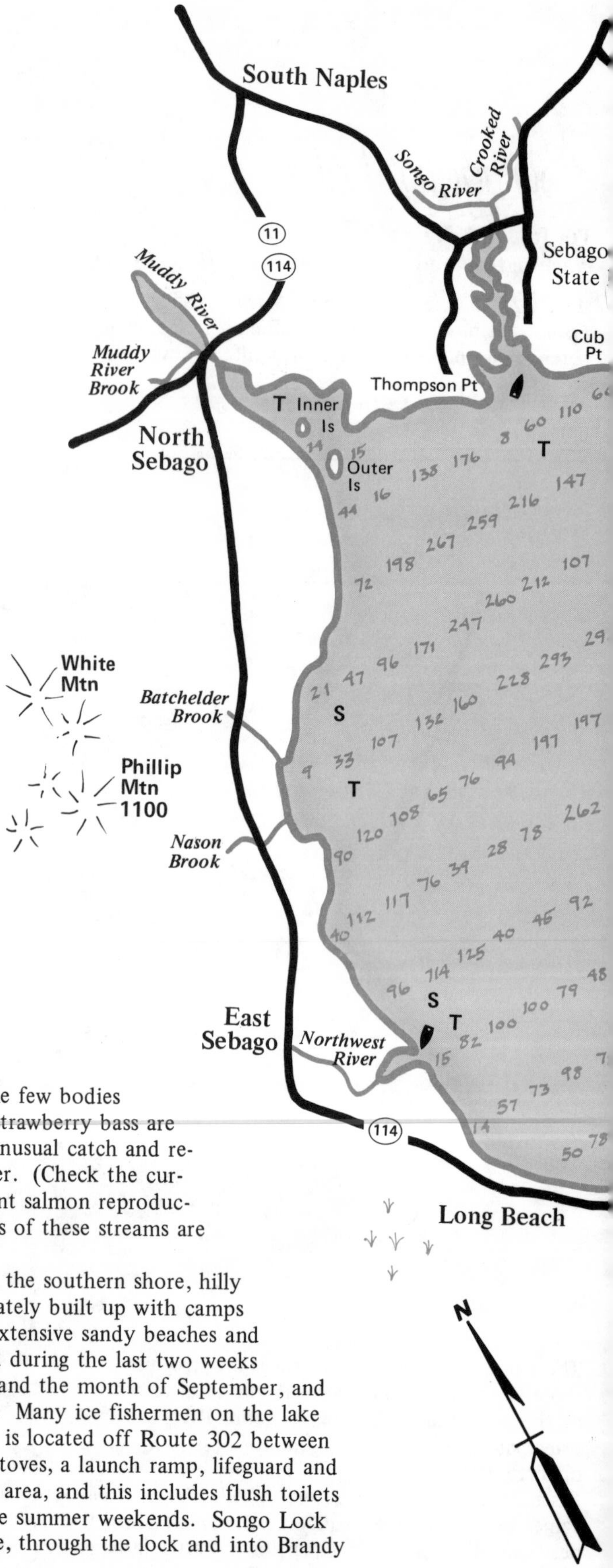

Sebago Lake is the glamor spot of southern Maine for a lot of good reasons. Its deep hole is the deepest of any New England lake. The third largest lake in New England, its Indian name means "big water." The landlocked salmon gets its scientific name *Salmo sebago* from Sebago Lake, one of the original four watersheds of this grand game fish.

The state's record landlocked salmon came from Sebago in 1907. The 22-pound, 8-ounce fish was caught by Edward Blakeley of Darien, Connecticut, while still fishing a redfin shiner. The lake also produced three other current state record fish, a 19-pound, 7-ounce brown trout caught in 1958, a 6-pound, 8-ounce pickerel in 1969, and a 7-pound, 8-ounce whitefish in 1958. The lake also produced a 15-pound, 12-ounce cusk in 1978, but that record has since been surpassed.

Situated close to the largest population centers in Maine and an easy drive from Massachusetts and New Hampshire, the Sebago region is one of the state's busiest resort areas, and every conceivable service a fisherman or vacationer could want is available in the surrounding communities. The lake has made a dramatic recovery of its salmon population since the 1950's, when it suffered from heavy DDT use for mosquito control. Besides the salmon fishery, lake trout have been stocked by the thousands and are utilizing the vast deep-water areas which previously harbored few fish. However, it would be a mistake to overlook Sebago as a producer of warmwater species, for its many weedy coves and rocky shoals are excellent for largemouth and smallmouth bass and pickerel. White perch and yellow perch as well grow to respectable sizes in the lake's fertile waters. Sebago is also one of the few bodies of water in the state to contain black crappie (calico or strawberry bass are colloquial names). Sebago Lake Station offers a highly unusual catch and release area for spawning landlocks in the month of October. (Check the current law book for the regulations.) The lake gets excellent salmon reproduction from the Crooked and Songo Rivers, and the mouths of these streams are two of the early ice-out areas which yield fish in April.

The shores of Sebago are mostly wooded and flat on the southern shore, hilly on the north. The eastern and western shores are moderately built up with camps and year-round homes. It is a typical glacial lake, with extensive sandy beaches and low bluffs of eroding glacial till. Ice-out can be expected during the last two weeks of April. The best coldwater fishing is in May and June and the month of September, and bass and pickerel fishing is good from June through July. Many ice fishermen on the lake specialize in whitefish and cusk. Sebago Lake State Park is located off Route 302 between Naples and South Casco. It offers sand beaches, tables, stoves, a launch ramp, lifeguard and bath facilities in the Casco area; camping is in the Naples area, and this includes flush toilets and hot showers. The camping area is often full on prime summer weekends. Songo Lock permits a boat trip up the Songo River from Sebago Lake, through the lock and into Brandy Pond and Long Lake.

The *Sebago Lake Map and Guide,* available from DeLorme Publishing Company, shows Sebago Lake and environs in full color and high detail, with text about recreation and history of the area.

Map **65**

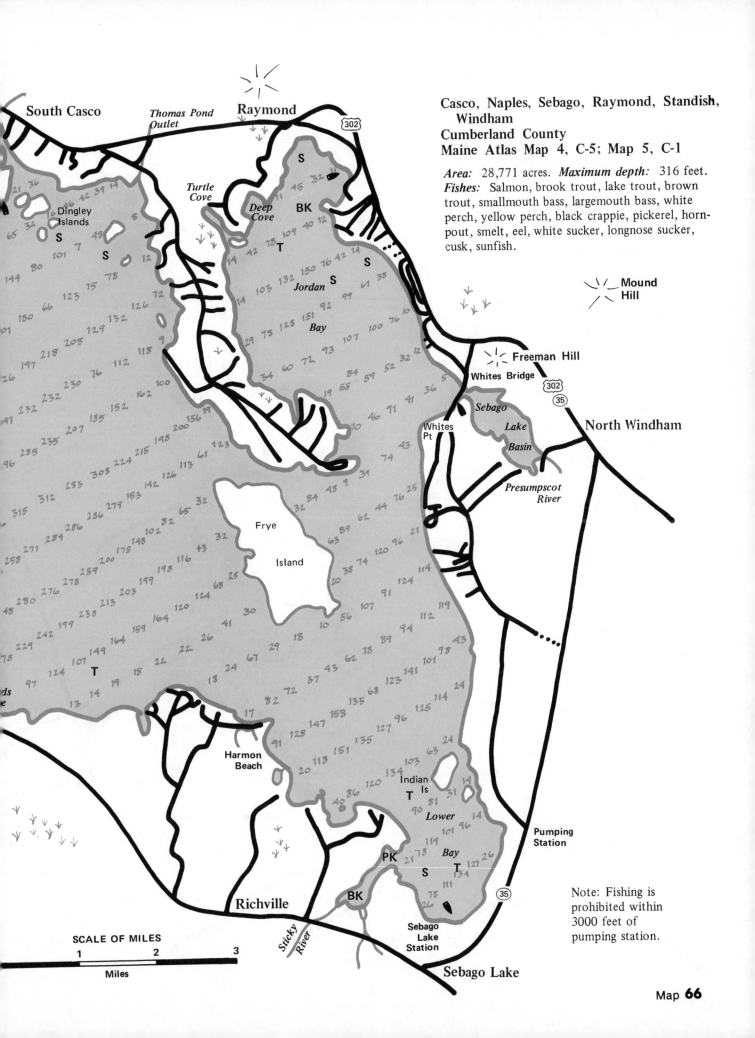

South Casco   *Thomas Pond Outlet*   Raymond   **302**

Casco, Naples, Sebago, Raymond, Standish,
Windham
Cumberland County
Maine Atlas Map 4, C-5; Map 5, C-1

Area: 28,771 acres. *Maximum depth:* 316 feet.
Fishes: Salmon, brook trout, lake trout, brown
trout, smallmouth bass, largemouth bass, white
perch, yellow perch, black crappie, pickerel, hornpout, smelt, eel, white sucker, longnose sucker,
cusk, sunfish.

**Mound
Hill**

*Turtle
Cove*

*Deep
Cove*

S

BK

T

Dingley
Islands

Jordan

S

Bay

S

Freeman Hill

Whites Bridge

*Sebago
Lake
Basin*

302
35

Whites
Pt

North Windham

*Presumpscot
River*

Frye

Island

Harmon
Beach

T

*Indian
Is*

T

Lower

Bay

**Pumping
Station**

S

PK

T

Richville

BK

Sebago
Lake
Station

35

*Sticky
River*

Note: Fishing is
prohibited within
3000 feet of
pumping station.

SCALE OF MILES

1   2   3

Miles

Sebago Lake

Map **66**

Sebec Lake

Willimantic, Bowerbank, Dover-Foxcroft
Piscataquis County, Maine Atlas Map 31, A-5; Map 32, A-1,2,3

Area: 6,803 acres. *Maximum depth:* 155 feet.
Fishes: Salmon, brook trout, lake trout, small-mouth bass, white perch, yellow perch, pickerel, smelt, eel, white sucker, cusk.

Sebec is respected as one of the best landlocked salmon lakes in the state. Most of the fishing is done at the west end. There are good numbers of lake trout in the deep areas and smallmouth bass along the rocky shorelines. Ice will be out by May 1; the best salmon fishing comes just after ice-out. The September fishing is good, too. The lake is surrounded by wooded hills, and the sections of rocky shoreline are found at the end of the lake near Dover-Foxcroft.

Peaks-Kenny State Park, located on Sebec Lake, is one of the least-utilized state parks in Maine. It is reached by Route 153 from Dover-Foxcroft. There is a sand beach, lifeguard, pic-nicking facilities and bathhouse, with showers at the park. Campsites are available. The park affords an excellent view of Boarstone and Barren Mountains, across the lake.

SCALE OF MILES

0   1

Miles

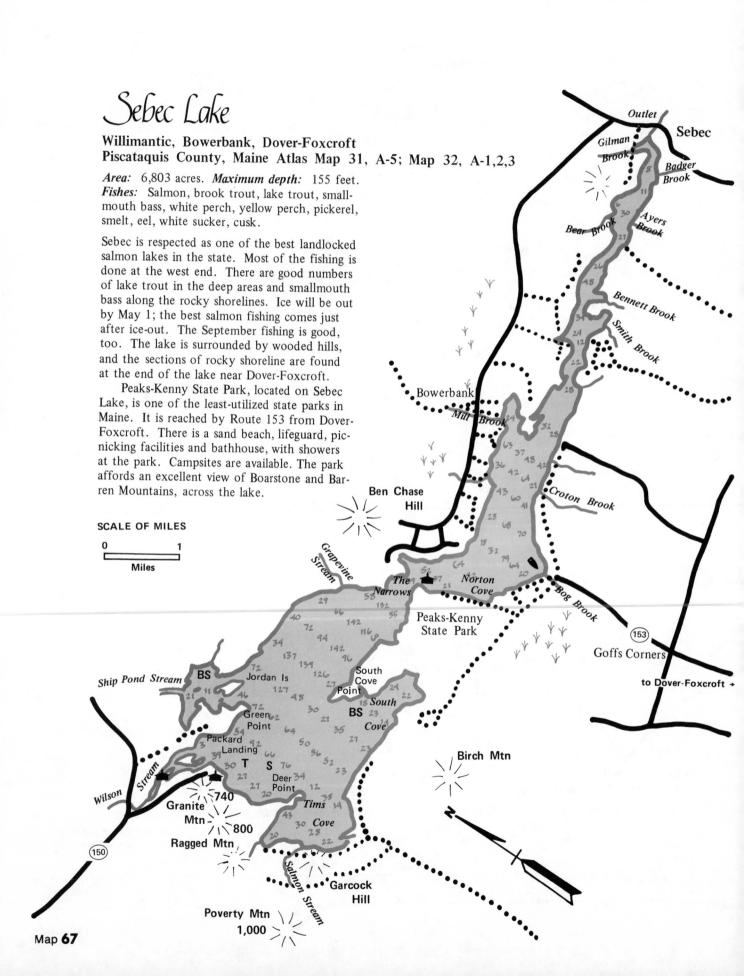

Map **67**

Sheepscot Pond

(Sheepscot Lake)
Palermo
Waldo County
Maine Atlas Map 13, B-4

N

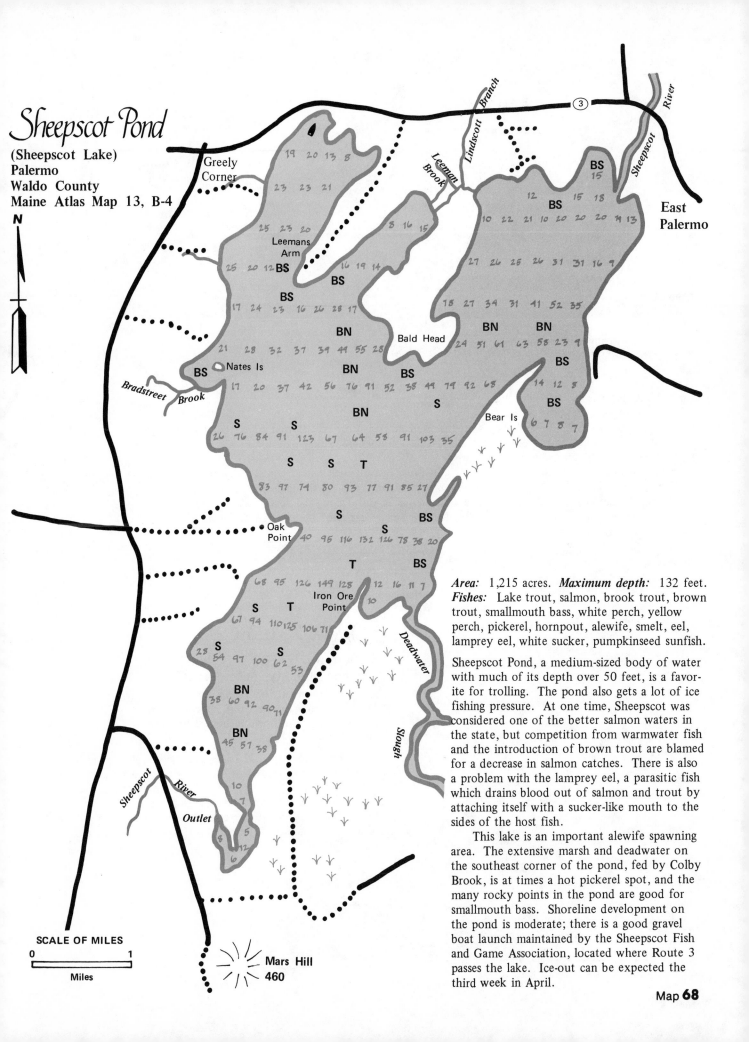

Greely Corner

19 20 13 8
23 23 21
25 23 20
Leemans Arm
25 20 12 **BS**
BS
17 24 23 16 26 28 17
BN
21 28 32 37 39 44 55 28
BS Nates Is
17 20 37 42 56 76 91 52 38 44 79 92 68
BN
S **S**
26 76 84 91 123 67 64 58 91 103 35
S **S** **T**
83 97 74 80 93 77 91 85 27
Bradstreet Brook
Oak Point
40 95 116 131 126 78 38 20
S
T **BS**
68 95 126 149 128 12 16 11 7
Iron Ore Point 10
S **T**
67 94 110 125 106 71
28 **S** **S**
54 97 100 62
53
BN
38 60 92 90 11
BN
45 57 38
10
7
Sheepscot River
Outlet
8 5
12
6

3

Lindscot Branch

Leeman Brook

BS 15
12 **BS** 15 18
10 22 21 10 20 20 20 14 13
27 26 25 26 31 31 16 9
18 27 34 31 41 52 35
BN **BN**
24 51 61 63 58 23 9
Bald Head
BS **BS**
14 12 5
BS
6 7 8 7
Bear Is

Sheepscot River

East Palermo

Deadwater

Slough

Area: 1,215 acres. *Maximum depth:* 132 feet. *Fishes:* Lake trout, salmon, brook trout, brown trout, smallmouth bass, white perch, yellow perch, pickerel, hornpout, alewife, smelt, eel, lamprey eel, white sucker, pumpkinseed sunfish.

Sheepscot Pond, a medium-sized body of water with much of its depth over 50 feet, is a favorite for trolling. The pond also gets a lot of ice fishing pressure. At one time, Sheepscot was considered one of the better salmon waters in the state, but competition from warmwater fish and the introduction of brown trout are blamed for a decrease in salmon catches. There is also a problem with the lamprey eel, a parasitic fish which drains blood out of salmon and trout by attaching itself with a sucker-like mouth to the sides of the host fish.

This lake is an important alewife spawning area. The extensive marsh and deadwater on the southeast corner of the pond, fed by Colby Brook, is at times a hot pickerel spot, and the many rocky points in the pond are good for smallmouth bass. Shoreline development on the pond is moderate; there is a good gravel boat launch maintained by the Sheepscot Fish and Game Association, located where Route 3 passes the lake. Ice-out can be expected the third week in April.

SCALE OF MILES
0   1
Miles

Mars Hill
460

Map **68**

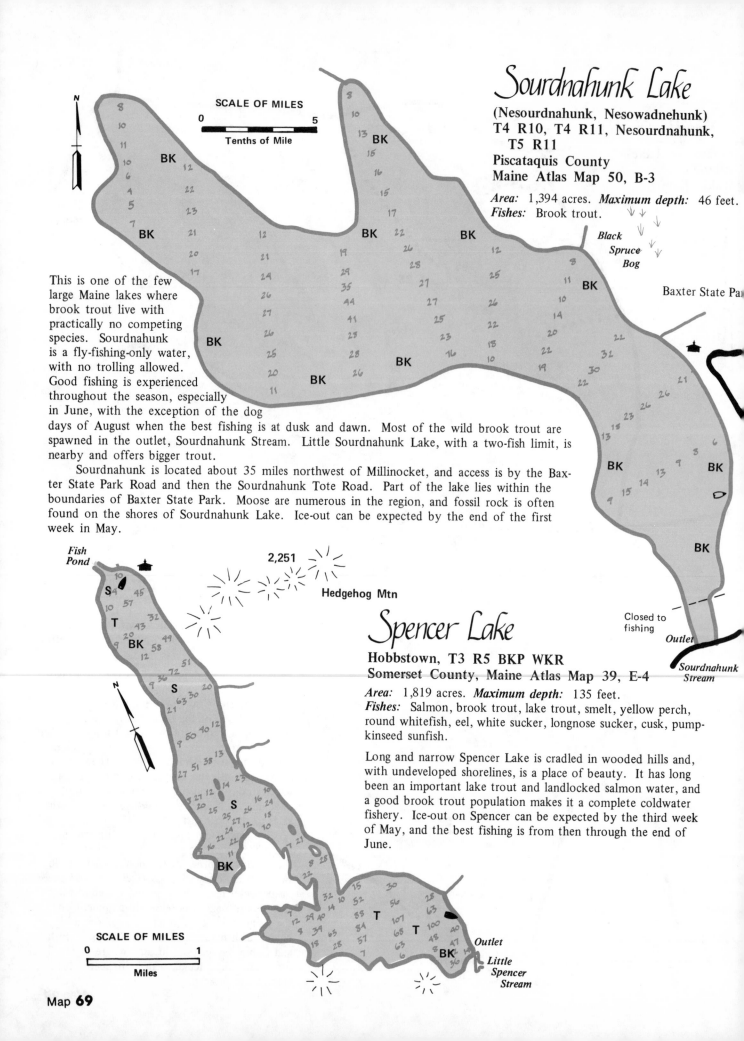

Sourdnahunk Lake

(Nesourdnahunk, Nesowadnehunk)
T4 R10, T4 R11, Nesourdnahunk,
 T5 R11
Piscataquis County
Maine Atlas Map 50, B-3

Area: 1,394 acres. *Maximum depth:* 46 feet.
Fishes: Brook trout.

SCALE OF MILES

0   5

Tenths of Mile

Black
Spruce
Bog

Baxter State Pa

This is one of the few large Maine lakes where brook trout live with practically no competing species. Sourdnahunk is a fly-fishing-only water, with no trolling allowed. Good fishing is experienced throughout the season, especially in June, with the exception of the dog days of August when the best fishing is at dusk and dawn. Most of the wild brook trout are spawned in the outlet, Sourdnahunk Stream. Little Sourdnahunk Lake, with a two-fish limit, is nearby and offers bigger trout.

Sourdnahunk is located about 35 miles northwest of Millinocket, and access is by the Baxter State Park Road and then the Sourdnahunk Tote Road. Part of the lake lies within the boundaries of Baxter State Park. Moose are numerous in the region, and fossil rock is often found on the shores of Sourdnahunk Lake. Ice-out can be expected by the end of the first week in May.

Closed to
fishing

Outlet

Sourdnahunk
Stream

Fish
Pond

2,251

Hedgehog Mtn

Spencer Lake

Hobbstown, T3 R5 BKP WKR
Somerset County, Maine Atlas Map 39, E-4

Area: 1,819 acres. *Maximum depth:* 135 feet.
Fishes: Salmon, brook trout, lake trout, smelt, yellow perch, round whitefish, eel, white sucker, longnose sucker, cusk, pumpkinseed sunfish.

Long and narrow Spencer Lake is cradled in wooded hills and, with undeveloped shorelines, is a place of beauty. It has long been an important lake trout and landlocked salmon water, and a good brook trout population makes it a complete coldwater fishery. Ice-out on Spencer can be expected by the third week of May, and the best fishing is from then through the end of June.

Outlet

Little
Spencer
Stream

SCALE OF MILES

0   1

Miles

Map **69**

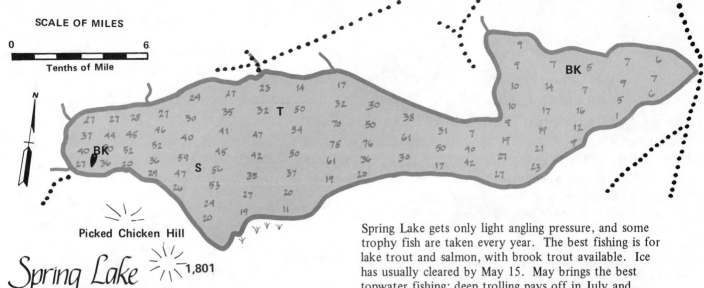

Spring Lake

T3 R4 BKP WKR
Somerset County, Maine Atlas Map 29, B-4

Area: 762 acres. *Maximum depth:* 78 feet.
Fishes: Salmon, brook trout, lake trout, smelt, eel, white sucker, longnose sucker.

Spring Lake gets only light angling pressure, and some trophy fish are taken every year. The best fishing is for lake trout and salmon, with brook trout available. Ice has usually cleared by May 15. May brings the best topwater fishing; deep trolling pays off in July and August. The land surrounding this remote lake is very hilly and heavily wooded. There are 10 cottages clustered on the east side of the lake. While most of the camps are private, boats can be launched for a small fee. Prior to May 15, the road is for four-wheel-drive vehicles only. After that, sedans can pass.

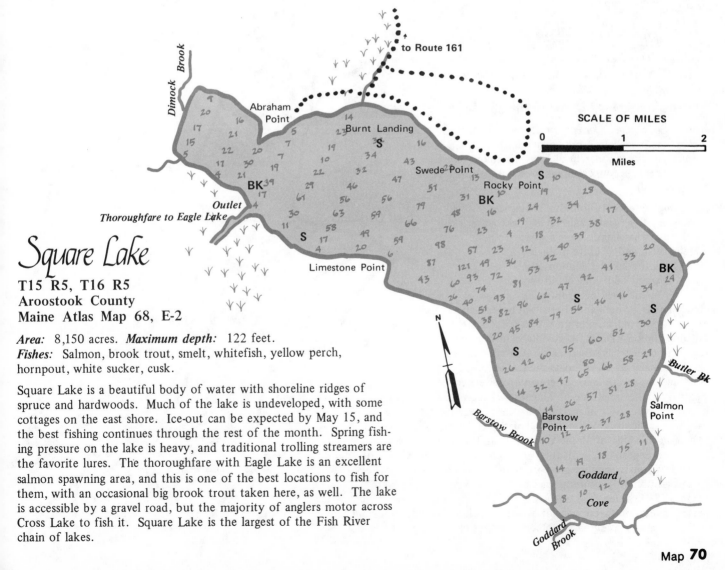

Square Lake

T15 R5, T16 R5
Aroostook County
Maine Atlas Map 68, E-2

Area: 8,150 acres. *Maximum depth:* 122 feet.
Fishes: Salmon, brook trout, smelt, whitefish, yellow perch, hornpout, white sucker, cusk.

Square Lake is a beautiful body of water with shoreline ridges of spruce and hardwoods. Much of the lake is undeveloped, with some cottages on the east shore. Ice-out can be expected by May 15, and the best fishing continues through the rest of the month. Spring fishing pressure on the lake is heavy, and traditional trolling streamers are the favorite lures. The thoroughfare with Eagle Lake is an excellent salmon spawning area, and this is one of the best locations to fish for them, with an occasional big brook trout taken here, as well. The lake is accessible by a gravel road, but the majority of anglers motor across Cross Lake to fish it. Square Lake is the largest of the Fish River chain of lakes.

Map **70**

Third Machias Lake

T43 MD, T42 MD, T5ND
Washington County
Maine Atlas Map 35, C-3

Area: 2,778 acres. *Maximum depth:* 35 feet.
Fishes: Smallmouth bass, white perch, yellow perch, pickerel, hornpout, eel, white sucker, pumpkinseed sunfish.

There are only a few camps on the heavily-wooded shores of this lake. There is no easy access to the lake -- but boats and motors are available, and arrangements must be made through the Colonial Sportsman's Lodge at Grand Lake Stream. Smallmouth bass is the primary game fish here, and the fishing is good from May 25 through August. Ice-out averages April 27. This lovely, island-studded lake drains into both the Machias and St. Croix Rivers.

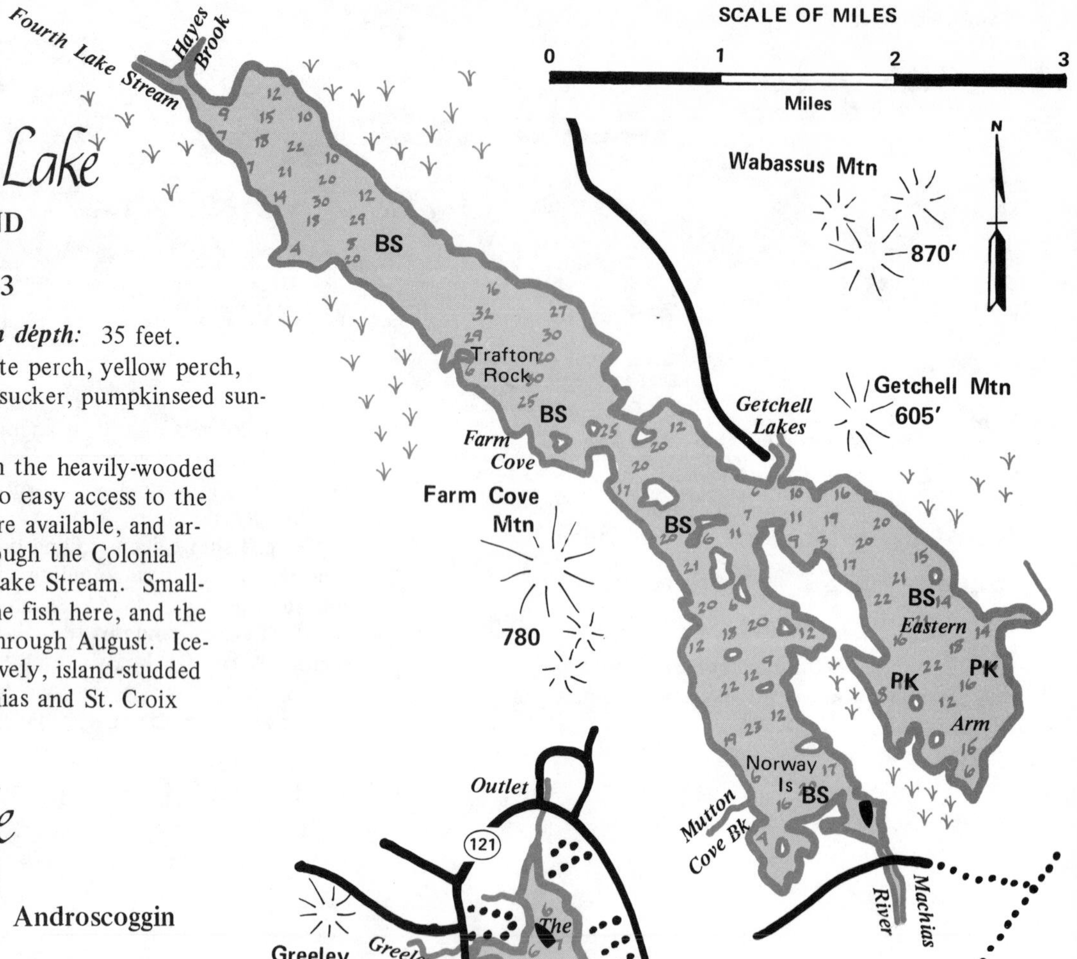

Thompson Lake

Oxford, Otisfield, Poland
Oxford, Cumberland and Androscoggin Counties
Maine Atlas Map 5, A-2; Map 11, E-2

Area: 4,426 acres. *Maximum depth:* 121 feet.
Fishes: Salmon, lake trout, smallmouth bass, largemouth bass, yellow perch, pickerel, hornpout, smelt, eel, white sucker, cusk, pumpkinseed sunfish, redbreast sunfish.

Some angling experts consider Thompson to be one of the finest salmon and lake trout waters in Maine. Here's what a Maine Fish and Wildlife biologist says about the lake: "Thompson offers a diversity of fishing to all types of anglers. In early spring, trolling for salmon along the rocky bars and shores can be extremely successful, and salmon up to 5-6 pounds are not uncommon. During the winter and summer, togue fishermen have their day -- it is common to check as many as 50-75 boats on a weekend day in July, and up to 200-300 fishermen on a weekend day in February. The small size of Thompson Lake togue has always been a problem, but in recent years the average size of togue caught is noticeably better. Some of the best smallmouth bass fishing in this area of Maine is available at Thompson Lake from June until September; with the right technique and knowledge, it is not difficult to catch a good string of bass. These fish show excellent growth at Thompson, and bass up to 3 pounds are quite common." Located near Sebago Lake, Thompson is in one of the most heavily populated areas of Maine, and shorefront development on the lake is considered a problem. Ice-out can be expected in the second week of April.

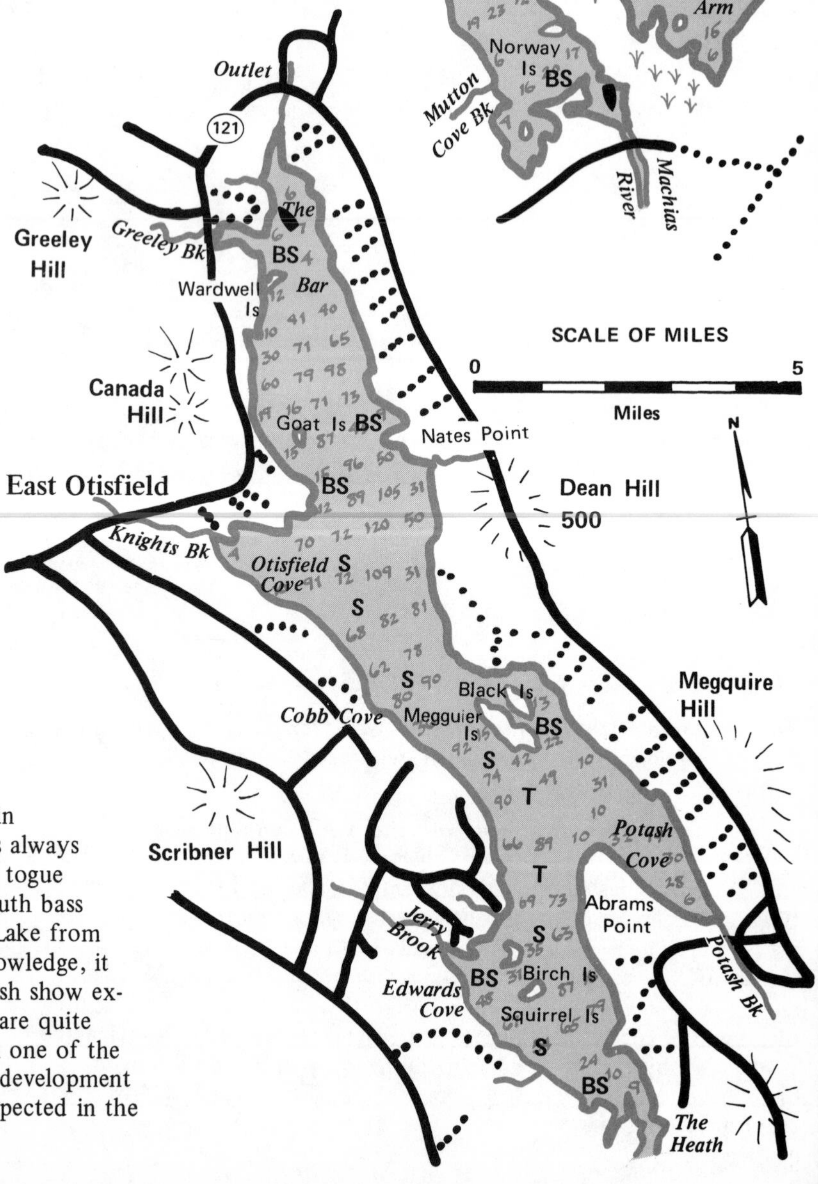

Map **71**

SCALE OF MILES

Wabassus Mtn

Getchell Mtn
605'

870'

Fourth Lake Stream

Hayes Brook

BS

Trafton Rock

BS

Farm Cove

Getchell Lakes

Farm Cove Mtn

BS

780

BS

BS

Eastern

PK

PK

Arm

Norway Is

BS

Mutton Cove Bk

Machias River

Outlet

121

Greeley Hill

Greeley Bk

The

BS

Bar

Wardwell Is

Canada Hill

Goat Is BS

East Otisfield

BS

Knights Bk

Otisfield Cove

S

S

Cobb Cove

S

Scribner Hill

Jerry Brook

Edwards Cove

BS

S

Nates Point

Dean Hill
500

SCALE OF MILES

Black Is

Megguier Is

BS

S

T

T

S

BS

Birch Is

Squirrel Is

S

Megquire Hill

Potash Cove

Abrams Point

Potash Bk

BS

The Heath

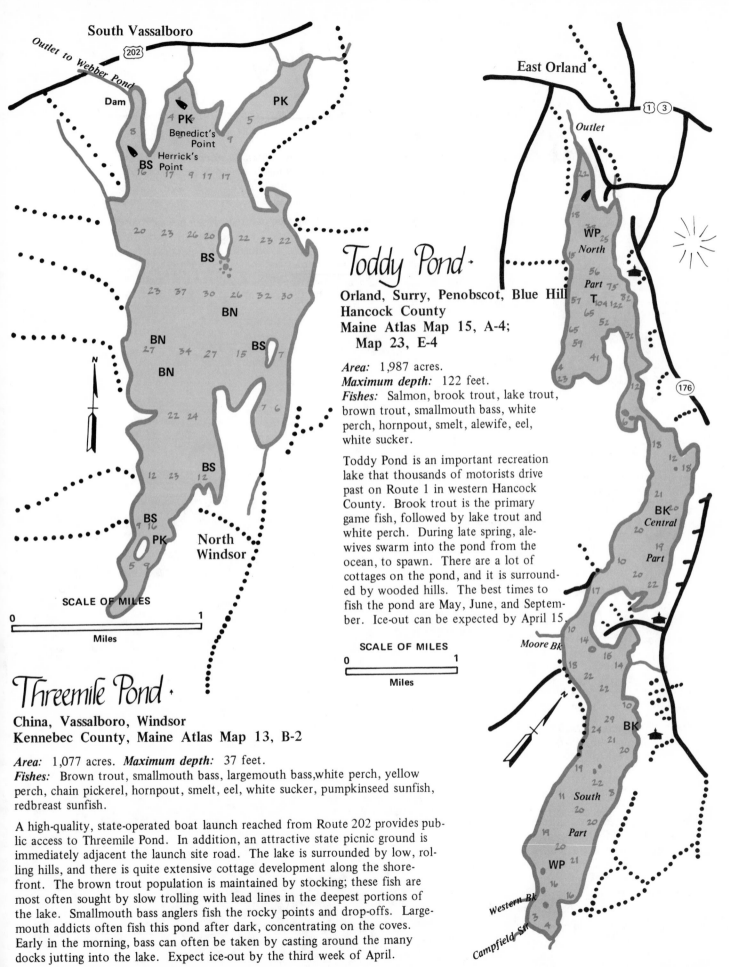

South Vassalboro

202

Outlet to Webber Pond

Dam

PK

PK
Benedict's
Point

Herrick's
Point

BS

BS

BN

BN

BS

BN

BS

BS
PK

North
Windsor

SCALE OF MILES

0   1

Miles

East Orland

1 3

Outlet

WP
North
Part
T

BK
Central

Part

Moore Bk

BK

South

Part

WP

Western Bk

Campfield Str

176

Toddy Pond

**Orland, Surry, Penobscot, Blue Hill
Hancock County
Maine Atlas Map 15, A-4;
Map 23, E-4**

Area: 1,987 acres.
Maximum depth: 122 feet.
Fishes: Salmon, brook trout, lake trout,
brown trout, smallmouth bass, white
perch, hornpout, smelt, alewife, eel,
white sucker.

Toddy Pond is an important recreation
lake that thousands of motorists drive
past on Route 1 in western Hancock
County. Brook trout is the primary
game fish, followed by lake trout and
white perch. During late spring, alewives swarm into the pond from the
ocean, to spawn. There are a lot of
cottages on the pond, and it is surrounded by wooded hills. The best times to
fish the pond are May, June, and September. Ice-out can be expected by April 15.

SCALE OF MILES

0   1

Miles

Threemile Pond

**China, Vassalboro, Windsor
Kennebec County, Maine Atlas Map 13, B-2**

Area: 1,077 acres. *Maximum depth:* 37 feet.
Fishes: Brown trout, smallmouth bass, largemouth bass,white perch, yellow
perch, chain pickerel, hornpout, smelt, eel, white sucker, pumpkinseed sunfish,
redbreast sunfish.

A high-quality, state-operated boat launch reached from Route 202 provides public access to Threemile Pond. In addition, an attractive state picnic ground is
immediately adjacent the launch site road. The lake is surrounded by low, rolling hills, and there is quite extensive cottage development along the shorefront. The brown trout population is maintained by stocking; these fish are
most often sought by slow trolling with lead lines in the deepest portions of
the lake. Smallmouth bass anglers fish the rocky points and drop-offs. Largemouth addicts often fish this pond after dark, concentrating on the coves.
Early in the morning, bass can often be taken by casting around the many
docks jutting into the lake. Expect ice-out by the third week of April.

Map **72**

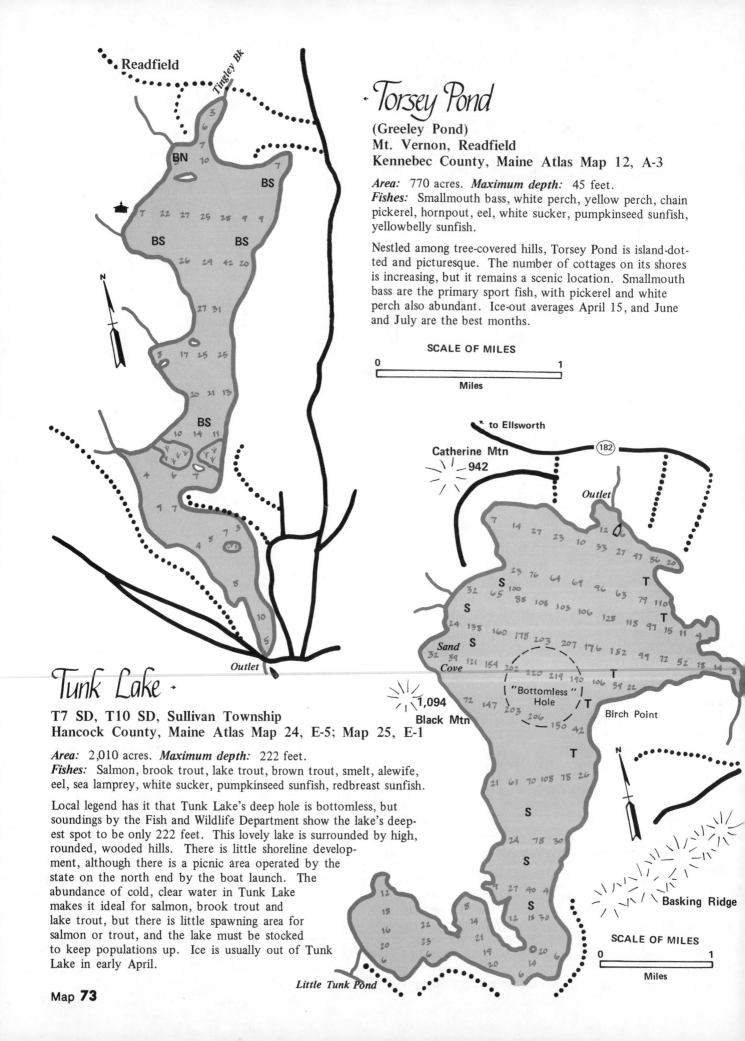

Torsey Pond

(Greeley Pond)
Mt. Vernon, Readfield
Kennebec County, Maine Atlas Map 12, A-3

Area: 770 acres. *Maximum depth:* 45 feet.
Fishes: Smallmouth bass, white perch, yellow perch, chain pickerel, hornpout, eel, white sucker, pumpkinseed sunfish, yellowbelly sunfish.

Nestled among tree-covered hills, Torsey Pond is island-dotted and picturesque. The number of cottages on its shores is increasing, but it remains a scenic location. Smallmouth bass are the primary sport fish, with pickerel and white perch also abundant. Ice-out averages April 15, and June and July are the best months.

SCALE OF MILES

0   1

Miles

Tunk Lake

T7 SD, T10 SD, Sullivan Township
Hancock County, Maine Atlas Map 24, E-5; Map 25, E-1

Area: 2,010 acres. *Maximum depth:* 222 feet.
Fishes: Salmon, brook trout, lake trout, brown trout, smelt, alewife, eel, sea lamprey, white sucker, pumpkinseed sunfish, redbreast sunfish.

Local legend has it that Tunk Lake's deep hole is bottomless, but soundings by the Fish and Wildlife Department show the lake's deepest spot to be only 222 feet. This lovely lake is surrounded by high, rounded, wooded hills. There is little shoreline development, although there is a picnic area operated by the state on the north end by the boat launch. The abundance of cold, clear water in Tunk Lake makes it ideal for salmon, brook trout and lake trout, but there is little spawning area for salmon or trout, and the lake must be stocked to keep populations up. Ice is usually out of Tunk Lake in early April.

SCALE OF MILES

0   1

Miles

Map **73**

Wassookeag Lake

Dexter
Penobscot County, Maine Atlas Map 32, D-1

Area: 1,062 acres. *Maximum depth:* 86 feet.
Fishes: Salmon, brook trout, lake trout, smallmouth
bass, white perch, yellow perch, chain
pickerel, hornpout, smelt, eel,
white sucker, cusk.

SCALE OF MILES

0   5

Tenths of Mile

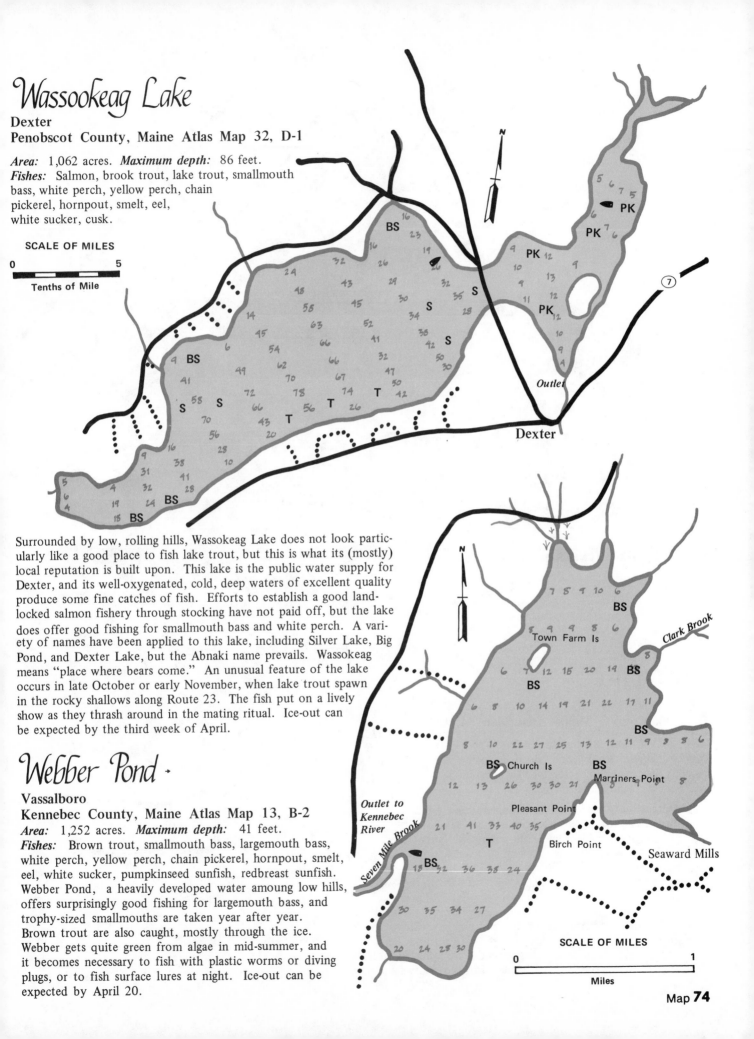

Surrounded by low, rolling hills, Wassookeag Lake does not look particularly like a good place to fish lake trout, but this is what its (mostly)
local reputation is built upon. This lake is the public water supply for
Dexter, and its well-oxygenated, cold, deep waters of excellent quality
produce some fine catches of fish. Efforts to establish a good landlocked salmon fishery through stocking have not paid off, but the lake
does offer good fishing for smallmouth bass and white perch. A variety of names have been applied to this lake, including Silver Lake, Big
Pond, and Dexter Lake, but the Abnaki name prevails. Wassookeag
means "place where bears come." An unusual feature of the lake
occurs in late October or early November, when lake trout spawn
in the rocky shallows along Route 23. The fish put on a lively
show as they thrash around in the mating ritual. Ice-out can
be expected by the third week of April.

Webber Pond

Vassalboro
Kennebec County, Maine Atlas Map 13, B-2
Area: 1,252 acres. *Maximum depth:* 41 feet.
Fishes: Brown trout, smallmouth bass, largemouth bass,
white perch, yellow perch, chain pickerel, hornpout, smelt,
eel, white sucker, pumpkinseed sunfish, redbreast sunfish.
Webber Pond, a heavily developed water among low hills,
offers surprisingly good fishing for largemouth bass, and
trophy-sized smallmouths are taken year after year.
Brown trout are also caught, mostly through the ice.
Webber gets quite green from algae in mid-summer, and
it becomes necessary to fish with plastic worms or diving
plugs, or to fish surface lures at night. Ice-out can be
expected by April 20.

SCALE OF MILES

0   1

Miles

Map 74

West Lake

T3 ND and T40 MD
Hancock County, Maine Atlas Map 34, C-4

Area: 1,344 acres. *Maximum depth:* 70 feet.
Fishes: Salmon, brook trout, lake trout, white
perch, yellow perch, pickerel, round whitefish,
white sucker, pumpkinseed sunfish.

West Lake is accessible via lumber company road
from Saponac, but the road is wet until June. The
salmon population is good, with four-pound fish fairly
common. This is a good place to troll a streamer in June
and September. West Lake makes an excellent day trip from
Nicatous Lodge on Nicatous Lake. Camp sites are on the woods
road running north off Route 9 or from the Enfield-Lincoln area.
A lot at the north end of the lake, on a spur road off the road to
Nicatous, has been set aside as a crude, but usable, landing. The
salmon fishing makes it well worth the effort to get back here. Ice-
out occurs by May 1. The lake is surrounded by low hills, with all
development confined to the north end. This is a pretty lake.

SCALE OF MILES

0   5

Tenths of Mile

Map 75

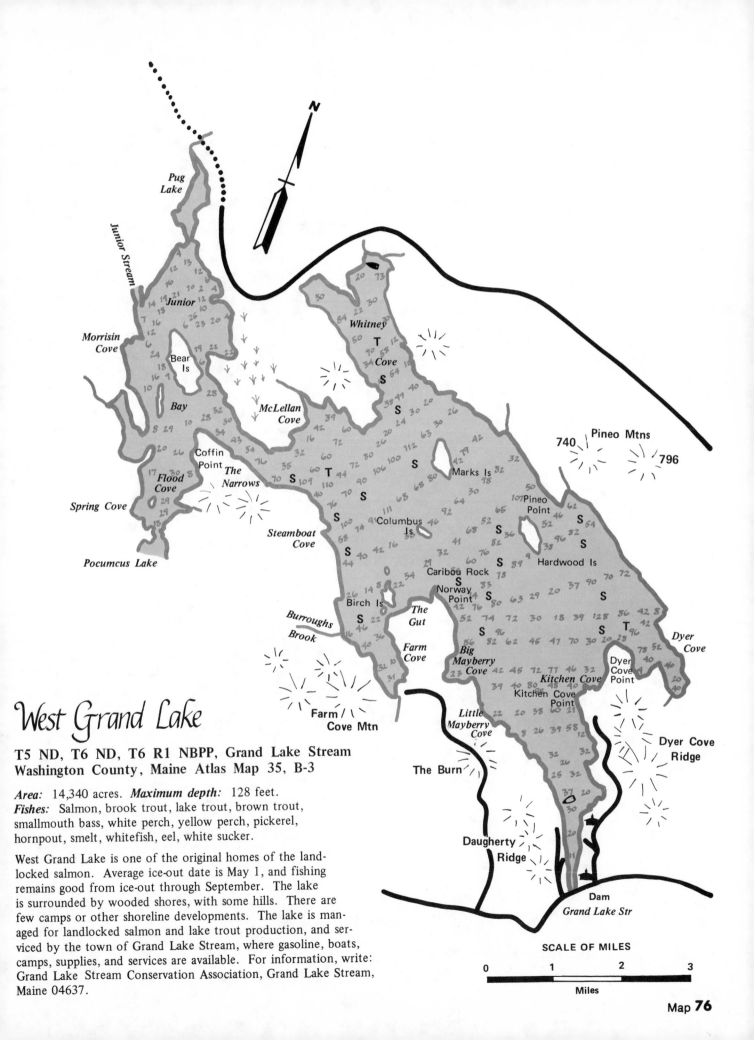

West Grand Lake

T5 ND, T6 ND, T6 R1 NBPP, Grand Lake Stream
Washington County, Maine Atlas Map 35, B-3

Area: 14,340 acres. *Maximum depth:* 128 feet.
Fishes: Salmon, brook trout, lake trout, brown trout, smallmouth bass, white perch, yellow perch, pickerel, hornpout, smelt, whitefish, eel, white sucker.

West Grand Lake is one of the original homes of the land-locked salmon. Average ice-out date is May 1, and fishing remains good from ice-out through September. The lake is surrounded by wooded shores, with some hills. There are few camps or other shoreline developments. The lake is managed for landlocked salmon and lake trout production, and serviced by the town of Grand Lake Stream, where gasoline, boats, camps, supplies, and services are available. For information, write: Grand Lake Stream Conservation Association, Grand Lake Stream, Maine 04637.

Map 76

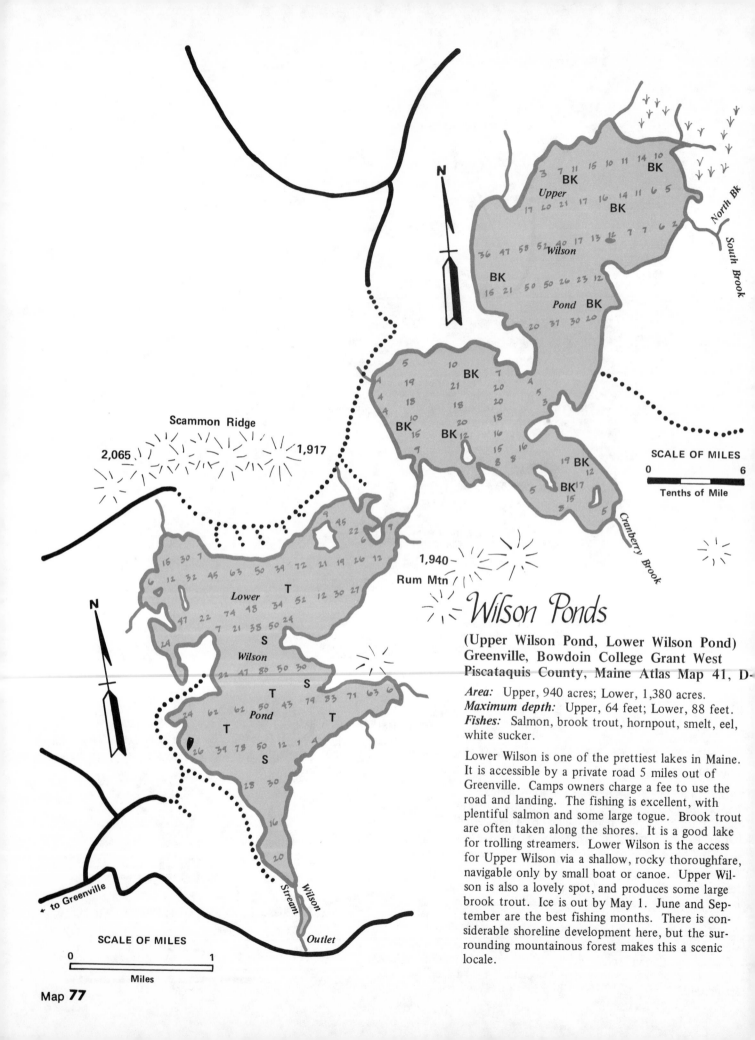

N

Upper

Wilson

Pond

BK BK BK BK BK BK

3 7 11 15 10 11 14 10
17 20 21 17 16 14 11 6 5
36 47 53 51 40 17 13 12 7 7 6 2
16 21 50 50 26 23 12
20 31 30 20

North Bk

South Brook

5 10 BK 7
19 21 20 4
4 13 18 20 5
4 10 20 18 3
BK 15 BK 12 16
7 15
8 8 16
19 BK
5 BK 12 17
15
3 5

Cranberry Brook

SCALE OF MILES

0   6

Tenths of Mile

Scammon Ridge

2,065   1,917

9 45 22 9
15 30 7 6
12 32 45 63 50 39 72 21 19 26 12
6 T
47 22 74 48 34 51 12 30 27
Lower S
7 21 38 50 24
Wilson
22 47 80 50 30
T S
T 62 62 50 43 79 83 71 63 6
24 *Pond* T
T 26 39 75 50 12 1 7
S
28 30
16
20

1,940

Rum Mtn

N

Wilson Stream

Outlet

← to Greenville

SCALE OF MILES

0   1

Miles

Wilson Ponds

**(Upper Wilson Pond, Lower Wilson Pond)
Greenville, Bowdoin College Grant West
Piscataquis County, Maine Atlas Map 41, D-**

Area: Upper, 940 acres; Lower, 1,380 acres.
Maximum depth: Upper, 64 feet; Lower, 88 feet.
Fishes: Salmon, brook trout, hornpout, smelt, eel,
white sucker.

Lower Wilson is one of the prettiest lakes in Maine.
It is accessible by a private road 5 miles out of
Greenville. Camps owners charge a fee to use the
road and landing. The fishing is excellent, with
plentiful salmon and some large togue. Brook trout
are often taken along the shores. It is a good lake
for trolling streamers. Lower Wilson is the access
for Upper Wilson via a shallow, rocky thoroughfare,
navigable only by small boat or canoe. Upper Wilson is also a lovely spot, and produces some large
brook trout. Ice is out by May 1. June and September are the best fishing months. There is considerable shoreline development here, but the surrounding mountainous forest makes this a scenic
locale.

Map 77

Wilson Pond

Wilton
Franklin County, Maine Atlas Map 19, D-5

Area: 480 acres. *Maximum depth:* 88 feet.
Fishes: Salmon, brook trout, lake trout, smallmouth bass, white perch, yellow perch, pickerel, hornpout, smelt, eel, white sucker, sunfish.

SCALE OF MILES

0   5

Tenths of Mile

N

Wilton

Wilson Stream

Outlet

The extreme southern tip of this attractive pond butts against a manufacturing mill in the town of Wilton, where the boat launch is located. There is a lot of deep, cold water in Wilson to support salmon, lake trout, and smelt. The Fish and Wildlife Department lists lake trout, smallmouth bass, yellow perch, and hornpout as the principal fisheries. Some of the perch, which feed heavily on smelt, reach jumbo proportions. The shoreline is wooded, with a number of fields, and there is extensive cottage development. Ice-out can be expected by the second week of May, which is the best time to fish Wilson Pond for trout and salmon. June is the best month for bass.

Wilson Stream
Bates Bk

Jackman

Wood Pond

(Big Wood Pond)
Attean, Dennistown, Jackman
Somerset County
Maine Atlas Map 39, B-4

Outlet

Gander Brook

Hog Is

Area: 2,150 acres.
Maximum depth: 72 feet.
Fishes: Salmon, brook trout, lake trout, yellow perch, hornpout, smelt, white sucker, longnose sucker, cusk, pumpkinseed sunfish.

Ice fishing for smelt and cusk is a winter feature of Wood Pond for area residents. There are at least four sets of sporting camps on this popular lake, the first of the series of waters fed by the Moose River. There is an 18-inch minimum length limit placed upon lake trout in the lake. The rocky, windswept shoreline and Sally Mountain to the west make Wood Pond an attractive place to be. Spawning areas for salmon and brook trout are found in Wood Stream and the Moose River. Ice-out can be expected by the first week of May, and the best fishing is from mid-May to mid-June.

Wood Stream

Sally Mtn

Moose River

Jackman Station

SCALE OF MILES

0   5

Tenths of Mile

N

Map **78**

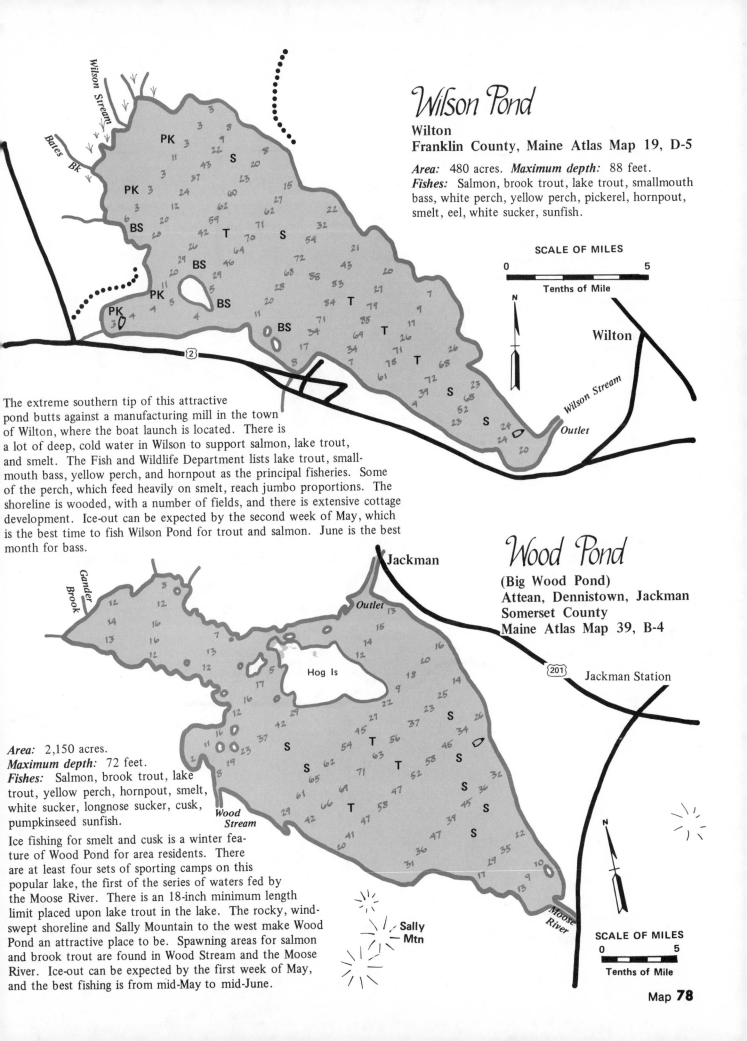

Wytopitlock Lake

T2 R4 WELS, Glenwood
Aroostook County
Maine Atlas Map 52, E-5

Area: 1,152 acres.
Maximum depth: 24 feet.
Fishes: White perch, yellow perch, chain pickerel, hornpout, eel, white sucker.

Wytopitlock Lake is an excellent spot for white perch and pickerel, just the location for an angler who wants to catch lots of fish or take his family on an outing. The best fishing is in June and July, with open water by May 5. The shoreline is swampy, with spruce and fir along the shores. There are some cottages. A high-quality state boat launch is located on the lake, accessible from Route 2A in Haynesville.

SCALE OF MILES

0   5

Tenths of Mile

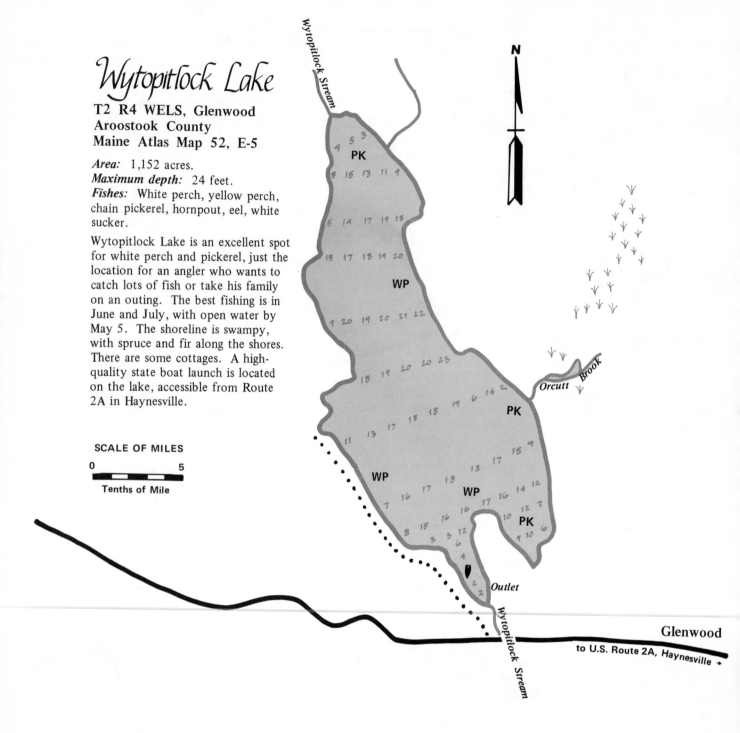

Map **79**

ABBREVIATIONS FOR FISH SPECIES

After the name and town/township location of each lake or pond listed are its principal fisheries, from coldwater to warmwater species. The following key spells out the abbreviations used:

S	Salmon
BK	Brook trout
T	Togue (lake trout)
BN	Brown trout
R	Rainbow trout
BL	Blueback trout
SU	Sunapee trout
BS	Bass
WP	White perch
PK	Pickerel
SM	Smelt
WF	Whitefish
CU	Cusk

HOW TO USE THE MAINE ATLAS AND GAZETTEER

TO LOCATE THESE LAKES AND PONDS

After the name of each lake or pond listed in this directory is the name of the town or township where it is located. To find the lake in the Maine Atlas and Gazetteer, check the "Index of Maine Place Names" in the Atlas and turn to the map number given for the town or township. (Note: In some editions of the Maine Atlas, some of the township numbers are listed with an extra "0"; Township T3 R12, for example, reads as "T03 R12".)

FISHING DIRECTORY OF MAINE LAKES AND PONDS

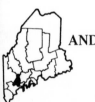

ANDROSCOGGIN

Allen Pond, Greene: BK, BS, WP, PK
Androscoggin Lake, Leeds: (see Map 2)
Auburn Lake, Auburn: (see Map 4)
Bartlett Pond, Livermore: BK
Bear and Little Bear Pond, Turner: BS, WP, PK
Berry Pond, Greene: BS, PK
Black Pond (Black Snake Pond), Turner: BK
Brettun's Pond, Livermore: BS, WP
Crystal Pond (Beals Pond), Turner: BS, WP, PK
Island Pond, Leeds: BS, PK
Little Wilson Pond, Turner/Auburn: BK, BS, WP
Long Pond, Livermore: BN, BS, WP, PK
Loon Pond (Spear Pond), Webster: BS, WP, PK
Lower Range Pond, Poland: (see Maps 56 and 57)
Middle Range Pond, Poland: (see Maps 56 and 57)
Moose Hill Pond, Livermore Falls: BS, PK
Nelson Pond, Livermore: BS, PK
No Name Pond, Lewiston: BS, WP, PK
Pleasant Pond, Turner: BK, BS, PK
Round Pond, Livermore: BN, BS, WP
Runaround Pond, Durham: BS, PK
Sabattus Pond, Greene/Webster/Wales: BS, WP, PK
Sandy Bottom Pond, Turner: BS, PK
Schoolhouse Pond, Livermore Falls: BS, PK
Taylor Pond, Auburn: BN, BS, WP, PK
Thompson Lake, Poland: (see Map 71)
Tripp Pond, Poland: BS, WP, PK
Upper Range Pond, Poland: (see Map 56)
Worthly Pond, Poland: BK

AROOSTOOK

B Lake, Smyrna/Hammond Plt.: BK
Basil Pond, Fort Kent: BK
Beau Lake, T19 R11/T20 R11/T20 R12: S, BK, T, WF, CU
Beaver Tail Pond, T14 R9/T14 R10: BK
Bennett Lake, Easton: BK
Big Machias Lake, T12 R8: S, BK, SM
Billings Pond, T11 R9: BK
Black Lake, T15 R9: BK
Black Lake, T15 R9: BK, BL
Black Lake, T16 R6: BK
Bourgoin Lake, St. Agatha/Frenchville: BK
Bradford Pond, Moro: BK
Bran Lake, St. Francis: BK
Caribou Pond, T11 R9/T11 R10: BK
Carlisle Pond, T8 R3: BK
Carr Pond, T13 R8: S, T, BK, WF
Carry Lake, Littleton: BK, R
Carry Pond, T16 R4: BK
Center Pond, T10 R8: BK
Chandler Pond, T9 R8: BK
Chase Pond (First) (Hourglass Pond), T14 R9: BK
Chase Pond (Second), T14 R9: BK, T
Chase Pond (Third), T14 R9: BK, T
Clayton Lake, T11 R14: BK
Clayton Lake, T12 R8: S, BK
Conroy Lake, Monticello: BK
Crater Pond, T15 R9: BK
Cross Lake, T16 R5: (see Map 17)

Cunliffe Lake, T12 R13: BK
Daigle Pond, New Canada Plt.: BK
Deboullie Pond, T15 R9: BK, BL
Deep Lake, Littleton: BK
Deering Lake, Weston/Orient: S, WP
Denny Pond, T15 R9: BK
Depot Lake, T13 R16: BK
Dickey Pond, T17 R5: BK
Dickwood Lake, Eagle Lake: BK
Drews Lake (Meduxnekeag Lake), New Limerick/Oakfield/Linneus: (see Map 19)
Eagle Lake, Wallagrass/Eagle Lake/T16 R5/T16 R6: S, BK, SM, CU
East Grand Lake, Weston/Orient: (see Map 20)
Echo Lake, Presque Isle: BK
Eyelet Pond, T11 R12/T12 R12: BK
Falls Pond (Fall Brook Lake), T18 R10/Allagash Plt.: BK
Farrar Pond, T11 R10: BK
Ferguson Pond, T14 R8: BK
Fish Lake (Fish River Lake), T13 R8/T14 R8: (see Map 22)
Galilee Pond, T15 R9: BK
Gardner Lake, T15 R9: BK, BL
Gilbert Pond (Jalbert Pond), St. John Plt.: BK
Girard Pond, Caswell Plt.: BK
Glazier Lake, T18 R10: S, BK, T, WF, CU
Greenlaw Pond, T12 R7, T12 R8: BK
Hafey Pond, T18 R11: BK
Hale Pond, Moro: BK
Hanson Brook Lake, Mapleton: BK
Horseshoe Pond, T11 R10: BK
Hunnewell Lake, St. John: BK
Island Pond, T14 R8: BK
Jones Pond, T20 R11/T20 R12: BK
Ketchum Lake, TD R2: BK
Lambert Pond, New Limerick: BK
Lindsay Lake, Easton: BK

Little Black Brook Lake, Caswell: BK
Little Black Pond (North), T15 R9: BK
Little East Lake, T17 R14: BK
Little Fall Brook Lake (Little Falls Pond),
  Allagash Plt.: BK
Little Gilbert Pond (Little Jalbert Pond), St.
  John Plt.: BK
Little Machias Lake, Nashville Plt.: S, BK
Logan Lake, Littleton/Houlton: BK
Long Lake, Littleton: BK
Long Lake, T17 R3/T17 R4/St. Agatha:
  S, BK, SM, CU
Long Lake, T11 R13/T12 R13: BK, SM
Long Pond, T11 R10/T11 R11: BK
Lost Pond, T11 R10: BK
Lost Pond, T15 R6: BK
Lower Hot Brook Lake, Bancroft: S, WP, PK
Lucifee Pond, T14 R8: BK
Madawaska Lake, T16 R4/Westmanland: S, BK,
  SM
Mattawamkeag Lake (Upper and Lower Matta-
  wamkeag Lakes), T4 R3/Island Falls: S, BS,
  WP, PK, SM
McClusky Lake, T14 R5/T15 R5: BK
McGowan Pond, T11 R8/T12 R8: BK
McKeen Pond, T14 R10: BK
McLean Lake, St. Francis: BK
Mink Marsh Pond, T11 R10: BK
Moccasin Pond, T14 R8: BK
Molunkus Lake, T1 R5W/Molunkus/Macwahoc:
  (see Map 42)
Monson Pond, Ft. Fairfield/Easton: BK
Mosquito Brook Pond, T14 R7: BK
Mud Lake (Pleasant Lake), Moro/T6 R6W: S, BK
Mud Lake, T17 R4/T17 R5: S, BK, SM
Mud Pond, T15 R9: BK
Musquacook Lake (First), T11 R12/T12 R12:
  (see Map 47)
Musquacook Lake (Second), T11 R11: (see Map
  47)
Musquacook Lake (Third), T11 R11: (see Map 47)
Musquacook Lake (Fourth), T11 R11/T10 R11:
  (see Map 47)
Negro Brook Lake (First), T16 R9: BK
Negro Brook Lake (Second), T16 R9: BK
Negro Brook Lake (Third), T16 R9: BK
Negro Brook Lake (Fourth), T16 R9: BK
Negro Brook Lake (Fifth), T15 R9: BK
Negro Brook Lake (Sixth), T15 R9: BK
Nickerson Lake, New Limerick/Linneus: S,
  WP, PK, SM
North Pond, T7 R3/T8 R3: BK
North Pond, T14 R9: BK
Number Nine Lake, T9 R 3: BK
Pennington Pond, T15 R6: BK
Perch Pond, T15 R9: BK
Pleasant Pond, Island Falls/T4 R3: (see Map 53)
Plunkett Pond, Benedicta/Silver Ridge: BS, WP,
  PK
Portage Lake, Portage Lake: S, BK, SM
Portland Lake, Bridgewater: BK, SM
Pratt Lake, T11 R9: S, BK
Presley Lake, T12 R17: BK
Presque Isle Lake, T9 R3: BK
Pushineer Pond, T15 R9: BK, BL
Read Lake, Merrill: BK
Rideout Pond, T19 R12: BK
Ritter Lake, Bridgewater: BK
Rockabema Lake, Moro: S, BK, SM
Ross Lake, Littleton/Monticello: BK
Round Pond, T14 R8: S, BK
Round Pond, T13 R12: BK
Round Mountain Pond, T11 R8: BK
Rowe Lake, T11 R8: S, BK
St. Croix Lake, T7 R4/T8 R4: BK
St. Froid Lake, Winterville/T14 R7: S,
  BK, SM, CU
Salmon Brook Lake, Perham: BK
Secret Pond, Moro: BK

Silver Lake, T15 R5: BK
Sly Brook Lake (First), New Canada Plt.: BK
Sly Brook Lake (Second), New Canada Plt.: BK
Sly Brook Lake (Third), New Canada Plt.: BK,
  BN
Soldier Pond, Wallagrass Plt.: S, BK, SM, CU
Spectacle Pond, T10 R8: BK
Squapan Lake, T10 R4/T11 R4/Masardis/Ash-
  land: S, BK, SM, CU
Square Lake, T15 R5/T16 R5: (see Map 70)
Squirrel Pond, T11 R10: BT
Stink Pond, T15 R9: BK
Timoney Lake, Oakfield/Smyrna: BK
Togue Pond, T15 R9: S, BK, T, SM, CU
Tote Road Pond, Moro: BK
Trafton Lake, Limestone: BK
Two Mile Pond, T16 R13/T16 R14: BK
Umcolcus Lake, T7 R5/T8 R5: S, BK
Umsaskis Lake, T11 R13: BK, T, SM, CU
Upper Pond, T15 R9: BK
Upper Hudson Pond, T11 R10: BK
Upper McNally Pond, T11 R10: BK
Wallagrass Lake (First and Second), St. John/
  Wallagrass/Eagle Lake/T16 R8: S, BK
Wallagrass Lake (Third), St. John Plt.: BK
Weeks Pond, T11 R8: BK
Wheelock Lake, St. John Plt.: BK
Wytopitlock Lake, T2R4/Glenwood: (see Map 79)

CUMBERLAND

Adams Pond, Bridgton: BK
Alden's Pond, Gorham: BK
Barker Pond, Sebago: BS, PK
Bay of Naples (Brandy Pond), Naples: BS, WP,
  PK
Bonny Eagle Lake, Standish: BS, WP, PK
Clark Pond, So. Portland: BK, PK
Coffee Pond, Casco: BK
Coffin Pond, Brunswick: BK
Crescent Lake, Raymond/Casco: BS, SU, PK, CU
Crystal Lake, Gray: BN, PK
Crystal Lake (Anonymous Pond), Harrison: T,
  BS, WP, PK
Dumpling Pond, Casco: BS, PK
Dundee Pond, Standish/Windham: BS, WP, PK
Forest Lake, Gray/Cumberland/Windham: BN,
  BS, PK
Great Pond, Cape Elizabeth: BS, PK
Hancock Pond, Sebago Lake: (see Map 26)
Highland Lake (Duck Lake), Windham/Falmouth:
  BN, BS, WP, PK
Highland Lake, Bridgton: (see Map 28)
Ingalls Pond (Fosters Pond), Bridgton: BK, BS,
  PK
Island Pond, Harrison/Waterford: BN, BS, PK
Lily Pond, New Gloucester: BK, BS, PK
Little Duck Pond, Windham: BK, SM
Little Sebago Lake, Gray/Windham: (see Map
  34)
Long Lake, Bridgton/Harrison/Naples S, BS,
  WP, PH, CU
Mild Pond, Portland: BS
Moose Pond, Bridgton: (see Map 45)
Moose Pond, Otisfield: BS, PK
North Gorham Pond, Windham/Standish: BS,
  WP, PK
Notched Pond, Gray/Raymond: BN, BS, PK
Nubble Pond, Raymond: BK, PK
Otter Pond, Bridgton: BS, PK
Panther Pond, Raymond: S, BS, WP, PK, SM,
  CU
Parker Pond, Casco: BS, WP, PK

Peabody Pond, Bridgton/Naples/Sebago: S, WP,
  PK, SM
Perley Pond, Sebago: BK, BS, PK
Pleasant Lake, Otisfield/Casco: S, T, BS, WP,
  PK, CU
Raymond Pond, Raymond: BN, BS, WP, PK,
  CU
Sabbathday Lake, New Gloucester: NB, BS
Sand Pond, Baldwin: BS, PK
Saturday Pond, Otisfield: BS, PK
Sebago Lake, Casco/Naples/Sebago/Baldwin/
  Standish/Raymond/Windham: (see Maps 65
  and 66)
Southeast Pond, Baldwin/Sebago: BS, WP, PK
Thomas Pond, Casco/Raymond: BN, BS, PK, WP
Thompson Lake, Otisfield: (see Map 71)
Trickey Pond, Naples: T
Upper Range Pond, New Gloucester: (see Map
  56
Watchic Pond, Standish: BN, BS, WP, PK
Wood Pond, Bridgton: BS, WP

FRANKLIN

Arnold Pond, Coburn Gore: S, BK, PK
Barnard Pond, Eustis: BK
Beal Pond (Trout Pond), Madrid: BK
Beaver Mountain Lake (Long Pond), Sandy River
  Plt./T2 R1: (see Map 6)
Beaver Pond, TD: BK
Blanchard Pond, Alder Stream: BK
Bug Eye Pond, Kibby/Chain of Ponds: BK
Caribou Bog, Chain of Ponds: BK
Chain of Ponds (Chain Lakes), Chain of Ponds:
  (see Map 11)
Clearwater Pond, Industry/Farmington: (see
  Map 14)
Cow Pond, Lang (T2 R3): BK
Dodge Pond, Rangeley: (see Map 19)
Dutton Pond (Shiloh Pond), Kingfield: BK
Eddy Pond, Sandy River Plt.: BK
Egypt Pond, Chesterville: R
Grindstone Pond, Kingfield: BK
Gull Pond, Dallas Plt.: BT
Harvey Pond, Madrid: BK
Hills Pond, Perkins Plt.: BK
Horseshoe Pond, Chesterville: BS, PK
Indian Pond, T1 R8: BK
Jim Pond, Jim Pond (T1 R5): S, BK, T, SM, WF
Johns Pond, Davis: BK
Kamankeag Pond, Davis: BK
Kennebago Lake, Davis (T3 R3)/Stetson (T3 R4):
  (see Map 30)
Kimball Pond, New Sharon: BK
Ledge Pond, Sandy River: BK
Little Jim Pond, T1 R5: (see Map 32)
Little Kennebago Lake, Stetson: (see Map 32)
Long Cove Pond, Phillips: BK
Long Pond, TD, TE: BK
Loon Lake, Rangeley/Dallas (T2 R2): BK
Lufkin Pond, Phillips: BS, WP
Midway Pond, Sandy River Plt.: BK
Mooselookmeguntic Lake (Lower Oquossoc Lake,
  Cupsuptic Lake, Lower Rangeley Lake), Range-
  ley/Rangeley Plt.: S, BK, SM
Mount Blue Pond, Avon: WP
Moxie Pond, TD: BK
Mud Pond, Berlin (No. 6): BK
Mud Pond, Jim Pond: BK
Norcross Pond, Chesterville: BS, WP, PK
North Pond, Chesterville: BS, PK
Otter Pond, Chain of Ponds: BK
Parker Pond, Jay: BS
Pinnacle Pond, Kingfield: BK

Podunk Pond, Carthage: BK
Porter Lake, Strong/New Vineyard: (see Map 54)
Quimby Pond, Rangeley: (see Map 56)
Rangeley Lake (Oquossoc Lake), Rangeley/
  Rangeley Plt./Sandy River Plt.: S, BK, SM
Redington Pond, Redington: BK, BN
Rock Pond, Chain of Ponds (T2 R6): BK
Rock Pond, Sandy River Plt.: BK
Ross Pond, Rangeley: BK
Round Pond, Rangeley: BK
Round Pond, TE: BK
Sabbath Day Pond, TE: BK
Saddleback Lake, Dallas (T2 R2): BK
Saddleback Pond, Sandy River (T2 R1): BK
Sand Pond, Chesterville: BS, WP
Sandy River Ponds (Upper, Middle, Lower),
  Sandy River Plt.: BK
Schoolhouse Pond, Phillips: BK
South Pond (Pine Tree Pond), Sandy River
  (T2 R1): BK
Spencer Pond, TD: BK
Staples Pond, Temple: BK
Stetson Pond, Phillips: BK
Stratton Brook Pond, Wyman: BK
Tea Pond, Jim Pond (T1 R5): S, BK, T
Tim Pond, T2 R4: BK
Toothaker Pond, Phillips: BK
Tufts Pond, Kingfield: BN
Tumbledown Pond, Berlin Twp. (No. 6): BK
Varnum Pond, Wilton/Temple: S, T, PK, SM
Webb Lake, Weld: S, BN, BS, WP
Wilson Pond, Wilton: (see Map 78)

HANCOCK

Abrams Pond, Eastbrook/Franklin: BS, WP
Alamoosook Lake, Orland: BS, WP, PK
Alligator Lake, T34 MD/T28 MD: S, BK
Aunt Betty Pond, Bar Harbor: BK
Beech Hill Pond, Otis: (see Map 6)
Birch Harbor Pond, Winter Harbor: BK, PK
Branch Lake, Ellsworth: (see Map 8)
Brewer Pond, Bucksport: WP, PK
Bubble Pond, Bar Harbor: BK
Burntland Pond, Stonington: BS
Chicken Mill Pond, Gouldsboro: BK
Craig Pond, Orland: S
Crystal Pond, T40 MD: BK
Debec Pond, Amherst: BK
Donnell Pond, T9 SD/Franklin: S, WP, PK
Duck Lake, T4 ND: S, BK, T
Dutton Pond, Amherst: BK
Eagle Lake, Bar Harbor: S, BK, T
Echo Lake, Mt. Desert: S, BK
First Pond (Billings Pond), Blue Hill: BK, WP
Flanders Pond, Sullivan: (see Map 23)
Floods Pond, Otis: (see Map 23)
Fourth Pond, Blue Hill: BK
Fox Pond, T10 SD: BK
Georges Pond, Franklin: BS, WP, PK
Giles Pond, Aurora: BK
Goose Pond, Dedham: BS, WP, PK
Graham Lake, Plantation No. 8/Ellsworth/Maria-
  ville/Waltham: BS, WP, PK
Great Pond, Plantation No. 33: BS, PK
Green Lake, Dedham/Ellsworth: (see Map 26)
Halfmoon Pond, Bar Harbor: BK
Hancock Pond, Bucksport: BK, PK
Harriman Pond, Dedham: BK
Hatcase Pond, Dedham: (see Map 27)
Heart Pond, Orland: BK
Hopkins Pond, Mariaville: (see Map 28)
Hurd Pond, Dedham: BK
Jacob Buck Pond, Bucksport: BK, PK

Jellison Hill Pond, Amherst: BK
Jones Pond, Gouldsboro: S, BS, PK
Jordan Pond, Mt. Desert Twp.: S, T
King Pond, Plantation No. 33: BK
Leonard Lake, Ellsworth: BS, WP, PK
Lily Pond, Deer Isle: BK
Little Long Pond, T10 SD: BK
Little Round Pond, Mt. Desert: BK, PK
Little Tunk Pond, Sullivan: BK
Long Pond, Bucksport: BS, WP, PK
Long Pond, Mt. Desert: BK
Long Pond (Great Pond), Mt. Desert/Southwest
  Harbor: S, BS, SM
Long Pond, Plantation No. 33/Aurora: BK
Long Pond, T10 SD: S, BK, SM
Loon Pond, T40 MD: BK
Lower Breakneck Pond, Bar Harbor: BK
Lower Hadlock Pond, Mt. Desert: BK, BN, WP
Lower Patten Pond, Ellsworth/Surry: S, BN, WP,
  PK
Lower Pistol Lake, T3 ND: S, WP, PK
Middle Lower Unknown Lakes, T4 ND: BS, WP,
  PK
Molasses Pond, Eastbrook: S, WP, PK
Moulton Pond, Dedham/Bucksport: BK
Mountainy Pond, Dedham: BS, WP, PK
Narraguagus Lake, T16 MD/T10 SD/T9 SD: BK,
  SM
Nicatous Lake, T3 ND/T40 MD/T41 MD: (see
  Map 48)
Norris Pond (Noyes Pond), Blue Hill: BK
Phillips Lake, Dedham: (see Map 52)
Pierce Pond, Penobscot: BS, WP
Pughole Pond, T41 MD: BK, WP
Rift Pond, Plantation No. 33: BK
Rocky Pond, Orland: BS
Rocky Pond, Otis: BS, WP, PK
Round Pond, Mt. Desert: BS
Round Pond, T10 SD/T7 SD: S, BK, SM
Seal Cove Pond, Tremont/Mt. Desert: BS, WP
Second Pond, Dedham: BK, WP
Simmons Pond, Hancock: BK
Somes Pond, Mt. Desert: BS, PK
Spring Lake, T3 ND: S, BK, WP, PK
Spring River Lake, T10 SD: S, BK
Sylsladobsis Lake (Lower Sylsladobsis, Dobsis,
  and Lower Dobsis), T4 ND: S, BS, WP, PK
Tilden Pond, T10 SD: BK
Toddy Pond, Orland/Surry/Penobscot/Blue Hill:
  (see Map 72)
Torry Pond, Deer Isle: BS
Tunk Lake, T7 SD/T10 SD/Sullivan : S, BK, T
Upper Breakneck Pond, Bar Harbor: BK
Upper Hadlock Pond, Mt. Desert: BK, BN
Upper Lead Mountain Pond, T22 MD/T28 MD:
  S, WP
Upper Middle Branch Pond, Aurora/T28 MD: S,
  WP
Upper Sabao Lake, T41 MD: BK, WP
Walker Pond, Brooksville/Sedgwick: BS, WP
Webb Pond, Eastbrook/Sullivan: BS, WP, PK
West Bay Pond, T7 SD/Gouldsboro: BK
West Lake, T3 ND/T40 MD: (see Map 75)
Wight Pond, Penobscot/Blue Hill: BS, WP, PK
Williams Pond, Bucksport: BS, WP, PK
Williams Pond, T28 MD: BK
Witchhole Pond, Bar Harbor: BK
Youngs Pond, Otis: BK

KENNEBEC

Androscoggin Lake, Wayne: BS, WP, PK, SM
Annabessacook Lake, Monmouth/Winthrop: BS,
  WP, PK

Basin Pond, Fayette: BK
Berry and Dexter Ponds, Wayne/Winthrop: BS,
  WP, PK
Black Pond, Vienna: BS, PK
Buker Pond, Litchfield: BN, BS, WP, PK
Burgess Pond, Fayette: BS, PK
Chamberlain Pond, Belgrade: BK
China Lake, China/Vassalboro: (see Map 13)
Cobbosseecontee Lake (Cobbossee Lake), Win-
  throp/Monmouth/West Gardiner/Litchfield:
  (see Map 15)
Cochnewagon Pond, Monmouth: (see Map 16)
Dam Pond, Augusta: BS, PK
David Pond, Fayette: BS, PK
Davis Pond, Vienna: BS
Desert Pond, Mt. Vernon: BK
East Pond, Oakland: (see Map 21)
Echo Lake (Crotched Pond), Fayette/Mt. Vernon/
  Readfield: (see Map 21)
Egypt Pond, Vienna: R
Emery Pond and Bean Pond, Sidney: BN
Fairbanks Pond, Manchester: BN, PK
Figure Eight Pond (Silver Pond), Sidney/Man-
  chester: BN
Flying Pond, Mt. Vernon: S, T, BN, BS, WP, PK,
  SM, CU
Gould and Wellman Ponds, Sidney/Belgrade: BN
Great Pond, Rome/Belgrade: (see Map 25)
Greeley Pond, Augusta: BS, PK
Hopkins Pond, Mt. Vernon: BS, PK
Hutchinson Pond (Sanborn, Hudson Ponds),
  Farmingdale/Manchester: BS, WP, PK
Ingham Pond, Mt. Vernon: BS, WP, PK
Jamies Pond (Jimmie Pond), Farmingdale/Man-
  chester: BS, PK
Jimmy Pond, Litchfield: BS, WP, PK
Kezar Pond, Winthrop: BS, WP, PK
Kimball Pond, Vienna: BK
Little Togus Pond, Augusta: BS, WP, PK
Long Pond, Rome/Belgrade/Mt. Vernon: (see
  Map 36)
Long Pond, Windsor: BS, WP, PK
Loon Pond, Litchfield: BS, WP, PK
Lovejoy Pond, Albion: WP, PK
Lovejoy Pond, Fayette/Readfield/Wayne: BS,
  WP, PK
Maranacook Lake, Readfield/Winthrop: (see
  Map 38)
Messalonskee Lake (Snow Pond), Belgrade/Sid-
  ney/Oakland: (see Map 40)
Mill Pond, Readfield: BS, PK
Minnehonk Lake, Mt. Vernon: T, BS, PK, SM,
  CU
Moose Pond, Mt. Vernon: BS, WP, PK
Mosher Pond, Fayette: BS, PK, WP
Mud Pond, Windsor: BS, WP, PK
Narrows Pond (Upper and Lower), Winthrop:
  S, T, BS, WP, PK, SM
Nehumkeag Pond, Pittston: BS, PK
North Pond, Rome: (see Map 49)
Parker Pond, Fayette/Vienna: (see Map 50)
Pattee Pond, Winslow: BS, WP, PK
Penny Pond, Belgrade/Sidney: BS
Pleasant Pond (Mud Pond), Litchfield/Gardiner:
  BS, WP, PK
Pocasset Lake, Wayne: BS, WP, PK
Purgatory Pond (Tacoma Lakes), Litchfield: BN,
  BS, WP, PK
Sand Pond (Tacoma Lakes), Monmouth/Litchfield:
  BN, BS, WP, PK
Schoolhouse Pond, Fayette: BS, PK
Spectacle Pond, Vassalboro/Augusta: WP, PK
Taylor Pond, Mt. Vernon: BS, PK
Threecornered Pond, Augusta: BS, WP, PK
Three Mile Pond, China/Vassalboro/Windsor:
  (see Map 72)
Tilton Pond, Fayette: BS, PK
Togus Pond, Augusta: BN, BS, WP, PK
Torsey Pond (Greeley Pond), Mt. Vernon/Read-
  field: (see Map 73

Ward Pond, Sidney: BS, PK
Watson Pond, Rome: BS, WP, PK
Webber Pond, Vassalboro: (see Map 74)
Whittier Pond, Rome: BS, PK
Whittier Pond, Rome: BS, PK
Wilson Pond, Monmouth/Wayne/Winthrop: BN, BS, WP, PK

KNOX

Alford Lake, Hope: S, BS, WP, PK, SM
Chickawaukie Pond, Rockland/Rockport: BN, BS BS, WP, PK, SM
Crawford Pond, Union/Warren: BN, BS, WP, PK
Crystal Pond, Washington: BN, BS, PK
Forest Lake (Forest Pond), Friendship: BK
Fresh Pond, North Haven: BS, WP
Havener Pond, Warren: BS, PK
Hosmer Pond, Camden: BS, WP, PK
Iron Pond, Washington: BK
Long Pond (Turners Lake), Isle au Haut: S, BK, SM
Megunticook Lake, Hope/Camden: S, BS, WP, PK, SM
North Pond, Warren: BN, BS, WP, PK
Rocky Pond, Rockport: BS, WP, PK
Round Pond, Union: BS, WP, PK
Sennebec Pond, Appleton/Union: BN, BS, WP, PK
Seven Tree Pond, Union/Warren: BS, WP, PK
South Pond, Warren: BN, BS, WP, PK
Washington Pond, Washington: BS, WP, PK

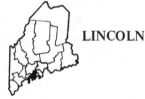

LINCOLN

Adams Pond, Boothbay: BS
Biscay Pond, Bremen/Bristol/Damariscotta: (see Map 8)
Boyd Pond, Bristol: BN, BS, WP, PK
Clark Cove Pond, Bristol: BN,
Cooks Pond, Nobleboro: BS, WP, PK
Damariscotta Lake, Jefferson/Nobelboro/New-castle: (see Map 18)
Deer Meadow Pond, Jefferson: WP
Duckpuddle Pond, Nobleboro/Waldoboro: BN, WP, PK
Dyer Long Pond, Jefferson: WP, PK
Gardiner Pond, Wiscasset: BS, PK
Hastings Pond, Bristol: BK
Havener Pond, Waldoboro: BS, PK
Horn Pond, Jefferson: PK
Ice Pond, Bristol: BS
Kalers Pond, Waldoboro: BN, PK
Knickerbocker Pond, Boothbay: BN, BS, WP
Lily Pond, Edgecomb: BS, WP, PK
Little Dyer Pond, Jefferson: BS, PK
Little Medomak Pond (Storer Pond), Waldoboro: BN, WP, PK
Long Pond, Somerville/Jefferson: BS, WP, PK
McCurdy Pond, Bremen: BS, WP. PK
Medomak Pond, Waldoboro: BS, WP, PK
Pemaquid Pond, Damariscotta/Bremen/Nobleboro: BN, BS, WP, PK, SM
Peters Pond (Gross Pond), Waldoboro: BK
Pinkham Pond, Alna: BN
Pleasant Pond (Clary Lake), Jefferson/Whitefield: BS, WP, PK
Ross Pond, Bristol: BK

Sidensparker Pond, Waldoboro: BS, WP, PK
Weary Pond, Whitefield: BS
Webber Pond, Bremen: BS, WP, PK
West Harbor Pond, Boothbay Harbor: BN, BS, WP
Wiley Pond, Boothbay: BK

OXFORD

Abbot Pond, Sumner: BK
Anasagunticook Lake (Canton Lake), Canton/Hartford: BN, BS, WP, PK
Aziscohos Lake (Azicoos, Sawyer Lakes), Lincoln/(T5 R2)/Parkertown (T5 R3)/ Lynchtown (T5 R4): (see Map 5)
Aziscohos Pond, Magalloway: BK
B Pond, Upton: BK, PK, SM
Back Pond, Lovell/Stoneham: BS, WP
Barker Pond, Hiram: BS, PK
Bear and Little Bear Ponds, Hartford: BS, WP, PK
Bear Pond, Waterford: BS, WP, PK
Beaver Pond, Denmark: BS, PK
Beaver Pond, Magalloway: BK
Bickford Pond, Porter: S, PK
Big Concord Pond, Woodstock: BS, WP, PK
Broken Ridge Pond, Albany: PK
Bryant Pond (Christopher Lake), Woodstock/Greenwood: BK
Bunganock Pond, Hartford: BS, PK
Burnt Meadow Pond, Brownfield: BK, PK
C Pond, C Surplus: BK
Clemons and Little Clemons Ponds, Hiram: BK, PK
Colcord Pond, Porter: S, T, BS, PK
Crocker Pond, Albany: BK
Cushman Pond, Lovell: BK, BS, PK
Ellis Pond (Silver Lake, Roxbury Pond), Roxbury/Byron: BS, PK
Farrington Pond, Lovell: BS, PK
Forest Pond, Canton: BS
Granger Pond, Denmark: BS
Hall Pond, Paris: BK
Hancock Pond, Denmark: (see Map 26)
Hicks Pond, Greenwood: BS, PK
Hogan Pond, Oxford: BS, WP, PK
Horseshoe Pond, Stoneham/Lovell: BS, PK
Howard Pond, Hanover: S, BK, T, SM
Hutchinson Pond, Albany: BN, BS, PK
Indian Pond, Greenwood: BK
Jaybird Pond, Hiram/Porter: BK
Jewett Pond, Waterford: BS, PK
Keewaydin Lake, Stoneham: S, BS, PK
Keoka Lake, Waterford: BK, BS, PK
Keys Pond, Sweden: BK, PK
Kezar Lake, Lovell: (see Map 30)
Kezar Pond, Fryeburg: BS, WP, PK
Labrador Pond, Sumner: BK, PK
Lincoln Pond, Parkertown (T5 R3): (see Map 31)
Little Beaver Pond, Magalloway: BK
Little Concord Pond, Woodstock: BK
Little Ellis Pond (Garland Pond), Byron: BK, SM
Little Labrador Pond, Sumner: BK, PK
Little Pennesseewassee Pond (Hobbs Pond), Norway: R, BS, SM
Long Pond, Denmark: BK
Long Pond (McWain Pond), Waterford: BS, PK
Lovewell Pond, Fryeburg: (see Map 37)
Lower Kimball Pond, Fryeburg/Chatham, N.H.: BS, WP, PK
Lower Richardson Lake (Wellekennebacook Lake),

Magalloway/Richardsontown (T4 R1)/'C': (see Map 58)
Marshall Pond, Oxford/Hebron: PK
Middle Pond, Lovell/Waterford: BS, PK
Mine Pond, Porter: BN, PK
Moose Pond, Denmark/Sweden: (see Map 45)
Moose Pond, Paris: PK
Moose Pond, Waterford: WP, PK
Mooselookmeguntic Lake (Cupsuptic Lake), Richardsontown (T4 R1)/Adamstown (T4 R2): S, BK, SM
Mud Pond, Greenwood: BS, PK
Mud Pond, Lower Cupsuptic: PK
Mud Pond, Waterford: BS, WP, PK
Nelson Pond, Canton: BS, PK
North Pond, Sumner: BK, BS
North Pond, Woodstock/Greenwood: BS, WP, PK
Otter Pond, Parmachenee: BK
Overset Pond, Greenwood: BN
Papoose Pond, Waterford: BS, WP, PK
Parmachenee Lake, Lynchtown/Parmachenee: S, BK, SM
Peat Pond, Fryeburg: BK,
Pennesseewassee Lake, Norway: BN, BS, WP
Pequaket Lake (Rattlesnake Pond), Brownfield: BK, BS, PK
Perley Pond, Denmark: BS, PK
Pickerel Pond, Denmark: PK
Pleasant Pond, Brownfield/Fryeburg/Denmark: BS, WP, PK
Pleasant Pond, Sumner: BS, PK
Pond in the River, Upton/C Surplus/'C': S, BK, WP, SM
Round Pond, Fryeburg: BK
Sand Pond, Denmark: BN, BS, PK, SM
Sand Pond, Norway: BS, PK
Shagg Pond, Woodstock: BK, SM
Songo Pond, Albany/Bethel: BK, BS, WP
South Pond, Greenwood: S, T, BS, WP, PK, WF
Southeast Pond, Hiram: BS, PK
Speck Pond, Grafton: BK
Spectacle Ponds, Porter: BS, PK
Stanley Pond, Hiram/Porter: S, BS, PK
Stearns Pond, Sweden: BN, BS, PK
Sturtevant Pond, Magalloway/T5 R1: S, PK, SM
Thompson Lake, Oxford: (see Map 71)
Trout Pond, Stoneham: BK
Twitchell Pond, Greenwood: BN, BS, WP, PK
Umbagog Lake, Magalloway/T5 R1/Upton: S, BK, PK, SM
Upper Richardson Lake (Molechunkamunk Lake) Richardsontown (T4 R1)/Magalloway (T5 R1): (see Map 58)
Virginia Lake, Stoneham: WP, PK
Washburn Pond, Sumner/Woodstock: BK
Wells Pond, Parmachenee: BK
West Richardson Pond (Richardson Pond), Adamstown (T4 R2)/Lincoln (T5 R2): S, BK
Whitney Pond, Oxford: BS, WP, PK
Worthly Pond, Peru: BN, BS, PK

PENOBSCOT

Ackley Pond, Mt. Chase: BK
Ben Annis Pond, Hermon: :WP, PK
Billfish Pond (Fillfish Pond), T6 R8/T6 R9: BK
Bottle Lake, T4 R1 (Lakeville): BS, WP, PK
Bowlin Pond, T5 R8: BK
Brewer Pond, Orrington/Holden: (see Map 9)
Burnt Pond, Clifton: PK
Cedar Lake, T3 R9/TA R8/TA R9: S, BK, WP, PK

Chemo Pond, Bradley/Eddington/Clifton: BS, WP, PK
Cold Stream Pond, Enfield/Lincoln/Lowell: (see Map 16)
Crooked Pond, Lincoln: BS, WP, PK
Cut Lake, T7 R6/T8 R6: BK
Davis Pond, Eddington/Holden: BS, WP, PK
Duck Lake, T4 R1 (Lakeville): BS, WP, PK
Endless Lake, T3 R9: S, BS, WP, PK
Escutasis Lake, Lowell/Burlington: BS, WP
Fields Pond, Orrington: BS, WP, PK
Fitts Pond, Clifton/Eddington: BK, PK
Folsom Pond, Lincoln: BS, WP, PK
Frost Pond, T6 R9: BK
Green Mountain Pond, T6 R6W: BK
Green Pond, Lee/T3 R1N: BK
Hammond Pond, Hampden: BS, WP, PK
Hatcase Pond, Eddington: (see Map 27)
Hay Lake, T6 R8: S, BK
Hay Pond, T6 R8: BK
Hermon Pond, Hermon: (see Map 27)
Holbrook Pond, Holden/Eddington: BS, WP, PK
Hopkins Pond, Clifton: (see Map 28)
Hot Pond, T6 R6/T6 R7: PK
House Pond, Lee: BK
Ireland Pond, T7 R8 WELS: BK
Jerry Pond, Millinocket/East Millinocket: BK
Jerry Pond, T5 R7: BK
Junior Lake, T5 R1/Lakeville: (see Map 29)
Katahdin Lake, T3 R8: BK
Keg Lake, Lakeville: BS, WP, PK
Kimball Pond, T5 R8: BK
Lawton Pond, Mt. Chase: BK
Lost Pond, T7 R7: BK
Lower Jo-Mary Lake, T3 Indian Purchase: S, T, WP, PK, CU
Lower La Pomkeag Lake, T8 R7: BK
Lower Shin Pond, T5 R7, Mt. Chase: S, BK, SM
Lunksoos Lake, T4 R7: BK
Matagamon Lake (Grand Lake, First and Second), T6 R8: (see Map 37)
Mattanawcook Lake, Lincoln: (see Map 39)
Middle Jo-Mary and Turkeytail Lakes, T4 Indian Purchase: S, WP, PK
Mill Privilege Lake, T5 R1/Carroll: BS, WP
Millimagassett Lake, T7 R8: S, BK, SM
Millinocket Lake, T1 R8/T2 R8: (see Map 41)
Mountain Catcher Pond, T6 R8/T6 R9: BK
Mower Pond, Corinna: BS, WP, PK
Nokomis Pond, Newport/Palmyra: BS, WP, PK
Peaked Mountain Pond, T4 R7: BK
Pemadumcook Chain of Lakes (South Twin and Elbow Lakes), T3 and T4 (Indian Purchase): (see Map 51)
Pickett Mountain Pond, T6 R6W: BK
Pleasant Lake (Stetson Pond), Stetson: BS, WP, PK
Pleasant and Mud Lakes, T6 R6W: S, BK
Puffers Pond, Dexter: BK, PK
Pushaw Lake, Glenburn/Old Town/Orono/Hudson: (see Map 55)
Round Pond, Soldiertown (T2 R7 WELS): BS, PK
Saponac Pond, Burlington/Grand Falls: BS, WP, PK
Sawtelle Deadwater, T6 R7: BK
Scraggly Lake, T5 R1: (see Map 64)
Sebasticook Lake, Newport: BS, WP
Seboeis Grand Lake, T7 R7/T8 R7: BS, PK
Smith Pond, T3 Indian Purchase: BK
Snowshoe Lake, T7 R7: S, BS, PK
South Branch Lake, Seboeis Plt./T2 R8: BS, WP, PK
Sweets Pond (Swetts Pond), Orrington: BS, WP, PK
Sysladobsis Lake (Dobsis Lake, Lower Dobsis, Lower Sysladobsis Lake), T4 R1/TS ND: S, BS, WP, PK
Trout Pond, Grand Falls Plt.: BK
Trout Pond, T2 R7 (Soldiertown): BK

Umcolcus Lake, T7 R6/T8 R6: S, BK, PK
Upper Cold Stream Pond, Lincoln/Burlington: S, T, WP, PK
Upper Jo-Mary Lake, Veazie Gore: S, T, WP, PK, WF, CU
Upper Shin Pond, T6 R6, Mt. Chase: S, BK
Upper Sysladobsis Lake, T4 R1: S, BS, WP, WF
Wassookeag Lake, Dexter: (see Map 74)
Weir Pond, T3 R1/Lee: BK, WP, PK
West Grand Lake, T5 R1: (see Map 76)
Wiley Pond, Patten: BK

 PISCATAQUIS

Abol Pond, T2 R9: BK
Allagash Lake, T7 R14/T8 R14: (see Map 1)
Alligator Pond, TA R11: BK
B Pond, TB R11: BK
Bartlett Pond, T10 R9: BK
Bear Pond, Bowerbank: BS, WP
Bear Pond, T2 R13: BK
Beaver Pond, TA R12: BK, CU
Bell Pond, Monson: BK
Bennett Pond, Parkman: BK, PK
Billfish Pond (Fillfish Pond), T6 R9/T6 R8: BK
Big Beaver Pond, T2 R11: BK
Big Beaver Pond (Aroostook Pond), T7 R9 WELS: BK
Big Bennett Pond, Guilford: BK
Big Benson Pond, T7 R9 /Bowerbank/Willimantic: S, BK, T
Big Boardway Pond (Big Boardman Pond), TA R11: BK
Big Bunker Pond, Shirley: BK
Big Duck Pond, East Middlesex: BK
Big Fisher Pond, T2 R12: BK
Big Greenwood Pond, Willimantic/Elliotsville: BK, T, SM, WF
Big Indian Pond, T3 R5: BK, T, SM, WF, CU
Big Lyford Pond, TAR 12/TAR 13: BK
Big Pine Pond, T3 R13: BK
Big Pleasant Lake, T9 R11/T10 R11: BK, WF
Big Pleasant Pond, TA R11: BK, T
Big Reed Pond, T8 R10: BK, BL
Big Squaw Pond, T3 R5: BK, SM
Boyd Lake, Orneville: BS, WP, PK
Buck Pond, T2 R11: BK
Burden Pond (Third Buttermilk Pond), Bowerbank: BK
Burnham Pond, T2 R6: BK
Carpenter Pond, T7 R11: BK
Caucomgomoc Lake, T6 R15/T6 R14/T7 R15/ T7 R14: (see Map 10)
Cedar Pond, TBR 10: BK
Celia Pond, T3 R10: BK
Center Pond, Sangerville: S, WP, PK
Chamberlain Lake, T6 R11/T6 R12/T7 R11/ T7 R12/T7 R13/T8 R13: (see Map 11)
Chandler Pond, T7 R10/T8 R10: S, BK
Chase Lake, T9 R10: S, BK, SM
Chesuncook Lake (Ripogenus Lake, Caribou Lake, Moose Pond), T3 R11/T3 R12/T2 R12/ T3 R13/T4 R12 T4 R13 T5 R12/T5 R13/ T6 R13: (see Map 12)
Church Pond, TA R10: BK
Churchill Lake, T9 R12/T9 R13/T10 R12: BK, T, SM, WF, CU
Clear Lake, T10 R11: BK, T, WF, CU
Cliff Lake, T8 R12/T9 R12: BK, T, WF
Clifford Pond, T2 R11: BK
Coffeelos Pond, T2 R11: BK
Cooper Pond, TA R10: BK, WP
Crawford Pond, TA R11: BK, T, CU
Crescent Pond, T9 R15: BK, T, CU

Daicey Pond, T3 R10: BK
Davis Pond (First), Guilford: S, WP, PK
Davis Pond (Second), Guilford/Willimantic: S, WP, PK
Debsconeag Lake (First), T2 R10: S, T, WP, SM, WF, CU
Deer Pond, T3 R13: BK
Doe Pond, Monson BK
Doughnut Pond, T2 R11: BK
Dow Pond, Sebec: BK
Draper Pond, T3 R10: BK
Duck Pond, T4 R11: BK
Dwelley Pond, T5 R10: BK
Eagle Lake (Big Eagle), T8 R13/T9 R13/T7 R12/ T8 R12: BK, E, SM, WF, CU
Ebemee Lake (Horseshoe, Pearl, East and West Ponds), T5 R9/ Brownville: S, BS, WP, PK
Echo Lake, T9 R11: BK, T
Elbow Pond, T3 R10: BK
Fifth Debsconeag Lake, T1 R11/T2 R11: BK
First Little Lyford Pond, T7 R10: BK
First West Branch Pond, TA R12: BK
Fitzgerald Pond (Mountain View Pond), T2 R6: BK
Fogg Pond, T8 R10: BK
Foss Pond, Kingsbury: BK, T
Fourth Debsconeag Lake, T1 R10/T1 R11: BK, T, PK
Fourth Lake, T7 R11: BK
Fowler Pond, T3 R11: BK
Frost Pond, T3 R11/T3 R12: BK
Garland Pond, Sebec/Dover-Foxcroft: BK
Gauntlet Pond, TB R10: BK
Grand Lake (see Matagamon Lake)
Greenleaf Pond, Abbot: BK, PK
Greenwood Pond, TB R11/T7 R10: BK
Grenell Pond, Greenville: BK
Grindstone Pond, Willimantic: BK
Hale Pond, T2 R10: BK
Harrington Lake, T3 R11/T4 R11: BK, T, SM, WF, CU
Harrow Lake, T10 R11/T10 R12: BK
Haymock Lake, T7 R11/T8 R11: BK, T, WF, CU
Hay Pond, T7 R11: BK
Hebron Lake, Monson: S, T, WP, SM
Henderson Pond, TA R11: BK
High Pond, T6 R9: BK
Holbrook Pond, T2 R11/T3 R11: BK
Horseshoe Pond, T8 R10: BK
Houston Pond, T6 R9/T7 R9: S, BK, T, SM, CU
Hurd Pond, T2 R10: BK, T
Indian Pond, Big Squaw Mtn.: (see Map 29)
Indian Pond, T7 R9: BK
Indian Pond, T7 R12: BK, T, WF
Island Pond (Chase Pond), T9 R10/T10 R10: S, BK, SM
Jackson Pond, T3 R10/T3 R11: S
Johnson Pond, T8 R14: BK, T, WF
Johnston Pond, TA R10: BK, SM
Jo-Mary Pond, TB R10: BK
Juniper Knee Pond, Elliotsville: BK
Kidney Pond, T3 R10: (see Map 31)
Kingsbury Pond, Kingsbury Plt.: S, WP, PK, SM
Lazy Tom Pond, T1 R13: BK
Leadbetter Pond, T9 R11: BK
Little Beaver Pond, T7 R9 WELS: S, BK
Little Benson Pond, Bowerbank: BK
Little Carpenter Pond, T7 R11: BK
Little Frost Pond, T3 R12: BK
Little Houston Pond, T6 R9: BK
Little Lobster Lake, T3 R14: BK
Little Mud Pond, Greenville: BK
Little Pillsbury Pond, T8 R11: BK
Little Pleasant Pond, T10 R11: BK
Little Sourdnahunk Lake, T5 R11: BK
Little Spencer Pond, East Middlesex Canal Grant: BK
Little Squaw Pond, T3 R5: BK
Lobster Lake, T3 R14/T3 R15/TX R14/East Middlesex Canal Grant: (see Map 35) Page 84

Long Pond, TA R11/T1 R11: BK
Long Bog, TA R12: BK
Long Pond, T7 R9/T7 R10/T8 R10/Elliotsville: S, BK, T, SM
Long Pond, T6 R9: BK, SM
Lower Bean Pond, T2 R11: BK
Lower Fowler Pond, T6 R9: BK
Lower Hudson Pond, T10 R10: S, BK, SM
Lower Jo-Mary Lake: T1 R9/T1 R10/TA R10: S, T, WP, PK, WF, CU
Lower South Branch Pond, T5 R9/Baxter State Park: BK
Lower Togue Pond, T2 R9: S, WP, PK, SM
Lower Wilson Pond, Greenville: (see Map 77)
Lucky Pond, T1 R14: BK
Matagamon Lake (Grand Lake First and Second), T6 R9: (see Map 37)
Mathews Pond, T8 R10: BK
McPherson Pond, T10 R10: BK
Middle Branch Pond, T5 R9: BK
Middle Elbow Pond, T10 R10: BK
Middle Fowler Pond, T5 R9: BK
Middle Jo-Mary and Turkeytail Lakes, TA R10: S, WP, PK
Millinocket Lake, T1 R9/T2 R9: (see Map 41)
Millinocket Lake, T7 R9/T7 R10/T8 R9: S, BK, SM
Mink Marsh Pond, T10 R10: BK
Mitchell Pond, T7 R9: BK
Moose Pond, T1 R9: BK
Moosehead Lake, Greenville: (see Map 44)
Mooseleuk Lake, T10 R9: BK
Monson Pond, Monson: S, BK, T, SM
Mountain Pond, TA2 R13/TA 12 R14/T8 R10 (West Bowdoin College Grant): BK
Mountain Catcher Pond, T6 R8/T6 R9: BK
Mud Greenwood Pond, Willimantic: BK
Mud Pond, T6 R12: BK
Munsungan Lake: T8 R9/T8 R10/T9 R10: S, BK, T, SM, WF, CU
Musquacook Lake (Fifth), T10 R11: BK
Musquacook Lake (Fourth), T10 R11: BK
Narrow Pond, T8 R14: BK
Nahmakanta Lake, T1 R11/T2 R11: (see Map 46)
North Pond, Elliotsville: BK
Norton Pond (Peters Pond), Brownville: BK
Onawa Lake, Elliotsville/Willimantic: S, BK, SM, CU
Otter Pond, T3 R13: BK
Peaked Mountain Pond, T10 R10/T10 R11: BK
Pemadumcook Chain of Lakes (Ambajejus, Pemadumcook, and North Twin), T1 R9/T1 R10: (see Map 51)
Penobscot Pond, T1 R11/T1 R12: BK
Piper Pond, Abbot: S, WP, PK, SM
Pretty Pond, T8 R11: BK
Priestly Lake, T10 R13: T
Prong Pond, TA2 R13/TA2 R14/Greenville: BK
Punchbowl Pond, Blanchard: BK
Rabbit Pond, Elliotsville: BK
Ragged Lake, T2 R13/T3 R13: S, BK, T, SM
Rainbow Lake, T2 R11: BK, BL, SM
Roach Pond (First), Frenchtown/TA R13/T1 R13: (see Map 60)
Roach Pond, Fourth), TA R12: BK, WF, CU
Roach Pond (Third), TA R12: BK, WF, CU
Rocky Pond, T2 R9: BK
Ross Lake (Chemquasabamticook Lake), T9 R14/T9 R15/T10 R15: BK, T, SM, WF
Round Pond, T2 R9: BK
Rum Pond, Greenville/T8 R10: BK, SM
Russell Pond, T4 R9: BK
Saddle Pond, T7 R9: BK
Sawyer Pond, Greenville: BK
Schoodic Lake, Lakeview Plt./T4 R9/Brownville: S, T, SM, WF, CU
Sebec Lake, Willimantic/Bowerbank/Dover-

Foxcroft: (see Map 67)
Seboeis Lake, Lakeview/T4 R9: S, BS, WP, PK
Second Buttermilk Pond, Bowerbank: BK
Second Debsconeag Lake, T2 R10: BK
Second Little Lyford Pond, T7 R10/T8 R10: BK
Second Roach Pond, TA R12/T1 R12: (see Map 60)
Second and Third West Branch Ponds, TA R12: BK
Secret Pond, Greenville: BK
Seventh Roach Pond, TA R11: BK
Shirley Pond, Shirley: BK, SM
Silver Lake, T6 R9: S, BS, WP, PK
Sixth Roach Pond, TA R12: S, CU
Slaughter Pond, T3 R11: BK
Smith Pond, Elliotsville: BK
Snake Pond, T7 R11: BK
Soper Pond, T8 R11/T8 R12: BK
Sourdnahunk Lake, T4 R10/T4 R11/T5 R10/T5 R11: (see Map 69)
Spectacle Pond, Monson: BK
Spencer Pond, T1 R14/East Middlesex Canal Grant: BK
Spider Lake, T9 R11/T9 R12: BK, T, WF, WF, CU
Spruce Mountain Pond, TB R11: BK
Telos Lake, T5 R11/T6 R11: BK, T, SM, WF, CU
Thanksgiving Pond, Blanchard: BK
Third Debsconeag Lake, T1 R10/T2 R10: BK, T, CU
Third Lake (Third Matagamon Lake), T7 R10: BK
Thissell Pond, T5 R11: BK
Trout Pond, TA R12: BK, WF, CU
Trout Pond, T3 R5: BK
Turtle Pond, Lake View: BS, PK
Upper Ebeemee Lake, T4 R9/TB R10: BS, WP, PK
Upper Elbow Pond, T10 R10: BK
Upper Island Pond, T10 R10: BK
Upper Jo-Mary Lake, TA R10/TB R10: S, T, WP, PK, WF, CU
Upper Portage Pond, T9 R11: BK
Upper Russell Pond, T9 R14: BK
Upper Soper Pond, T8 R11: BK
Upper South Branch Pond, T5 R9/Baxter State Park: BK
Upper Togue Pond, T2 R9: S, PK
Upper Wilson Pond, Greenville/Bowdoin College Grant, West: (see Map 77)
Wadleigh Pond, T8 R15: BK, BL
Webster Lake, T6 R10/T6 R11: BK, T, SM
Whetstone Pond, Blanchard/Kingsbury: T, SM
Woodman Pond, T2 R11: BK
Yoke Ponds, TA R11: BK

SAGADAHOC

Caesar Pond, Bowdoin: BS, PK
Center Pond, Phippsburg: WP, BS
Nequasset Lake, Woolwich: (see Map 48)
Pleasant Pond (Mud Pond), Richmond: BS, WP, PK
Sewell Pond, Arrowsic: WP, PK
Silver Lake, Phippsburg: BN
Wat-tuh Lake, Phippsburg: BS, PK
Winnegance Pond (Winnegance Creek), Phippsburg/West Bath: BS, WP, PK

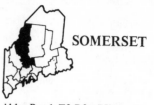

SOMERSET

Alder Pond, T3 R3: BK
Attean Pond, Attean: (see Map 3)
Austin Pond, Bald Mountain (T2 R3): BK
Baker Lake, T7 R17: S, BK
Baker Pond, T1 R2: BK
Baker Pond, Caratunk (Spaulding): S, BK
Barrett Pond, Holeb: BK
Basin Pond, T2 R2 (Pierce Ponds): BK
Beans Pond, Pleasant Ridge Plt.: BK
Beck Pond, T3 R5: BK
Big Indian Pond, St. Albans: BN, WP, PK
Bill Morris Pond, T3 R5: BK
Black Brook Pond, Moxie Gore: BK
Black Hill Pond, Embden: BK
Brassua Lake, T1 R1/T2 R1/T1 R2/T2 R2: (see Map 9)
Butler Pond, Kingfield/Lexington: BK
Canada Falls Lake, T2 R3/T3 R3/T2 R4: BK, WF
Center Pond, T2 R3 NBKP (Soldiertown): BK
Chase Pond, Moscow: BK
Clearwater Pond, Attean: BK, CU
Clish Pond, T5 R20: BK
Cold Stream Pond, T2 R6/T2 R7/T3 R7: BK
Crocker Pond, Dennistown: BK
Daymond Pond, Moose River: BK
Dead Stream Pond, 10,000 Acre Tract /West Forks/Chase Stream: BK
Demo Pond, Rockwood Strip: BK
Desolation Pond, T8 R16: BK
Dimmick Ponds (Big and Little Dimmick Ponds), Caratunk (Spaulding): BK
Dixon Pond, Pierce Pond: BK, SM
Dole Pond, T3 R5: BK,WF, CU
Duncan Pond, T4 R4: S, BK, T, SM
Durgin Pond, T2 R6: BK
East Pond, Smithfield: (see Map 21)
East Carry Pond, Carrying Place: BK
Ellis Pond, T1 R6: BK
Embden Pond, Embden: (see Map 22)
Fifth St. John Pond, T5 R17/T6 R17: BK
Fish Pond (Big Fish Pond), Holeb: BK
Fish Pond, Thorndike (T3 R2): S, BK, T, WF, SM
Fogg Pond, Long Pond: BK
Foley Pond, T4 R18: BK
Fourth St. John Pond, T5 R17: BK, WF
Grace Pond, Upper Enchanted: BK
Grass Pond, Pierce Pond: BK
Hall Pond, T4 R4: BK
Hancock Pond, Embden/Lexington: T, BS
Hayden Lake (Wesserunsett Lake), Madison: BS, WP, PK
Heald Pond, Moose River Plt.: S, BK, SM
Heald Ponds (Little Heald Pond), Caratunk (Spaulding): BK
Holeb Pond, Attean/Holeb: BK, CU
Horseshoe Pond, T1 R6: BK
Indian Pond, Big Squaw/Sapling/Indian Stream/Chase Stream: (see Map 29)
Iron Pond, T5 R6/Hobbstown: BK
Island Pond, T1 R6: BK
Jackson Pond, Concord: BK
Jewett Pond, Pleasant Ridge Plt.: BK
Jones Pond, T4 R3: BK
Kilgore Pond, Pierce Pond/Bowtown: BK
King and Bartlett Lakes, T4 R5: BK
King Pond, Bowtown: BK
Kingsbury Pond and Mayfield Pond, Mayfield/Brighton Plt.: S, WP, PK, SM
Knights Pond, Moxie Gore/Squaretown: BK

Lake George, Skowhegan/Canaan: BN, BS, PK
Little Austin Pond, Bald Mountain: BK
Little Big Wood Pond, Attean/Dennistown: S, BK, T, SM
Little Chase Stream Pond, T2 R7 (Misery): BK
Little Jim Pond, T4 R5: (see Map 32)
Little King Lake, T4 R5: BK
Little Otter Pond, T2 R1: BK
Loon Pond, Attean/Holeb: BK
Long Pond (Martin Pond), The Forks Plt.: BK, R
Long Pond, Forsythe/Holeb: BK
Long Pond (Little Long Pond), T1 R6: BK
Long Pond, T3 R5: BK, T, WF, SM
Long Pond, T3 R1/Jackman: S, BK, SM, CU
Long Pond, Taunton/Raynham: S, BK, SM, WF
Lost Pond, T5 R16: BK
Lost Pond, Pleasant Ridge: BK
Luther Pond, Thorndike: BK
Mac Dougall Pond, Caratunk Plt.: BK
Mary Petuche Pond, T4 R4: BK
McKenny Pond, Holeb: BK
Middle Carry Pond, Carrying Place: BK
Mill Pond (Clear Pond), Pleasant Ridge Plt.: BK
Misery Pond, T2 R7: BK
Moore Pond, T4 R7: BK
Moose Pond, Bowtown: BK
Moose Pond, Hartland/Harmony: (see Map 45)
Morrill Pond, Hartland: BK
Mosquito Pond, The Forks: BK
Mountain Dimmick Pond, Caratunk Plt.: BK
Moxie Pond, The Forks Plt./East Moxie: S, BK, SM
Nokomis Pond, Palmyra/Newport: BS, WP, PK
North Pond, Mercer/Smithfield/Rome: (see Map 49)
Oaks Pond, Skowhegan: BN, WP, PK
Otter and North Otter Ponds, Bowtown: BK
Otter Pond, T2 R1: BK
Palmer Pond, T2 R2: BK
Parlin Pond, T2 R6/Parlin Pond: S, BK, SM
Penobscot Lake, T3 R4/T3 R5/T4 R4/T4 R5: BK, BL
Pickerel Pond, Pierce Pond, Bowtown: BK, PK
Pierce Pond, Bowtown/Pierce Pond: S, BK, PK, SM
Pleasant Pond, Caratunk/ The Forks Plt.: BK
Rancourt Pond, Dennistown: BK
Ripley Pond, Ripley: BK
Rock Pond, T5 R6: BK
Roderique Pond, T2 R1: BK
Round Pond, T1 R6: BK
Rowe Pond, Pleasant Ridge Plt.: BK
Russell Pond, T5 R16: BK
Sandy Pond, Embden: PK
Seboomook Lake, T1 R4/T2 R4: S, BK, WF, CU
Sibley Pond, Canaan/Pittsfield: WP, PK
Smith Pond, Brighton: BN, WP, PK
Smith Pond, Parlin Pond/Misery: BK
Spectacle Pond, King and Bartlett: BK
Spencer Lake, Hobbstown (T4 R6)/T3 R5: (see Map 69)
Split Rock Pond, Pierce Pond: BK
Spring Lake, T3 R4: (see Map 70)
Spruce Pond, Lexington: BK
St. Francis Lake, TB R16: BK
Sugar Birth Pond, Dennistown: BK
Supply Pond, Jackman/Moose River: BK
Ten Thousand Acre Pond, T1 R6: BK
Tomhegan Pond, T1 R3/T2 R3: BK, CU
Trickey Pond, T3 R3: BK
Turner Pond, Forsythe: BK
Turner Pond, T7 R16: BK
Upper Misery Pond, T2 R7: BK
Wentworth Pond (Ironbound Pond), Solon/Athens: S, BS, WP, SM
West Carry Pond, Carrying Place: BK, T, SM
Whites Pond, Palmyra: BS, WP, PK

Wood Pond, Attean/Dennistown/Jackman: (see Map 78)

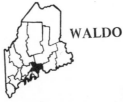

WALDO

Basin Pond, Monroe: BK, PK
Bowler Pond (Belton Pond), Palermo: BK, BS, WP, PK
Cargill Pond, Liberty: BS, PK
Coleman Pond, Lincolnville: BS, WP, PK
Dutton Pond, Knox: BN, WP, PK
Halfmoon Pond, Brooks: BK
Halfmoon Pond, Searsport/Prospect: BK, BS
Jump Pond, Palermo: BS, WP, PK
Knight Pond, Northport: BS, WP, PK
Megunticook Lake, Lincolnville/Camden/Hope: S, BS, WP, PK
Mixer Pond, Knox/Morrill: BK, BN
Moody Pond, Lincolnville: BK, PK
Norton Pond, Lincolnville: BK, BS, WP, PK
Passagassawaukeag Lake (Randall Pond), Brooks: BS, WP, PK
Pitcher Pond, Lincolnville/Northport: BS, WP, PK
Quantabacook Pond, Searsmont/Morrill: BS, WP, PK
Saban Pond, Palermo: BS
Sanborn Pond, Palermo: BS
Sandy Pond (Freedom Pond), Freedom: BS, WP, PK
Sheepscot Lake (Sheepscot Pond), Palermo: (see Map 68)
St. George Lake (Lake St. George), Liberty: (see Map 62)
Stevens Lake, Liberty: BS, WP, PK
Swan Lake, Swanville/Searsport/Frankfort: BK, BS, SM
Tilden Pond, Belmont: BS, WP, PK
Toddy Pond, Swanville/Brooks: BS, WP, PK
Trues Pond, Montville: BS, PK
Unity Pond (Lake Winnecook), Burnham/Unity/Troy: S, BS, WP, PK, SM

WASHINGTON

Baskahegan Lake, Brookton/Topsfield: BS, WP, PK
Big Lake, Indian/ Grand Lake Stream/T27 ED, No. 21: (see Map 7)
Bog Lake, Northfield: S, BS, WP, PK
Boyden Lake, Perry/Robbinston: S, PK
Cathance Lake, Cooper/No. 14: (see Map 10)
Clifford Lake, T26 ED/T27 ED: BS, WP, PK
Coleback Lake, Charlotte: S, SM
Crawford Lake, Crawford/No. 21 : (see Map 17)
Crooked Brook Flowage, Danforth: BS, WP, PK
Dead Pond, T25 MD: BK
Eastern Lake, Robbinston: BK
East Grand Lake, Danforth/T9 R4: (see Map 20)
East Monroe Pond, T43 MD: BK
East Musquash Lake, Topsfield S, PK
East Pike Brook Pond, T18 MD: BK
Farrow Lake, Topsfield: S, PK
Gardner Lake, East Machias/Marion/Whiting: (see Map 24)
Goulding Lake, Robbinston: BS, WP, PK

Howard Lake, Calais/Robbinston: BS, WP, PK
Indian Lake, Whiting: S, PK
James Pond, Charlotte: BK
Keeley Lake, Marshfield: BK
Keenes Lake, Calais: BK
LaCoute Lake, Vanceboro: BK
Lambert Lake, T11 R3N/T1 R3: S, PK
Ledge Pond (Bald Eagle Pond), Charlotte: BK
Lily Lake, Trescott: BK
Lily Lake, T30 MD: BK, PK
Little Cathance Lake, No. 14: BK
Little Lily Lake, Marshfield/East Machias: BK
Little Pickerel Pond, Brookton : BS, PK
Long Lake, Indian/Princeton/Plt. 21: BS, WP, PK
Love Lake, T19 ED/Crawford: S, BK, BS, WP, PK
Lower Hot Brook Lake, T8 R4/Danforth: BS, WP, PK
Lower Oxbrook Lake, T6 ND/T6 R1: BK, WP, PK
Marks Lake, Marshfield: BK, BS
Meddybemps Lake, Alexander/Baring/Baileyville/Meddybemps: (see Map 39)
Monroe Lake, T43 MD: BK
Montegail Pond, T19 MD: BK
Mopang Lake, T29 MD: S, WP
Nash's Lake, Calais: S, PK
Orie Lake, T6 R1/T7 R2: BK
Patrick Lake, No. 14/Marion: WP, PK
Peaked Mountain Pond, T19 MD/Northfield/Centerville: BK, PK
Peep Lake, T30 MD: BK, R
Penman Pond, T26 ED/T31 MD: BK
Pennamaquam Lake, Charlotte/Pembroke: BS, PK
Pineo Pond, Deblois: BK
Pleasant Lake, T7 R2/T6 R1: (see Map 52)
Pleasant Lake, Alexander: S, WP, PK
Pleasant River Lake, Beddington/T29 MD: S. BS
Pocomoonshine Lake, Princeton/Alexander: (see Map 53)
Pocumcus Lake, T5 ND/T6 ND: S, BS, WP
Possum Pond, T26 ED: BK
Pug Lake, T26 ED: BS, WP, PK
Rocky and Sunken Lakes, Marion/Edmunds/Whiting: BK
Rocky Lake, T18 ED: BS, WP, PK
Round Lake, Charlotte: BS, PK
Round Pond, Steuben: S, BK
Salmon Pond, T30 MD: BK
Scraggly Lake, T6 R1: (see Map 64)
Second Marks Lake, Marshfield: BK
Shattuck Lake, Robbinston/Calais: BK
Simpson Pond, Roque Bluffs: BK
Six Mile Lake, Marshfield/Whitneyville: BK
South Myers Pond, Columbia: BK
Spednik Lake, T9 R4N/T10 R3N/T11 R3N/Vanceboro: S, BS, WP, PK, CU
Sunken and Rocky Lakes, Marion/Whiting: BK
Sysladobsis Lake, T5 ND: S, BS, WP, PK
Third Machias Lake, T43 MD/T42 MD/T5 ND: (see Map 71)
Unnamed Pond, T31 MD: BK
Unnamed Pond, T36 MD: BK
Upper Hot Brook Lake, T8 R4/Danforth: BS, WP, PK
Upper Oxbrook Lake, T6 R1/Talmadge: BK, WP
Vining Lake, Cooper/Plt. No. 14: BK
Wabassus Lake, T5 ND/T6 ND/T43 MD: BS, WP, PK
West Grand Lake, T6 R1/T6 ND/Grand Lake Stream/T5 ND: (see Map 76)
West Monroe Pond, T43 MD: BK
West Musquash Lake, T6 R1/Talmadge: S, BK, T
West Pike Brook Pond, T18 MD: BK
Western Lake, Robbinston: BK

Page 86

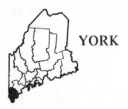

YORK

Adams Pond, Newfield: PK
Alewife Pond, Kennebunk: PK
Balch Pond, Acton/Newfield: WP, PK, BS
Bartlett Pond, Lyman/Waterboro: BS, PK
Bauneg Beg Lake, Sanford/North Berwick: BS, PK
Bonny Eagle Lake, Buxton: BS, WP, PK
Bunganut Pond, Lyman: BS, PK
Deer Pond, Hollis: BN, PK
Ell Pond, Sanford/Wells: BK, R
Estes Lake, Sanford/Alfred: BS, WP, PK
Granny Kent Pond, Shapleigh: BS, PK

Great East Lake, Acton: (see Map 24)
Hansen Pond, Acton/Shapleigh: BS, PK
Holland Lake (Sokokis Lake), Limerick: BS, PK
Horn Pond, Newfield/Acton: BN, BS, PK
Horne Pond (Pequawket Lake), Limington: BK, SM
Isinglass Pond, Limington/Waterboro: BK, PK
Kennebunk Pond, Lyman: BN, WP
Killick Pond, Hollis: BS, PK
Leigh's Mill Pond, South Berwick: BN, WP, PK
Little Ossipee Lake, Waterboro: (see Map 33)
Lone Pond, Waterboro: BK
Long Pond, Parsonsfield: S, BS, PK
Middle Branch Pond, Waterboro: BS, PK
Moody Pond, Waterboro: BK
Moose Pond, Acton: BK, BS, PK
Mousam Lake, Acton/Shapleigh: (see Map 46)
Northeast Pond, Lebanon: BN, BS, WP, PK
North Shapleigh Pond, Shapleigh/Newfield: BS, PK
Parker Pond (Barker Pond), Lyman: BK, PK

Pickerel Pond, Limerick: BS, PK
Pinkham Pond (Hidden Lake), Newfield: BS, PK
Poverty Pond, Newfield/Shapleigh: BN, PK
Province Lake, Parsonsfield: BS, PK
Roberts and Wadley Ponds, Lyman: BS, PK
Round Pond, Lyman/Dayton: BK
Sand Pond, Limington: BK, BS, PK
Scituate Pond, York: BS
Shaker Pond, Alfred: BS, WP, PK
Square Pond, Shapleigh/Acton: BN, BS, WP, PK
Sunken Pond, Sanford: BK
Swan Pond, Lyman: BN, BS, WP
Town House and Milton Ponds, Lebanon: BN, BS, WP, PK
Turner Pond (Mirror Lake), Newfield: BS, PK, WF
Ward's Pond, Limington: BS, PK
Warren Pond, South Berwick: BK
West Pond, Parsonsfield: BS, PK
Wilcox Pond, Biddeford: BK
Wilson Pond, Acton: BN, BS, PK
York Pond, Eliot: BS, PK

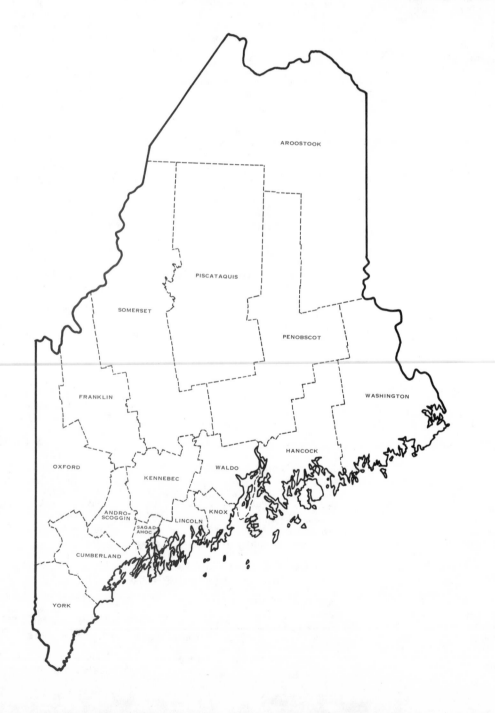